# THE WORKS

## OF

# CORNEILLE

*and*

# RACINE

# The Works
## of
# Corneille and Racine

*With an introduction*
*by*
PAUL LANDIS

BLACK'S READERS SERVICE

ROSLYN, NEW YORK

PRINTED IN THE UNITED STATES OF AMERICA

# CONTENTS

# INTRODUCTION

Nothing in the literature of modern Europe speaks with a stranger language to Anglo-Saxon ears, or has more difficulty being heard than the French classic tragedy of Corneille and Racine. Nothing more forcibly represents the abysmal gulf which even in the modern world may exist between the habits of thought of two civilized peoples than the attitude of the French towards Shakespeare and that of English speaking peoples towards these corresponding dramatists of France. Although little by little both peoples have come to recognize the merit of the other's premier poet, such recognition remains for the most part intellectual, and in general it is still true that to the French mind Shakespeare is "a barbarian of genius," and to those brought up on English literature Racine is almost the opposite, a cultivated mediocrity.

We who are accustomed to the rich variety of Shakespeare, who thrill with unnamable emotions at the imaginative incoherence of Lear, who delight to laugh and shudder at once at the heartless humor of the grave-diggers, are likely to remain unmoved by the meticulously worded passion of Phædra, and our admiration for even the most violent of Corneille's tirades expresses itself in regret that he would not permit himself the freedom of our own Elizabethans. We have learned from our master the mad beauty of words flung out in artless frenzy, and tragedy for us is a grand symphony in which the lines are often a burning obbligato to an accompaniment of thunder and lightning and the wind on the heath. Even Hamlet, the most intellectual of our tragic heroes, would be less moving for us without the grisly horse-play and the moonless battlements of Elsinore.

All this somber orchestration of life and nature is lacking in French classic tragedy. Even when the characters are glamorous with the luster shed by Homer, we are discouraged at the start by the frigid announcement: "The scene is at Buthrotum, a city of Epirus, in a room in the palace of Pyrrhus." As we read on we discover that the action is as little startling as the setting. Nothing really happens in this room; only endless talk, some impassioned duologues and soliloquies, and more long analytical confessions to characterless confidants. Clearly we are not meant to get from these plays the same sort of thrill which we derive from Shakespeare.

Nevertheless, there is about these decorous tragedies a peculiar and matchless beauty, if one develops the ability to see it. As with all drama, the first necessity for appreciation is a recognition of the conventions of the theater for which the plays were written. The French theater of the seventeenth century accepted on what it thought was the authority of Aristotle the three unities of time, place, and action. As was the case in fifth century Athens, these conventions were in a measure supported by the physical limitations of the theaters; but with the French by far the most potent force in maintaining the unities was the example of Greek and Latin drama and the criticism of Aristotle. Corneille deliberately accepted the principle that the action of the play must take place in a single day, that it must be carried on in one circumscribed locality, and that it must be concerned with a single situation. That he chafed under these limitations and that he was not always able entirely to adjust his matter to their requirements is evident from his plays. Both *The Cid* and *Cinna* require more than one room to accommodate the action, and *The Cid,* in order to maintain the unity of time, relates the events of what is probably the most crowded day in all recorded time. In those twenty-four hours Roderick declares his love, fights his first duel, kills his sweetheart's father, repels in a tremendous battle a national invasion, wins a trial by combat, and in the course of all this loses and regains the favor of his king and the lady of his heart. Here, if anywhere in drama, it is necessary to accept Mr. Belloc's principle that if a thing is true you must accept it no matter how incredible it may seem. Once the conventions of the unities have been accepted, these difficulties disappear, and especially in the hands of Racine, these very restrictions become the instruments of power.

No literary artifice can long persist in so popular an art as the drama unless it possesses some deep and fundamental virtue, and this, in the case of the unities, is the aid they give to dramatic concentration. After all it is the moment, not the story, that is dramatic, and the drama of Corneille and Racine concentrates on the moment. In a sense these plays do not really tell a story at all. Whereas Shakespeare traced the degradation of Macbeth from the first timid, conscience-stricken yielding to ambition to the utterly heartless courage with which he met his death, Racine in *Britannicus,* also a study in degradation, concerns himself only with the culminating moment at which Nero by his first assassination became a tyrant. It is as if Macbeth ended with the murder of Duncan. We are not shown the birth and growth of Phædra's guilty passion for Hippolytus, but only the maddening day when Theseus' return brought all their tangled lives to ruin. There can be no doubt that the latter method is better adapted to the brief time of a stage presentation, and that the former is more the method of the novel.

In action so concentrated as this, what happens is of less importance than the mental reactions of the characters. In fact the action is practically confined to the mind. Once this is realized, it becomes clear that the "room in the palace of Pyrrhus," is simply a place where tortured souls display their strength and agony. Any room would have done as well, and the very poverty of the scene helps to concentrate the attention upon the psychological analysis. This is not really Epirus, but anywhere; these are not Homeric Greeks, but man and woman. Paradoxically, this narrowing of the scene and action gives to the characters a universality difficult to attain in the more varied panoramas of romantic plays. It may seem at first that there is no life here; but presently we come to realize that in thinking so we are mistaking movement for life, and that here is life stripped of all its trappings, life and nothing else. Abbé Dimnet relates that a great French teacher once asked a pupil whose dramas he preferred, Racine's or Hugo's. "Hugo's," answered the boy, "there is more life in them." Half to himself the teacher murmured: "More bustle." It is a confusion which our present-day civilization renders more and more prevalent.

Actually the classic tragedies move from first to last with a feverish intensity. It is only at the moment when passion has been heated to incandescence that we see it, and in these plays we see it rather than feel it. In the last analysis they were written to be witnessed, not read. This, of course, is true of all real drama, but of French classic tragedy it is more true than of most, that the reader who comes nearest to appreciating them is the one who reads as an actor. In one way or another these plays must be acted to be enjoyed.

The two dramatists whose works are here chosen to represent French classic tragedy were almost contemporaries. Corneille (1606-1684) belonged to the first generation of the seventeenth century, and Racine (1639-1699) to the second; and Corneille's reputation was established before Racine began to write. *The Cid* was written in 1636, and *Cinna* in

1640. *Andromache* was first produced in 1667, *Britannicus* in 1669, and *Phædra* in 1677. The greater part of their lives overlapped, and the rivalry between them was often intense and generally disastrous to the elder poet. Corneille set the fashion, and *The Cid* has been called "perhaps the most epoch-making play in all literature." With what difficulty he forced his material almost to conform to the unities has been pointed out. *Cinna* is much more successful in this respect, but even here there are difficulties. Racine took the form established by Corneille and made of these unities, next to his verse, his greatest instrument of power.

It is not necessary here to judge between them. Racine is generally esteemed the greater, and, all things considered, the judgment must stand. His plays are more closely knit; his verse, at its best incomparable, never descends to the banalities of which Corneille is sometimes guilty; and above all, his characters present their emotional states, whereas those of Corneille often ask you to take their feelings for granted and talk about them rather than display them. But Corneille, too, has his virtues. Nothing in Racine is finer structurally than the dexterity with which Corneille in *Cinna* first throws the sympathy to Cinna, then to Augustus, and finally extracts and unites the virutes of both. And it would be hard to find anywhere a more powerful exposition of the confusion of good and evil, strength and weakness, egotism and humility, that can exist in the heart of a noble man than Augustus' great soliloquy.

Finally, what is often attacked as Corneille's greatest weakness becomes for some of us, once it is appreciated, his noblest virtue. "Admiration," say his detractors, "is not a tragic passion." Aristotle, it must be admitted, bears them out; but to us it matters very little whether *The Cid* and *Cinna* are proper tragedies or not. Admiration is at least a noble and unselfish passion, and one, unfortunately, rather out of fashion in the world in which we live. It has its roots in a conception of man as a being capable of nobility, and that is an idea that the race cannot afford to lose.

The passion-swept heroines of Racine plumb the depths of the human spirit, and under their spell, in the words of Mr. Strachey, "we plunge shuddering through infinite abysses, and look, if only for a moment, upon eternal light." That is true tragedy, and it must be admitted that Corneille does not move in that sphere. But we of the Freudian era who have been nourished on psychoanalysis, though we have had precious few glimpses of eternal light, have become used to plunging into abysses. For us, sturdy old Corneille has a more salutary message than his more poetically gifted rival. We may be bored sometimes by his stiffness, and we may agree with Voltaire that Roderick offers Chimene his head much too often for dramatic effect, but we cannot read with understanding without a thrill of pride at man's capacity for self-mastery. Here is a world in which personal honor is not a chemical reaction of gland secretions, but a self-instituted, self-administered rule of life. Here is a world which believes that man is master of himself and responsible for good and evil in his own conduct; a world in which nothing—not even life and love—is so precious as one's honor as a man. It is an old-fashioned, classical world, to be sure, but the knowledge that destroys it may be bought at too high a price.

PAUL LANDIS.

Urbana, Illinois
1931

# THE CID

by

PIERRE CORNEILLE

# CHARACTERS

Don Ferdinand ......*First King of Castile*
Donna Urraque .....*Infanta of Castile*
Don Diegue .........*Father of Roderick*
Don Gomez .........*Count of Gormaz, father of **Chimene***
Don Roderick ......*Lover of Chimene*
Don Sancho ........*in love with Chimene*
Don Arias ⎫
⎬ *Castilian Gentlemen*
Don Alonzo ⎭
Chimene ...........*Daughter of Don Gomez*
Leonora ...........*Maid to the Infanta*
Elvire .............*Maid to Chimene*
A Page to the Infanta

The scene is in Seville.

# ACT I

## Scene I

*(Enter Chimene and Elvire)*

*Chimene.* Is this the truth, Elvire? Have you disguised
Or held back anything my father said?

*Elvire.* My heart still thrills with thinking of his words;
He honors Roderick as you adore him,
And if I read your father's heart aright
He will command you to return his love.

*Chimene.* Tell me again, I pray, a second time,
Why you believe he will approve my choice;
Teach me anew the hope that I may cherish—
So sweet a tale is never heard too much.
Nor can you pledge too often to our loves
Freedom to come from hiding into day.
What did he say about the secret plot
Which Roderick and Sancho made with you?
Did you not make too clear what difference
Between these lovers draws me all to one?

*Elvire.* Not I! I made of yours a pliant heart,
Not kindling hope nor quenching it in either,
Not viewing either with too stern an eye,
Nor yet too gentle, waiting to obey
Your father's wishes when you take a husband.
That caught his heart; his lips, his whole expression
Gave quick and eloquent assurance of it.
But since you wish that I repeat his words

3

Over and over for you—thus he spoke:
"She shows her duty; both are worthy men,
Both sprung of noble blood, both brave and faithful,
Youths in whose eyes one easily may read
The shining virtues of their ancestors.
Roderick especially bears upon his face
No features but bespeak a man of courage,
Sprung of a house so rich in warriors,
Born every one in the very lap of glory.
His father's valor and the matchless age
To which his strength endures are marvelous;
The lines his deeds have graven on his brow
Speak still of that which formerly he was.
I hope for such a son as was his father,
And loving him, my daughter gives me joy."
The council-chamber called him then; he left
Breaking his speech off when he'd scarce begun.
And yet from these few words I think he holds
His favor balanced between both your lovers.
The king would choose a tutor for his son,
And this high post will fall upon your father.
His choice is certain, and his noble spirit
Cannot admit the fear of rivalry.
His deeds have marked him peerless, he will have
No rival for a post so well deserved.
Don Roderick has gained his father's word,
Straight on adjournment to propose the matter.
I let you judge if all will not be well,
And all your hopes rest presently fulfilled.

   *Chimene.* It seems my troubled heart is still unapt
For happiness, heavy with doubting still.
Such alteration may one moment bring
That in great joy I fear a greater sorrow.

*Elvire.* You'll see your fears dissolve in happiness.

*Chimene.* Well, come what may, we will await the issue.

### Scene II. *Infanta and Leonora, Page*

*Infanta.* Go quickly, page, and tell Chimene I think
She waits too long today to come to me,
And that my love complains of this delay.

*Leonora.* Madam, each day you press the selfsame wish;
I see you thoughtful, sad; each time we meet
You ask the daily progress of her passion.

*Infanta.* Have I not reason? Her young heart is pierced
By shafts I leveled at her breast. Her lover,
Roderick, was my lover first; she holds
His love but by my gift. So I, who forged
These lasting lovers' chains, feel rightfully
Desire to see the end of all their pains.

*Leonora.* Madam, their dear delight in one another
Finds, as I read your heart, no echo there.
This love which crowns them both with happiness—
Does it oppress your noble head with sorrow?
And does the anxiety you feel for them
Render you sad at seeing them so happy?
But I am bold. I overstep discretion.

*Infanta.* My sorrow doubles while I hold it hidden!
Hear, hear at last how I have battled, hear
What trials my heart has still to undergo.
Love is a tyrant sparing none. This youth,
This gallant lover whom I give away—
I love him!

*Leonora.* You!

*Infanta.*　　　　　Here, feel my beating heart,
See how it flutters at its conqueror's name,
How well it knows its master.

*Leonora.*                    Pardon, madam,
I would not fail in gentle courtesy,
Though I o'erstep respect to censure you.
A royal princess but forgets herself
To take a simple cavalier to heart.
What would the king say? What would all Castile?
Have you remembered who your father is?

    *Infanta.* So well I know it that I would shed this blood
Rather than bring dishonor to my rank.
I might well say that in a noble soul
Merit alone should light the flame of love;
And if my passion sought to find excuse,
A thousand noble names would sanction it.
Yet would I not pursue where honor falls.
A heart surprised does not destroy my courage.
Always I am the daughter of a king
And none but kings are fit to mate with me.
When once I saw my heart fail of defense,
Myself rejected what I dared not take.
I drew the bonds of love about Chimene,
And lit their passions to extinguish mine.
Wonder no longer that my harassed soul
Awaits impatiently their wedding day.
You see how much my peace depends upon it.
Love lives on hope, and dies when hope is dead;
It is a flame which sinks for lack of fuel.
And spite of all the sorrows I have borne,
If Roderick once is wedded with Chimene,
My hope is dead, my wounded spirit healed.
Till then I suffer torture, until then
Roderick will still be dear to me.
I will to lose, yet lose regretfully.
That is the secret sorrow of my heart.

With shame I see my heart compelling me
To sigh for that which yet I hold in scorn;
I feel my soul divided, though my will
Is strong, my heart is all aflame. That wedding
Is death to me; I fear, yet long for it;
I dare not hope for more than partial joy.
Honor and love are both so dear to me
I die if either wins or either yields.

   *Leonora.* Madam, I have no more to say. I sigh
With you and suffer with your sorrow.
I cannot blame you more, but only pity.
Yet since in grief at once so sweet and bitter
Your royal spirit, beautiful as strong,
Can conquer its desires, it will bring
Once more sweet peace into your troubled heart.
There lies your hope, there and in friendly time;
There is too much of justice still in heaven
To torture longer such a noble heart.

   *Infanta.* My sweetest hope is hope's own swift defeat.

*(Enter Page)*

   *Page.* Chimene awaits your pleasure as you wished.

   *Infanta.* Go entertain her in the gallery.

*(Exit Page)*

   *Leonora.* Will you remain to brood upon your sorrow?

   *Infanta.* No, give me but a moment to compose
My thoughts and hide my grief. I'll follow you.

*(Exit Leonora)*

Just Heaven, whence only I must look for help,
Bring to its end this suffering of mine,
Restore my peace, and keep my honor strong;
Let me in others' joy find happiness.
Three hearts are waiting for this wedding day.
Hasten its coming, or give my heart more strength.

The bond which joins these lovers will destroy
My chains and put an end to all my pain.
But I delay too long—I'll find Chimene,
And in her presence comfort for my grief.

### SCENE III. *The Count and Don Diegue*

*Count.* You have prevailed; the favor of the king
Has raised you to a post that should be mine.
You shall be tutor to Castile's young prince.

*Diegue.* This mark of honor placed upon my house
But shows to all how just he is, how well
He can bestow rewards for service done.

*Count.* Great as kings are, they are but men like us,
Able to be deceived like other men;
All courtiers may discern from this preferment
How poorly present service may be paid.

*Diegue.* Well, speak no more about a preference
So galling to your spirit. Kindness may,
As much as merit, have brought the prize to me.
We owe at least so much to royal power
As not to weigh the judgments of the king.
Add to the king's, I beg, another honor—
And join in marriage bonds your house and mine.
You have an only daughter, I a son.
This marriage would forever bind our houses
In more than friendship. Will you grant this honor?

*Count.* Roderick's aspirations should be higher,
And this new splendor of your office serve
To puff his mind with swelling vanity.
Perform your duties, sir, instruct the prince;
Show him how a province should be ruled
To make a people tremble at his word,

To fill good men with love, rascals with fear;
Add to all these a soldier's virtues, too,
Teach him to laugh at hardships, peerlessly
To ply the trade of Mars, to spend long days
And nights on horseback, to sleep fully armed;
To force a stronghold, and the battle won,
To owe the glory to himself alone.
Instruct him by example; his young eyes
Must see in you a model of perfection.

*Diegue.* Your envious soul speaks in your sneering words;
He needs but scan the story of my life,
And learn from that long tale of glorious deeds
How to subdue a nation, storm a fort,
Command an army, and to make a name
Whose wide renown shall rest on mighty deeds.

*Count.* Living examples are the only guides;
A prince learns not his lesson from a book.
What, after all, avails your length of years
When all can scarcely match one day of mine?
Valiant you have been; I am valiant now!
On my strong arm this kingdom rests secure;
When my sword flashes, Aragon retreats,
Granada trembles; by my mighty name
Castile is girded round as by a wall.
Without me you would serve an alien law,
And find your enemies become your kings.
Each day, each flying hour exalts my fame,
Adds victory unto victory, praise to praise.
Under the guarding shadow of my arm
The prince would prove his mettle on the field,
Learn from the sight of conquest how to conquer,
And quickly reach the heights; with me he'd see—

*Diegue.* I know, you serve the king, your master, well;
You have done battle under my command,
And since the stiffening currents of old age
Have chilled my strength, your valor fills my place—
Enough, what I have been, you are today.
And yet when there is reason for a choice
The king still marks some difference between us.

    *Count.* That which was mine by right, you've stolen from me.

    *Diegue.* He who defeats you has the greater merit.

    *Count.* Who best can use an honor most deserves it.

    *Diegue.* To be refused is not good proof of merit.

    *Count.* You've won by trickery, being an old courtier.

    *Diegue.* My high renown was my sole partisan.

    *Count.* Say rather, the king honors your old age.

    *Diegue.* If so, the king has measured age by deeds.

    *Count.* If deeds are years, I am by much your elder.

    *Diegue.* Who failed to get this honor was not worthy.

    *Count.* I unworthy? I?

    *Diegue.*             Yes, you!

    *Count.*                    Old man,
Your insolence shall have its due reward

               *(Gives him a blow)*

    *Diegue.* (*drawing his sword*)
Come finish this affront and take my life,
First of my house to wear the blush of shame.

    *Count.* What do you mean to do, weak as you are?

                  *(Disarms him)*

    *Diegue.* O God! my withered strength fails me at need.

    *Count.* Your sword is mine, but you would be too vain
If I should take this trophy of your fall.
Adieu, go read the prince, in spite of sneers,

The history of your life for his instruction.
This chastisement of insolence will serve
To furnish it with no small ornament.
     (*Exit Count*)


## SCENE IV. *Don Diegue*

 *Diegue.* Rage and despair! O villainous old age!
Have I lived so long to suffer this disgrace?
Shall laurels gained with slowly whitening locks
In years of warlike toils fade in a day?
And does the arm all Spain has wondered at,
Whose might has often saved the king his throne,
And kept the rod of empire in his grasp,
Betray me now and leave me unavenged?
O sad remembrance of my vanished glory!
O years of life, undone in one short hour!
New honor, fatal to my happiness!
New eminence, from which my honor falls!
Must the Count's triumph add the final pang,
To die without revenge, or live in shame?
The office, Count, is yours, yours the high place
Of tutor to my prince, that dignity
Demands a man of honor and your hand,
In spite of the king has rendered me unworthy.
And you, brave instrument of my exploits,
But useless ornament of feeble age,
Sword, once so feared, which now in this affront
Served only to parade my impotence—
Go, quit henceforth the least of mortal men,
Pass to avenge me into worthier hands.

### SCENE V. *Don Diegue and Roderick*

*Diegue.* Roderick, have you courage?

*Roderick.*                                        Any man
Except my father soon should learn I have.

*Diegue.* O welcome fire! wrath that soothes my hurt!
In this swift anger speaks my own young blood,
And youth revives in me. Go, go, my son!
Go, scion of my house, repair my wrong!
Go and avenge me.

*Roderick.*          Avenge you, sir? For what?

*Diegue.* For an affront so cruel as to deal
A fatal thrust to the honor of our house.
A blow! His insolence had cost his life
Save that my nerveless arm betrayed my will.
This sword, which I can never wield again,
I pass to you for vengeance unto death.
Against this arrogance set up your courage;
Only in blood can such a stain be cleansed.
Kill or be killed! But to deal fairly with you,
This enemy is worthy of your steel;
Begrimed with blood and dust, I've seen him hold
A terror-stricken army at his will,
And break a hundred squadrons by his charge;
And, to say all, more than a brave commander,
More than a valiant warrior, he is—

*Roderick.* In mercy speak!

*Diegue.*                              The father of Chimene!

*Roderick.* Chimene!

*Diegue.*                    Nay, answer not, I know your love;
But who can live disgraced, deserves not life.
Is the offender dear? Then worse the offense.
You know my wrong; its quittance lies with you;

I say no more; avenge yourself and me!
Remember who your father is—and was!
Weighed down with fate's misfortunes heaped upon **me**
I go to mourn them. Speed, you, to my vengeance.

## Scene VI. *Roderick*

NOTE: This scene is in lyrical stanzas. Translation by
Florence Kendrick Cooper.

*Roderick*. My heart's o'erwhelmed with woe.
A mortal stroke that mocks my tender trust
Makes me avenger of a quarrel just,
  And wretched victim of an unjust blow.
Though crushed in spirit, still my pride must **cope**
With that which slays my hope.
So near to love's fruition to be told—
  O God, the strange, strange pain!—
My father has received an insult bold,
  The offender is the father of Chimene.

  'Mid conflicts wild I stand.
I lift my arm to strike my father's foe,
But Love with mighty impulse urges "No!"
  Pride fires my heart, affection stays my **hand;**
I must be deaf to Passion's calls, or face
A life of deep disgrace.
Whate'er I do, fierce anguish follows me—
  O God, the strange, strange pain!
Can an affront so base unpunished be?
  But can I fight the father of Chimene?

  To which allegiance give?—
To tender tyranny or noble bond?—
A tarnished name or loss of pleasures fond?
  Unworthy or unhappy must I live.

[*To his sword.*] Thou dear, stern hope of souls **high-born**
    and bold
And fired with love untold,
But enemy of my new dreams of bliss,
    Sword, cause of all my pain,
Was 't given me to use for this, for this?—
    To save my honor, but to lose Chimene?

    I must seek death's dread bourne.
To weigh my duty and my love is vain.
If I avenge his death, her hate I gain,
    If I no vengeance take, I win her scorn;
Unfaithful must I prove to hope most sweet,
Or for that hope unmeet.
What heals my honor's wounds augments **my grief,**
    And causes keener pain;
Be strong, my soul! Since death's my sole relief,
    I'll die, nor lose the love of my Chimene.

    What, die without redress?
Seek death—so fatal to my future fame?
Endure that Spain shall heap on me the shame
    Of one who failed in honor's sorest stress?
All for a love whose hope my frenzied heart
Already sees depart?
I'll list no longer to the subtle plea
    Which but renews my pain;
Come, arm of mine, my choice turns now to thee,
    Since naught, alas! can give me back Chimene.

    Yes, love my will misled.
My father—life and name to him I owe—
Whether of grief or from a mortal blow
    I die, my blood all pure and true I'll shed.

Too long I've dallied with a purpose weak;
Now vengeance swift I seek.
The flush of shame mounts hotly to my brow,
    That I can deem it pain
To save my father's house. I haste e'en now
    To seek—woe's me!—the father of Chimene.
              *(Exit Roderick)*


## ACT II

### Scene I. *The Count and Arias*

*Count.* I grant you that my somewhat hasty **blood**
Took fire too soon and carried me too far;
But what is done is done: the blow was struck.

*Arias.* Let your proud spirit yield to royal will.
The king is deeply moved; his anger roused
Will make you suffer penalties extreme.
You have no just defense to plead before him;
The deed was gross, the aged victim great;
No common rule that serves 'twixt man and man
Will meet the high demand exacted here.

*Count.* The king can use my life as suits his will.

*Arias.* You add the fault of anger to your deed.
The king still loves you well; appease his wrath;
You know his will, you will not disobey?

*Count.* To disobey—a little—were no crime,
Should it preserve the fame that I most prize.
But even were it such, my valiant service
Were more than cause for overlooking it.

*Arias.* For deeds, however high and glorious,
A king can never be a subject's debtor.
Better than any other, you should know

Who serves his king well, does his simple duty.
This haughty confidence will cost you dear.

  *Count.* I will believe you when I pay the price.

  *Arias.* You owe your monarch's will more reverence.

  *Count.* I can outlive a single day's displeasure.
Let the whole state be armed to hurl me down—
If I be made to suffer, Spain will fall.

  *Arias.* Have you so little fear for sovereign power?

  *Count.* Why should I fear a sceptred hand whose grasp
Is weaker than my own? He knows my use;
My head, in falling, will shake off his crown.

  *Arias.* Let reason rule your action; be advised.

  *Count.* I wish no further counsel; all is said.

  *Arias.* What shall I tell him then? I must report.

  *Count.* That I cannot consent to my disgrace.

  *Arias.* Remember that you brave a tyrant's power.

  *Count.* The die is cast, I'll speak no more about it.

  *Arias.* Adieu, then, since I cannot change your will.
Even on your laureled head the bolt may strike.

  *Count.* I wait it without fear.

  *Arias.*                              But not without disaster.

  *Count.* Then old Diegue will be well satisfied.
Who fears not death need surely not fear threats.
I have a heart to bear the worst disgrace;
Reduced to poverty, I yet can live;
Life without honor I could not endure.

### Scene II. *Roderick and the Count*

  *Roderick.* Grant me a word, Count.

  *Count.*                              Speak.

  *Roderick.*                                      Resolve my doubt:
Do you know Don Diegue?

  *Count.*                    I do.

*Roderick.*　　　　　　　　Speak low,
And listen. Do you know that this old man
Was once the heart and glory of his time?

*Count.* Perhaps.

*Roderick.*　　　And do you know the fire in my eyes
Is his own blood?

*Count.*　　　Well, what of that?

*Roderick.* Four paces off I'll teach you what of that.

*Count.* Presumptuous youngster!

*Roderick.*　　　　　　　Speak more quietly.
True, I am young, but in a well-born soul
Valor waits not upon advancing years.

*Count.* Young upstart, would you measure swords with
　　me?
You, who were never seen to wield a sword?

*Roderick.* I am not one that needs a second proof;
My very trial blows are master-strokes.

*Count.* Know you to whom you speak?

*Roderick.*　　　　　　　I do. Another
Might tremble at the mention of your name;
The palms which crown your head would seem to spell
The sentence of my doom, but I attack
Boldly against your ever-conquering arms.
Where courage leads, power is bound to follow.
A father's honor is a triple shield;
Unconquered yet, you are not invincible.

*Count.* Your fearless words reveal a fearless heart.
I've watched your growing powers from day to day;
And seeing in you the glory of Castile,
With pride I marked you for my daughter's hand.
I know your love, and I am charmed to see
That duty is a dearer mistress still,
And love cannot reduce your warlike zeal.

Your noble spirit wins my high esteem;
And proves that I was not deceived when I,
Seeking a perfect knight for son, chose you.
But pity stirs within me at your words;
I admire your courage, and lament your youth.
Let not your maiden effort be your last;
I cannot fight a combat so unequal;
No glory could be mine from such a triumph;
No honor comes of victory without risk.
None would believe you could have stood against me,
And nothing but regret would fall to me.

   *Roderick.* Insulting pity follows scorn! Who dares
Destroy my honor, fears to take my life!

   *Count.* Withdraw.

   *Roderick.*           Let us go on with no more words.

   *Count.* Are you so tired of life?

   *Roderick.*               Do you fear death?

   *Count.* Come! you do your duty. He would be
A base son who survives his father's honor.

### Scene III. *Infanta and Chimene*

   *Infanta.* Nay, do not weep! Be comforted, Chimene.
This sorrow should disclose your spirit's strength.
After this transient storm a calm will fall,
And happiness, deferred and clouded now,
Will be the brighter for it. Do not weep.

   *Chimene.* My heart, worn out with trouble, dares not hope.
A storm so sudden and so terrible,
Brings to so poor a bark the threat of wreck;
Ere I set sail, I perish in the harbor.
I loved; I was beloved; and both our fathers
Approved our loves, but even while I told
My charming tale, they fell to quarreling

And changed my story to a tale of woe,
O cursèd wrath, detestable ambition,
Twin tyrants even of the greatest souls!
Pride, pitiless to all my dearest wishes,
You cost me heavily in sighs and tears.

*Infanta.* You need not fear this hasty wrath of theirs;
Born in a moment, it will vanish so.
The king already seeks to make a peace;
And I, you know, would try the impossible
To dry your tears and heal your suffering.

*Chimene.* Nothing can reconcile them now. Such wounds
Are mortal, and admit no reparation.
Prudence pleads and power commands in vain;
If peace be gained 'tis only outwardly.
The fires of hate, compressed within the heart,
Burn fiercer and will break at last in flame.

*Infanta.* When love has bound Chimene and Roderick
In sacred marriage, hatred will depart;
Your fathers will forget, and happiness
Will silence discord in sweet harmony.

*Chimene.* I long for such an end, but dare not hope.
Diegue is haughty; and I know my father.
I would hold back these tears, but I must weep;
The past is torture, and the future, fear.

*Infanta.* What do you fear? An old man's feebleness?
*Chimene.* Roderick is brave.
*Infanta.*                    He is too young.
*Chimene.* Brave men are heroes in their maiden blow
*Infanta.* You should not fear his boldness overmuch;
He cannot wound you whom he loves so well;
Two words from your sweet lips will check his wrath.

*Chimene.* How shall I speak them? If he do not yield,
'Tis but an added burden to my heart;

And if he yield, what will men say of him—
His father's son to suffer such affront!
I stand confused, uncertain which to choose;
His too weak love, or his too stern refusal.

  *Infanta.* In such a noble soul as yours, Chimene,
No thought unworthy can find room to dwell.
But if, until this trouble be resolved,
I make a prisoner of this gallant youth,
Preventing thus the dread results you fear,
Would it offend your proud and loving heart?

  *Chimene.* Ah, madam, then my cares are quieted.

### Scene IV. *Infanta, Chimene, Page*

  *Infanta.* Page, summon Roderick hither; I would see him.
  *Page.* He and the Count de Gormaz—
  *Chimene.*                              Dear God, I tremble!
  *Infanta.* Speak!
  *Page.*              Together they have left the palace.
  *Chimene.* Alone?
  *Page.*              Alone; and muttering angrily.
  *Chimene.* They have come to blows! All words are useless
    now;
Madam, forgive my haste—my heart is breaking.

### Scene V. *Infanta and Leonora*

  *Infanta.* Alas, that such inquietude is mine!
I weep for her, but Roderick holds my heart.
My peace is gone, the flames of love revive!
The fate that parts Chimene from him she loves
Renews alike my sorrow and my hope.
Their separation, cruel though it be,
Stirs in my heart a secret ecstasy.

*Leonora.* Surely the noble virtue of your soul
Yields not so soon to passion's baser power.

*Infanta.* Nay, do not call it base, since in my heart
Strong and triumphant, it controls my will.
Honor my love, for it is dear to me.
My nobler pride forbids it—yet I hope.
My heart without defense against my folly
Flies to a lover that Chimene has lost.

*Leonora.* Is thus your high resolve made impotent?
Does reason lay her wonted sceptre down?

*Infanta.* How weak in such a strait is reason's power!
When such sweet poison has inflamed the heart,
The patient loves his painful malady,
And takes unwillingly the healing draught.

*Leonora.* Be not beguiled by love's sweet wiles. We all
Know well how far beneath you Roderick stands.

*Infanta.* Too well, myself, I know it, but my heart
Is subject to the flattery of love.
If from this combat Roderick comes the victor,
And this great warrior falls beneath his blow,
What other plea will love have need of? Who
Could stand against the conqueror of the Count?
My fancy sets no bounds to his exploits;
Whole kingdoms soon would fall beneath his sway;
I see him on Granada's ancient throne;
Trembling, the subject Moors obey his will;
Proud Aragon acknowledges him king;
And Portugal receives him, while the seas
Bear his high destiny to other lands.
In Afric's blood his laurels shall be dyed,
And all that's said of the greatest conquerors
I hear of Roderick, this victory won.
Then in his love my highest glory lies.

*Leonora.* Nay, madam, 'tis your fancy makes you dream
Of conquests that may never be begun.

*Infanta.* Roderick's offended—the Count has given the af‹
front—
They have gone forth together—needs there more?

*Leonora.* Even should they fight—since you will have it
so—
Will Roderick prove the knight you picture him?

*Infanta.* Nay, I am weak; my foolish mind runs wild;
Love spreads its snares for victims such as I.
Come to my chamber, and console me there.

### SCENE VI. *King, Arias, Sancho*

*King.* Pray, is this haughty Count bereft of sense?
Dares he believe his crime is pardonable?

*Arias.* I have conveyed to him your strong desire;
And nothing gained from long and earnest pleas.

*King.* Great heaven! Have I a subject in my realm
So rash that he will disregard my wish?
He gives affront to Don Diegue, insults
His king, and in my court gives law to me.
Warrior and chief, however great he be,
I know a way to school his haughty pride.
Were he the god of battles, valor's self,
He yet shall pay obedience to his sovereign.
Though he deserved the insolence he showed,
It was my will to grant him leniency.
Since he abuses mercy, from this hour
He is my prisoner, all resistance vain.

(*Enter Alonzo*)

*Sancho.* Perhaps a brief delay will calm his mind.
Fresh from the quarrel, he was first approached,
Boiling with passion. Sire, a soul like his,

So hasty and so bold, belies itself
In its first impulse. He will see his fault,
But cannot yet admit himself the offender.

*King.* Be silent, Sancho, and be warned henceforth.
He who defends the guilty shares the guilt.

*Sancho.* Sire, I am silent. But grant me yet the grace
To say one further word in his defense.

*King.* What can you say for such a reckless man?

*Sancho.* A soul accustomed to great deeds cannot
Abase itself so far as to submit:
He cannot think of it without disgrace,
And that word only has the Count resisted.
He feels his duty something too much forced;
He would obey you were his spirit less.
Command his arm, bred among war's alarms,
To right this wrong upon the field of honor;
He will give satisfaction, Sire, and I,
Let come who will, till then, will answer for him.

*King.* You fail in due respect; but you are young,
And I forgive the zeal of youthful courage.
A king whose prudence shows him higher objects
Must be more careful of his subjects' blood.
I shepherd mine; my care preserves their lives,
As the head preserves the limbs which do it service.
Your right, therefore, cannot be right for me;
You speak as soldier, I must act as king.
Whatever he says, whatever he dares believe,
Obeying me, the Count forsakes not honor.
Besides, this insult touches me, he stained
The honor of him I made my son's instructor:
To assail my choice is to cast blame on me,
And aim attack at sovereign power itself.
Speak no more. Ten vessels have been sighted

Flying the flags of our old enemy;
They dared appear in the very river's mouth.

*Arias.* The Moors have learned perforce to know you well;
So often conquered, they have no more heart
To risk themselves against so great a chief.

*King.* Never will they see without some jealousy
My sceptre rule in Andalusia;
This lovely land which they too long possessed
They look on always with an envious eye.
That was the only reason why I placed
Castile's throne years ago here in Seville,
That I might be more ready and more promptly
Resist whatever they might undertake.

*Arias.* At the cost of many mighty chiefs they know
How victory is assured us by your presence.
You can have naught to fear.

*King.*                              Nor to neglect.
Danger breeds best on too much confidence;
And you must know with what an easy sweep
A rising tide may bear them to our walls.
Still, I should be at fault did I disturb
The people's hearts with terror at a rumor.
The useless fear caused by a false alarm
Would trouble the whole city through the night.
A double guard upon the walls and port
Will be enough.

### SCENE VII. *King and Alonzo*

*Alonzo.* Sire, the Count is dead.
Diegue has taken vengeance through his son.

*King.* As soon as I had heard of this affront
I feared revenge, and hoped I might prevent it.

*Alonzo.* Chimene approaches, bathed in bitter tears,

And at your royal feet would plead for justice.
  *King.* Much as my heart is moved to pity her,
The Count's offense appears to have deserved
This punishment of his audacity.
And yet, however just may be his fate,
I must regret the loss of such a leader.
After so long a service to my state,
His blood a thousand times poured out for me,
Although his pride excites my wrath, his death
Bereaves me and enfeebles my position.

SCENE VIII. *King, Chimene, Diegue*

  *Chimene.* Justice, Sire!
  *Diegue.*                    Ah, Sire, let me speak!
  *Chimene.* Behold me at your feet.
  *Diegue.*                            I clasp your knees.
  *Chimene.* I cry for justice, Sire.
  *Diegue.*                            Hear my defense.
  *Chimene.* Punish the insolence of this reckless youth;
He has struck down your sceptre's chief support.
He has killed my father.
  *Diegue.*                    He avenged his own.
  *Chimene.* A king owes justice to his subjects' blood.
  *Diegue.* Just vengeance does not call for punishment.
  *King.* Rise, both of you and speak of this more calmly.
Chimene, I share your sorrow, and I feel
Deep in my heart an equal grief. You sir,
Speak later. Do not interrupt her plea.
  *Chimene.* My father, Sire, is dead; my eyes have seen
His blood in great drops flowing from his side,
That blood which has so often saved your walls,
That blood which won so many a battle for you,
That blood, still smoking with the heat of rage,

I saw poured out for other lives than yours.
Unshed amid the thousand risks of war,
Roderick spilled it in your very court.
All weak and pale I hastened to the spot;
I found him lifeless. Pardon, Sire, my grief;
My voice will not recount this tale of death,
The rest is better told with sighs and tears.

    *King.* Take courage, child, and be assured, today
Your king would serve you in a father's stead.

    *Chimene.* My grief is too much honored. Sire, I told you
I found him lifeless; and to move me more
The blood that issued from his mangled side
Wrote out my duty for me in the dust;
His valor, brought to such a low estate,
Cried out to me and drove me here to you,
That through my voice that dreadful gaping mouth
Might plead its cause to the most just of kings.
Permit not, Sire, such outrage to be done
Under your sway, before your very eyes;
Permit not that the noblest be exposed
So freely to the blows of insolence;
That one rash youth may triumph o'er their glory,
Bathe in their blood and mock their memory.
So brave a warrior, slain and unavenged,
Must cool the ardor of the rest who serve you.
My father, Sire, is dead; I plead for vengeance
More for your sake than for my own relief.
Your loss is great when such a man is killed;
Revenge him with another, blood for blood:
A victim, not for me, but for your crown,
Your person, and your majesty; a victim
I beg of you to show to all the state
The madness of a deed so arrogant.

*King.* Answer her, Don Diegue.

*Diegue.*                            He should be envied

Who when his strength is spent lays down his life.

Old age reserves a melancholy fate

For noble souls before their life is done.

I, who have won such glory by my deeds,

I, whom victory has so often followed,

I see myself today too long alive,

Insulted, vanquished, and doomed still to live.

What never combat, siege, nor ambuscade,

Granada never, never Aragon,

Not all your enemies, nor all my rivals

Could do, the Count has done in jealous rage

Within your court, almost before your eyes,

Against your choice, and proud of the advantage

My age and feebleness bestowed on him.

Sire, thus these hairs grown white beneath the helmet,

This blood so many times poured out to serve you,

These arms, before, the terror of your foes,

Had gone to the grave borne down with infamy,

Had not my son proved worthy of his father,

Worthy of his country, worthy of his king.

He lent his hand to me; he killed the Count;

He gave me back my honor, cleansed my shame.

If to show courage and resentment, if

To avenge a blow deserves some punishment,

On me alone the tempest ought to fall:

When the arm has failed, one punishes the head.

Whether or not his action be a crime,

I am the head, and he is but the arm.

Chimene laments that he has killed her father,

The chance had ne'er been his could I have done it.

Then sacrifice this head which years have bowed,

And spare the arm with power to serve your throne.
Let my blood flow to satisfy Chimene:
I offer no resistance, suffer gladly,
And far from murmuring at your stern decree,
Dying with honor, die without regret.

    *King.* Of deep and serious import is this deed,
And in full council to be gravely met.
Don Sancho, lead Chimene back to her home.
You, Don Diegue, shall have my court for prison,
Held by your word of honor. Go, someone,
And bring his son to me. I shall do justice.

    *Chimene.* Justice, great king, demands a murderer die.

    *King.* Go, take some rest, my child, and calm yourself.

    *Chimene.* The thought of rest can but increase my pain.


# ACT III

## Scene I. *Elvire and Roderick*

    *Elvire.* Roderick, what have you done? Why come you here?

    *Roderick.* I run the course of my sad destiny.

    *Elvire.* Whence springs this new audacity, this pride,
Which brings you to the spot you fill with mourning?
Have you come to brave the spirit of the Count?
Did you not kill him?

    *Roderick.*        His life was my disgrace.
My honor bade my hand commit the deed.

    *Elvire.* But to seek refuge in the dead man's house?
What murderer ever found asylum there?

    *Roderick.* I came to place myself before my judge.
Look not on me with such astonishment;
I, who have killed, come here to plead for death.

My judge is my belovèd, my Chimene;
I merit death in meriting her hate,
And, like a welcome favor, I would take
My sentence from her lips, death from her hand.

*Elvire.* Oh, rather flee her eyes, flee from her passion;
Save her the anguish of your presence now,
And do not bare yourself to that wild madness
Which the first rage of grief has stirred within her.

*Roderick.* No, no, this dear heart which I brought to sorrow,
Cannot feel too much anger at my deed,
And could i double it to speed my death,
I should escape a hundred deaths to come.

*Elvire.* Chimene is at the palace bathed in tears,
And she will not return without an escort.
Flee, Roderick, flee, relieve me of my fear.
What will be said if they should find you here?
Would you have slander add to her distress,
Saying she gave her father's murderer refuge?
Soon she will be here—she comes—I see her—
For her honor's sake, at least conceal yourself.

## Scene II. *Sancho and Chimene*

*Sancho.* Yes, you deserve a sacrifice of blood.
Your wrath is just; your tears have cause to flow.
And I would not attempt by force of words
To soften one or to console the other.
But if in any way I can assist you,
Command my sword to punish this assassin;
Command my love to avenge your father's death:
I shall have double strength in serving you.

*Chimene.* Unhappy me!

*Sancho.*                     I pray, accept my service.

*Chimene.* I should offend the king who promised justice

*Sancho.* You know with what a languid step she moves
How often guilt escapes her tardy hand.
Her slow and doubtful course costs many tears.
Permit a knight to avenge you with his sword;
That is a surer path to punishment.

*Chimene.* That is the last resort; if it must come,
And if your pity for me still is strong,
You shall be free to avenge my injury.

*Sancho.* This is the only happiness I ask;
If I may hope for it, I go content.

### Scene III. *Chimene, Elvire*

*Chimene.* At last I am free, at last I may give way,
And let you see the sharpness of my grief;
At last, now, I can give my sad sighs breath,
Open my heart and tell you my distress.
My father is dead, Elvire, and the first sword
Which Roderick ever wielded cut him down.
Weep, weep, my eyes, and drown yourselves in tears!
One half my life has done to death the other,
And by this blow has made me cry for vengeance
For what is gone on what remains to me.

*Elvire.* Be calmer, madam.

*Chimene.*               This is not the time,
In the midst of grief like mine, to speak of calm.
How shall my sorrow ever be appeased
If I may not hate the hand that called it forth?
What may I hope for but eternal torture,
Who punish crime, yet love the criminal?

*Elvire.* He killed your father, and you love him still!

*Chimene.* Love is a word too feeble, I adore him.
My passion wars against my just resentment;

I find my lover in my enemy,
And Roderick, in spite of all my anger,
Does battle with my father in my heart,
Attacks him, drives him, yields, defends himself,
Now strong, now weak, and now at last triumphant:
But in this combat between love and anger,
He wins my heart, but cannot share my soul;
And though my love has power over me,
I do not hesitate to follow duty.
I go unwaveringly where honor leads.
Roderick is dear to me, I mourn his fate:
My heart defends him, but my spirit knows
I am a daughter, and my father's dead.

    *Elvire.* And you will hunt him down?
    *Chimene.*                      Ah, cruel thought!
Ah, cruel chase to which I am compelled!
I seek his death, yet fear to have my wish;
My death will follow his, for which I sue.
    *Elvire.* Stop, madam, stop these dark imaginings;
Lay not upon yourself so harsh a law.
    *Chimene.* My father dead and almost in my arms,
Shall I not hear his blood cry out for vengeance?
And shall my heart, deceived by shameful charms,
Believe my duty paid with futile tears?
Could I be bought by love, however great,
To stifle honor under shameful silence?
    *Elvire.* Madam, believe me, it were pardonable
To hate less hotly one so lovable,
So dear a lover: You have done enough,
You have seen the king, press not your purpose further,
Be not so adamant in this strange humor.
    *Chimene.* Honor demands that I pursue my vengeance;

However love deceive us with desire,
Excuse is shameful to a noble soul.

    *Elvire.* Roderick cannot cause you pain. You love him.
    *Chimene.* I do.
    *Elvire.*          Then, after all, what is your purpose?
    *Chimene.* To save my honor, and end this weariness;
Pursue him, kill him, and die after him.

### Scene IV. *Roderick, Chimene, Elvire*

    *Roderick.* You need not take the trouble of pursuit
To satisfy your honor with my life.
    *Chimene.* Elvire, where are you, who is this I see?
Roderick in my house! before my eyes!
    *Roderick.* Spare not my blood; without resistance taste
The sweetness of my death and your revenge.
    *Chimene.* Ah me!
    *Roderick.*         Hear me, I beg.
    *Chimene.*                 Go! Go!
    *Roderick.*                   One moment.
    *Chimene.* Go, let me die.
    *Roderick.*            Permit me but a word.
Then let me have your answer with this sword.
    *Chimene.* This sword, still stainèd with my father's blood!
    *Roderick.* Chimene...
    *Chimene.*           Oh, take away the hateful thing
That speaks your crime and taunts me with your life.
    *Roderick.* Look on it, then, that you may hate me more;
Inflame your anger, and so speed my doom.
    *Chimene.* 'Tis soiled with my own blood.
    *Roderick.*               Plunge it in mine,
And thereby cleanse it of the stain of yours.
    *Chimene.* A cruel sword whose blade can kill a father
And slay his daughter by its very sight.

Take it away. I may not look on it.
You bid me listen, and you strike me dead.

   *Roderick*. I do your will, yet cherish still the wish
Of ending at your hands my wretched life;
Do not expect that love will stir in me
A base repentance for a worthy deed.
The fatal issue of too swift a wrath
Disgraced my father and brought shame to me.
You know how a man of courage takes a blow:
I shared the affront, and I sought out the author;
I found him, and upon his head avenged
My father and my honor; I should do it
All again, were all again to do.
And yet against my father and myself
My love for you long battled with my duty.
Judge of its power, when I could hesitate
To take revenge for such a bold affront.
Bound to bring you grief or suffer insult,
I thought perhaps my arm had been too swift,
Accused myself of too much violence;
Your beauty might have turned the balance still,
But for the thought, stronger than all your charms,
That without honor, no man could deserve you;
That spite of all the love you bear for me,
Who loves me noble, would despise me base;
And that to yield, to hear the voice of love,
Would render me unworthy of your choice.
Again I say, though not without a sigh,
And with my latest breath would I repeat:
I did you wrong, but had I not erased
This insult, I had proved unworthy of you;
Now, honor and my father satisfied,
I come to you to pay my final debt.

You see me here to offer you my life.
Half my duty done, I do the rest.
I know your father's death makes you my foe;
I have no wish to rob you of your victim.
Shrink not from offering up the blood of him
Who glories in the shedding of your father's.

    *Chimene.* Ah, Roderick, 'tis true, although your foe,
I cannot blame you that you shunned disgrace;
And, somehow, even in my sorrow, I
Do not accuse you, but bemoan my woe.
I know that after such an insult, honor
Demands revenge from any noble heart.
You did your duty as a man of spirit,
But, doing so, alas, you showed me mine.
I saw how by its victory your valor
Avenged your father and sustained your honor.
The same care falls to me, I have my honor
To be sustained, my father to revenge.
Alas, your part in this drives me to madness;
My father dead by any other cause,
My heart had taken in the sight of you
The only comfort which it could have found.
In grief I still had felt your sympathy,
When your dear hand had wiped away my tears.
But now in losing him, I lose you too;
Honor demands this victory o'er my love,
And dreadful duty, like a murderer,
Drives me to work your ruin and my own.
For do not hope that my affectionate heart
Will weaken in its will to punish you.
Although our love incline me in your favor,
Nobility in me must equal yours.
As by your very crime you showed yourself

Worthy of me, I could not show myself
Worthy of you unless I sought your death.
  *Roderick.* Delay no longer what your honor bids you;
It asks my head, I offer it to you;
Make it a sacrifice to your revenge;
The sentence and the death-stroke will be sweet.
After my crime to wait upon slow justice
Removes the glory from my punishment.
I shall die happy, dying by your hand.
  *Chimene.* Go! I am not your executioner.
I am your foe. You offer me your life.
I cannot take it as a gift from you.
I should attack you, you defend yourself;
Some other hand than mine must take your life.
My part is to pursue you, not to punish.
  *Roderick.* However our love persuades you in my favor
Your spirit must be equal to my own.
It is not meet, my dear Chimene, that you
Avenge your father by some borrowed arm:
My hand alone avenged my father's shame,
And only yours should take revenge on me.
  *Chimene.* Ah, cruel. Why so stubborn on this point?
You are avenged without my aid, and yet
You wish to give me yours. No. I shall follow
Your example; I have too much courage
To let you share in what will be my glory.
My father and my honor would owe nothing
Either to your love or to your wretchedness.
  *Roderick.* O stubborn rule of honor! Can I not
Obtain this final mercy? In the name
Of your dead father, of our mutual love
Either in pity or in vengeance, kill me.

Your wretched lover will be less unhappy
In dying so than living in your hate.

   *Chimene.* Leave me. I do not hate you.
   *Roderick.*                         'Tis your duty.
   *Chimene.* I cannot.
   *Roderick.*             Have you then so little fear
Of blame and slander? When my deed is known,
And known that even still your love endures,
What will not malice and false rumor say?
O keep them silent, and with no more words,
Save your good name by putting me to death.

   *Chimene.* It will shine brighter that I let you live,
And blackest slander's voice, I hope, will raise
My fame to heaven and lament my woes,
Knowing I love you and pursue you still.
Go, drive me not to grief's extremity,
That I must kill him whom I so adore.
Shroud your departure in the dark of night.
If you are seen my honor is destroyed.
'Tis scandal's only chance to stain my name
If it be known that I have seen you here:
Go—give it not this reason to attack me.

   *Roderick.* O let me die.
   *Chimene.*              Go! Go!
   *Roderick.*                    What will you do?
   *Chimene.* Although the furies of love disturb my wrath,
My father's vengeance calls for all my zeal.
Yet though I go to serve so cruel a duty
My only hope is—nothing to achieve.

   *Roderick.* O miracle of love!
   *Chimene.*                 O weight of woe!
   *Roderick.* What sufferings and tears our fathers cost us!
   *Chimene.* Roderick, who had thought—

*Roderick.*                                    Who would have
   dreamed—

*Chimene.* That joy so near us should so soon be lost?

*Roderick.* Or that, so near to port, against all signs,
So swift a storm would wreck our every hope?

*Chimene.* Ah, mortal grief!

*Roderick.*                               Oh, useless, vain regrets.

*Chimene.* Go. Go. I beg you. I shall hear no more.

*Roderick.* Adieu. I go to drag a dying life
Till by your own hand it is taken from me.

*Chimene.* If I succeed, I pledge my faith that I
Will never breathe a moment after you.
Adieu, and go that none may see you leave.

                    (*Roderick exit*)

*Elvire.* Madam, whatever evils heaven send you—

*Chimene.* Trouble me not, pray, leave me with my grief.
I long for night and silence for my tears.

### SCENE V. *Diegue, Roderick*

*Diegue.* We never taste a perfect happiness:
Our best successes all are mixed with sorrow;
With all achievements come some heavy cares
To mar the purity of our delight.
In the midst of happiness my heart is troubled;
My joy o'erflows and yet I quake with fear.
I see him dead whose hand insulted me;
I may not see the hand that has avenged me.
Broken as I am, I wander through the city:
The little vigor which old age has left me,
Consumes itself in futile search for him.
Each moment everywhere in this sad night
I think I see him, and embrace a shadow.
Till love, deceived so often by his ghost,

Conceives suspicions which increase my fear.
I cannot find the traces of his flight.
I fear the dead Count's friends and followers;
Their number terrifies and stuns my mind.
If Roderick be alive, he lives in prison.

(*Enter Roderick*)

Just Heaven, is this another apparition,
Or do I see at last my only hope?
'Tis he, my son; my vows are heard, my fears
Are dissipated and my longings over.

 At last, my Roderick, Heaven has restored you!
 *Roderick.* Alas.
 *Diegue.*    Mar not with sighs my new delight.
Let me find words to praise you as I would,
My valor sees in you no cause to blush.
You are its worthy scion and your daring
Restores in you the heroes of my race:
Your ancestors they are, and you my son.
Your earliest sword-thrust equals all of mine.
Your youth, inspired by a noble ardor,
By this one effort equals my renown.
Prop of my age and crown of all my fortune,
Lay your redeeming hand on these white hairs.
Come kiss this cheek, where still you can behold
The mark of that affront which you avenged.

 *Roderick.* The honor is your due: I could no less.
Sprung from your blood and nourished by your care,
My heart rejoices that my sword's first stroke
Brought joy to him to whom I owe my life.
But be not angry with me if I dare
To take my satisfaction in my turn.
Let me at last give voice to my despair;
Which has too long been stifled by your words.

I feel no mean regret for having served you;
But give me back the joy this blow has cost me.
My arm for you was raised against my love
And by that stroke I lost my heart's desire.
Tell me no more; I have lost all for you;
That which I owed you, I have paid too well.

   *Diegue.* Nay, hold your victory more high than this.
I gave you life, you gave me back my glory.
As much as honor is more dear than life,
So much more now I owe you in return.
But drive this weakness from your noble heart,
We have one honor only. Mistresses
Are plentiful! Love is a pleasant toy,
But honor is a master to be served.

   *Roderick.* What do you tell me?

   *Diegue.*                  That which you should
   know.

   *Roderick.* My outraged honor turns upon myself:
And you dare press me to the shame of treason.
An equal infamy and shame pursues
The craven soldier and the faithless lover.
Wrong not my faith, I pray. Let me be noble
Without the blot of perjury: the bonds
Which hold me are too strong to be so snapped.
My faith is pledged, though I may hope no more.
And since I cannot leave nor win Chimene
The death I seek will be my sweetest pain.

   *Diegue.* This is no time for you to seek for death.
Your country and your king have need of you.
The enemy's fleet has entered the great river
To sack the country and surround the town.
The Moors have come upon us. At any moment
Night and the tide may bear them silently

Under our very walls. The court is shaken,
The people terrified; in every quarter
Rises the tumult of their fear. It chanced
That in this general crisis, happily
Five hundred friends who heard of my affront
Offered their service to avenge my quarrel.
Your zeal outsped them, but their valiant hands
Shall now be bathed in Moorish blood. Go take
The place which honor offers at their head.
This noble band calls you to be its chief.
Lead the assault on these old enemies:
And there, if you would die, die gloriously.
Embrace the chance since it is offered you,
To make your king owe safety to your death:
But rather come back crowned with victory.
Bound not your glory by a deed of vengeance:
Carry it farther. Let your bravery force
The King to pardon and Chimene to silence.
If you still love her, know that she will yield
Only if you return a conqueror.
But we waste time in words. I hold you here
When I would give you wings. Come follow me,
And show your king he has regained in you,
All that he lost when you struck down the Count.


## ACT IV

### SCENE I. *Chimene, Elvire*

*Chimene.* This news is true? You are sure of it, Elvire?
   *Elvire.* You would not credit how the people cheer him
And raise to heaven with a single voice
The praise of this young hero's glorious deeds.

Before his charge the Moors found only shame;
The attack was swift, the flight was swifter still;
Three hours of battle left our warriors
A glorious victory and two captured kings.
Nothing could stop the onset of our chief.

    *Chimene.* And Roderick's hand worked all these miracles!

    *Elvire.* Two captive kings bear witness to his deeds,
Conquered and captured by his hand alone.

    *Chimene.* What is the source of this strange news, Elvire?

    *Elvire.* The people, everywhere they sound his praises
As author and protector of their joy,
Their guardian angel and their liberator.

    *Chimene.* And the king? What thinks he of this victory?

    *Elvire.* Roderick dares not yet appear before him.
But Don Diegue, beside himself with joy,
In the Conqueror's name presents the crownèd kings
In captive chains and begs our noble prince
To grant his savior audience and pardon.

    *Chimene.* Is he not wounded?

    *Elvire.*                    That I have not heard.
Why, madam, you grow pale. Your cheek is blanched!

    *Chimene.* Let me revive again my weakening wrath.
Shall I forget myself in thoughts of him?
The people praise him, and my heart agrees!
Honor is mute and duty powerless!
Silence, my love, let me recall my anger:
Though he has captured kings, he killed my father.
These mournful weeds wherein I read my woe,
These are the first results of his new valor.
However others praise so great a heart,
Here everything recalls to me his crime.
You weeds which speak the power of my wrath,
Veil, crêpe, and garment, ornaments of mourning,

Sad pomp in which his earliest triumph wrapped me,
Against my passion keep my honor firm.
And when my love becomes too powerful
Tell to my heart my melancholy duty;
And bid me meet this hero without fear.

*Elvire.* Calm yourself, madam. See, the Infanta comes.

### SCENE II. *Chimene, Elvire, Infanta*

*Infanta.* I come not to console your sorrow, rather
I would my sighs might mingle with your tears.

*Chimene.* Share rather in the general rejoicing
And taste the happiness which Heaven has sent us.
I, I alone can claim the right to weep.
The danger Roderick has warded off,
The public safety which his arms have won,
Are cause for tears today to none but me.
He has saved the city, he has saved the king.
To me alone his valorous arm is deadly.

*Infanta.* 'Tis true, Chimene. He has worked miracles.

*Chimene.* Already the grievous news has reached my ears.
And I can hear him everywhere proclaimed,
Luckless in love as he is great in war.

*Infanta.* Why should this happy news be sad for you?
This youthful Mars they praise was once your joy.
He held your heart. He lived at your command,
And praise for him does honor to your choice.

*Chimene.* They all have cause to praise him, but for me
His glory is new torture, my distress
Grows only keener with his rising fame;
I see in it the hero I have lost.
Ah, cruel anguish of a lover's heart,
I love him more the more I see his worth;

While duty drives me ever firmly on
In spite of love to hunt him down to death.

 *Infanta.* But yesterday this duty did you honor
And in your will to follow it you seemed
So brave, so great of heart that all the court
Admired your courage and bemoaned your love.
But—would you have a faithful friend's advice?

 *Chimene.* I should be base indeed did I not hear you,

 *Infanta.* What yesterday was right, today is not.
Roderick has become our sole support,
The hope and love of an adoring people,
Castile's defense, and terror to the Moors.
The king himself agrees, that in this youth
Your father lives again. If, finally
I tell you in a word my thought, I say
You seek the public ruin in his death.
To avenge your father, is it right that you
Betray your country to its enemies?
Is vengeance against us a just pursuit?
What is our crime that you should punish us?
'Tis not that I would have you wed this man,
Made hateful to you by a father's death,
Nay, rather would I have you crush desire,
Rob him of love, but leave for us his life.

 *Chimene.* Such mercy is not in my power to grant:
My duty which I follow knows no bounds.
Although my love still pleads for him, although
The people worship and a king adores him,
Although the bravest warriors flock around him,
Still will my cypress overspread his laurels.

 *Infanta.* 'Tis noble that in vengeance for a father
We follow duty against one so dear;
But it is nobler still to sacrifice

A private injury to the public good.
'Twill be enough to quench the flame of love,
For him there is no greater punishment,
Believe me, than such exile from your heart.
Your country's weal makes this demand of you.
Besides, what can you hope for from the king?

*Chimene.* He may refuse, but I may not be silent.

*Infanta.* Think, my Chimene, think what you wish to do.
Adieu! Let solitude assist your choice.

*Chimene.* My father is dead. There is no choice for me.

SCENE III. *King, Diegue, Arias, Roderick, Sancho*

*King.* Great son is he of an illustrious family,
Always the strength and glory of Castile,
Son of so many valorous ancestors,
Whose feat at arms already equals theirs.
I have no power to give you just reward;
My strength is less than your deserts. Our country,
Delivered from so cruel an enemy,
My sceptre by your hand made firm in mine,
The Moors defeated ere my call to arms
Could raise the populace in my defense:
Such deeds as these leave to your king no means
Nor hope of paying you what you deserve.
Let these two captive kings of yours reward you:
Their Cid they both have named you in my presence,
And Cid in their tongue is the same as king:
I shall not envy you this sovereign title.
Henceforward be the Cid, to that great name
Let all do service, let Granada tremble,
And let Toledo quake on hearing it.
And let it be a sign to all who live
Beneath my sway how much I owe to you.

*Roderick.* Spare, Sire, my shame! Your majesty esteems
Too highly the poor service I have done.
And makes me blush before so great a king
Whose generous honor is so undeserved.
Too well I know how much I owe your empire,
The blood which gives me life, the air I breathe;
When in your service I shall lose both these,
I shall have only done a subject's duty.

   *King.* Not everyone whom duty binds to serve me
Acquits himself with such high bravery;
And when his courage is not superhuman
It cannot win to such a rare success.
Endure our praise, and with your own lips tell me
The true tale of our glorious victory.

   *Roderick.* Sire, you have learned that when this danger
     threatened,
Striking the city with a deadly fear,
A band of followers in my father's house
Besought my spirit still so wildly troubled—
Pardon, Sire, my boldness, that I dared
To lead them without your authority:
The danger threatened; they were armed for battle,
To show myself at court had risked my life,
And if it must be lost, I chose to die
Leading the charge against your enemies.

   *King.* I pardon you the fury of your vengeance.
The country saved speaks now in your defense:
Chimene, hereafter, pleads a cause forlorn,
And I shall listen but to comfort her.
Say on.

   *Roderick.* Under my head the band advanced
With stern defiance written on their brows.
Five hundred we set out, but quick recruits

Made us three thousand ere we reached the port,
So much the frightened populace took heart
Seeing with what courageous look we marched!
Two thirds I hid as soon as we arrived
In vessels lying at the river's mouth.
The rest, their number growing every hour,
And burning with impatience, stay with me;
Couched on the ground without the slightest noise,
They pass a good part of the night; the guard
At my command does likewise, and assists
My strategy by keeping under cover.
I let them think the orders which I give,
And which they see me follow, come from you.
At last upon the rising tide the pale,
Uncertain starlight shows us thirty sails;
And darkly riding on the ocean's swell,
The Moors sweep to the harbor with the sea.
We let them enter; all seems tranquil, still;
No soldiers at the port or on the walls—
Our silence leads them on. They cannot doubt
That they have taken the city by surprise.
Fearlessly they anchor and debark
And rush headlong into our waiting arms.
We spring from every ambush and at once
A thousand cries of battle rise to heaven.
Our shouts are answered from the ships, our fellows
Leap forth in arms; the Moors are paralyzed;
Terror-struck ere half of them have landed.
They know themselves for lost before the battle.
They came for pillage and encountered war.
We pressed them on the water and on land,
Before they could resist or form their ranks
Streams of their blood were flowing on our soil.

But soon their princes rally them; their courage
Is born again; their terror is forgotten.
The shame of dying without having fought
Stops their disorder and restores their heart.
Firmly they draw their scimitars against us,
And our blood mingles horribly with theirs.
Shore, river, fleet, and port are battle fields
Where death is victor. Oh, how many deeds,
How many exploits worthy of renown
Are wrought ingloriously within the shadows,
Where each, sole witness of what blows he deals,
Knows not upon which side the favor falls!
I rushed about encouraging our men,
Made some advance, and others reinforced,
Drew up the newcomers and urged them on,
And knew not who was victor until dawn.
But then the daylight shows our victory.
The Moors perceive their loss; their courage fails;
And seeing reinforcements come to aid us,
Their fear of death o'ercomes their zeal to war.
They gain their ships, cut cables, and their cries
Of terror fill the heavens; they retreat,
Broken and orderless, without a thought
Whether their kings can flee with them or not.
The flood tide bore them hither, on the ebb
They sailed away, while in the van their kings
And some few wounded warriors fight on
To sell their lives as dearly as they can.
Vainly I call upon them to surrender;
They hear me not; but seeing at their feet
Their soldiers lie and knowing that henceforth
They fight alone, they call for our commander;
I show myself; they yield, and both of them

I straightway send to you; the battle ended
For want of combatants. So in your service ...

SCENE IV. *King, Diegue, Roderick, Arias, Alonzo, Sancho*

*Alonzo.* Chimene approaches, Sire, to sue for justice.
*King.* Unhappy news, and most untimely duty!
Go, I would not force your sight on her.
To pay you fully I must send you hence.
But before going, let your king embrace you.
(*Exit Roderick*)
*Diegue.* Chimene would save him from her own pursuit.
*King.* They say she loves him still, and I shall test her.
Put on a mournful air.

SCENE V.
(*King, Diegue, Arias, Sancho, Alonzo, Chimene, Elvire*)

*King.* Rejoice, Chimene.
Success, at last, has answered all your prayers.
Though Roderick has triumphed o'er our foes,
Their swords have robbed us of him, he is dead;
Give thanks to Heaven which has avenged you thus.
(*Aside to Diegue*)
Mark how her color changes with the news.
*Diegue.* Look, Sire, she swoons, and by this weakness
shows
Her perfect love. Her sorrow has betrayed
The secrets of her heart, and left no room
To doubt the endurance of her passion's flame.
*Chimene.* What, Roderick is dead?
*King.* No, no, he lives,
And with unchanging passion loves you still.
Forget the anxious grief that mourns for him!

*Chimene.* Sire, one swoons from joy, as well as grief.
The soul surprised with happiness grows weak,
And sudden gladness overcomes the senses.

*King.* You ask us to believe the impossible?
Chimene, your sorrow showed itself too clearly.

*Chimene.* Then add this deeper pain to my distress,
And call my faintness the result of grief.
My righteous wrath has brought me to this pass.
His death removed his life beyond my grasp:
If he should die from wounds which he received
In battle for his country, my revenge
And all my plans to take his life were lost.
So fine an end for him, were my misfortune:
I ask his death, but not a glorious one.
Not one which lifts him in a blaze of glory:
Not in a bed of honor, but on a scaffold;
Not for his country's sake, but for my father,
His name dishonored and his memory stained.
'Tis no sad fate to perish for one's country,
That is the doorway to eternal fame.
I can enjoy his victory without shame.
It saves the State and gives me back my victim—
But noble, famous among all the warriors,
A chief with laurels crowned, instead of flowers,
In short one fitting to be sacrificed
To him who was my father. But alas,
My hope exceeds my reason. Roderick
Need dread no more from me. How can my tears,
Which men despise, work any harm to him?
He holds the freedom of your empire—all
That he would do, he can beneath your laws.
He triumphs over me as o'er his foes
And justice stifled in their blood bestows

Another trophy on their conqueror.
We join his train and in despite of law
Follow his chariot with two captive kings.

 *King.* My child, your words display too great a violence.
One must weigh all when one would render justice.
Your father has been killed; he was the aggressor;
And equity itself commands my mercy.
Before condemning me for showing it,
Look in your heart. There Roderick is master;
Your love gives secret thanks unto your king
Whose favor saves your lover's life for you.

 *Chimene.* For me! my foe! the object of my wrath!
My sorrow's source! my father's murderer!
My just revenge is such a little thing
I should rejoice that I must give it up!
Since you deny this justice to my tears,
Permit me, Sire, to make resort to arms.
By arms alone he wronged me and by arms
I ought to work my vengeance for his crime.
Of all you cavaliers I ask his head.
On him who brings it I bestow my hand:
Let them do battle, and the conflict over,
I wed the conqueror if Roderick loses.
Let this be published, Sire, as your decree.

 *King.* This ancient custom honored in these parts,
Under pretense of punishing a wrong,
Deprives the State of its best fighting men.
Often by a false success the weight
Falls on the innocent; the base escape.
Roderick is too precious to the state
To risk his life in this ordeal of arms.
Whatever such a noble heart could do,
The flying Moors have borne away his crime.

*Diegue.* What, Sire? For him alone reverse the laws
Which all the court have seen so often honored!
What will the people think, or envy say,
If he retreat behind your sheltering arm
And so excuse his failure to appear
Where men of honor seek a worthy death?
Such favors would but tarnish his renown:
Let him enjoy his victory without shame.
The Count was insolent; he punished him;
The courage he showed then he should maintain.

*King.* Since that is your desire, let it be so;
But there will be a thousand clamoring
To take the place of every vanquished champion,
For what Chimene has promised to the victor,
Will make of all my knights his enemies.
To fight them all would be no justice; therefore,
He shall go only once into the lists.
Choose whom you will, Chimene, but choose with care;
And afterwards ask nothing more of me.

*Diegue.* Excuse not those who tremble at his strength.
But leave an open field, where none will enter.
After what Roderick has done today,
Who has the courage to oppose his arm?
To risk himself with such an adversary?
Who is so valiant and so insolent?

*Sancho.* Leave the field open; I will face him. I
Am insolent enough and brave enough.

*(To Chimene)*

Madam, grant this favor to my love,
You know you have already promised it.

*King.* Chimene, do you accept this champion?

*Chimene.* Sire, I promised him.

*King.*                 Tomorrow, then.

*Diegue.* No, Sire, there is no reason for delay;
He who is brave enough is always ready.

*King.* To go from battle into trial by combat?

*Diegue.* Roderick has rested telling you his tale.

*King.* I bid him rest at least an hour or two;
And lest this combat form a precedent,
That all may see with what reluctance I
Permit this fray in which I have no pleasure,
I and my court shall not be witnesses.

(*To Arias*)

You shall judge between these combatants.
See that they both observe the laws of honor,
And afterwards bring me the conqueror.
Whoever he be, the prize will be the same.
He shall receive Chimene from my own hand,
And she shall plight her troth as his reward.

*Chimene.* What, Sire, impose on me so stern a law?

*King.* You murmur, but your love will not complain
If Roderick emerge the conqueror.
Cease your complaints against my mild decree:
The victor of these two shall be your husband.


# ACT V

## Scene I. *Roderick, Chimene*

*Chimene.* What! Roderick before my eyes! This boldness
Will cost my honor! Go! Go! Go!

*Roderick.* I go to die, madam, but ere I go
I come to offer you a last good-bye;
The changeless love which binds me to your will
Demands my homage even as I die.

*Chimene.* You go to die!

*Roderick.*           I seek the happy moment
When with my life I satisfy your wrath.

   *Chimene.* You go to die! Is Sancho then so great
That he can terrify your valiant heart?
What renders you so weak or him so strong?
Before the combat Roderick speaks of death!
Who neither feared my father nor the Moors,
Despairs before he goes to meet Don Sancho!
Does courage so desert you in your need!

   *Roderick.* I go to punishment not to a combat.
Since you desire my death, my faithful heart
Knows no desire to preserve my life.
My heart is firm, but I can find no joy
In saving that which only brings you pain.
This night already had brought death to me
Had I been fighting for myself alone.
But for my king, his people, and my country,
I have been brave not to defend myself.
Life is not yet so hateful to my soul
That I would leave it stained with treachery:
Now it is only of myself I think,
You seek my death and I accept the sentence.
Your anger chose another hand to serve it.
I was not worthy to meet death at yours.
They shall not see me giving blow for blow.
I cannot strike the arm that fights for you.
I shall rejoice to think his blows are yours.
Since 'tis your honor that his arms maintain,
I'll bare my bosom gladly to his sword,
Worshiping as yours the hand that slays me.

   *Chimene.* If that same duty, sad and just at once,
Which drives me 'gainst my will to seek your death,
Lays on your love such stern restraint that you

Must stand defending 'gainst my champion.
Forget not, in this blindness, that your glory
Will not survive your life; it matters not
With what a brilliance Roderick has lived,
Who sees him dead will think of him as vanquished.
Your honor is more dear to you than I,
Since for its sake you shed my father's blood,
And though you loved me, gave up hope to win me:
I see you count that hope so little worth
That you would yield without a show of fight.
What inconsistency your valor shows!
Why have you any, if you have no more?
Think you of honor but to do me wrong?
Have you no courage but in hurting me?
And will you so disgrace my father's name
By being vanquished after having killed him?
Accept not willingly the death I seek,
And if you would not live, defend your honor.

    *Roderick.* The Count is dead. The Moors, defeated, fly.
Must I do more to prove my right to glory?
My fame demands not that I save myself.
I need no further proof that I am brave,
That I am powerful, that under heaven
Nothing is dearer to me than my honor.
No, in the coming combat, Roderick,
Whatever you may think, can meet his death
And never risk his honor; never fear
That anyone will dare impeach his courage,
Or say that he has met his conqueror.
Men will say only: "He adored Chimene,
He could not live the object of her hate.
He yielded willingly to that stern fate,
Which forced his mistress to pursue his death.

She sought his life; to his great soul it seemed
Refusal of her wish were criminal.
He lost his love to keep his honor bright
And to avenge his mistress gave his life;
Preferring still, whatever hope he cherished,
His honor to Chimene, Chimene to life.
And thus my death upon the field of honor
Far from destroying glory, will enhance it.
And on my voluntary death will follow
Honor which only that could bring to you.

   *Chimene.* Since life and honor have no power to stay
This rush to death, dear Roderick, if ever
I loved you, in return defend yourself
And save me from Don Sancho; fight for me.
Fight to save me from an odious fate
That will deliver me to one I hate.
Shall I say more? Go plan for your defense.
Fulfill my duty, silence my complaints.
And if you love me still, return as victor
From this encounter where Chimene is prize.
Adieu. I blush with shame to tell you this.

                                        (*Exit Chimene*)

   *Roderick.* What enemy can daunt me now! Come on,
Navarre, Castile, Morocco, come, you Knights,
The bravest of all Spain, join arms against me.
Oppose a solid army to my hand.
Against so sweet a hope your strength combined
Were all too small to conquer me alone.

### SCENE II. *Infanta*

NOTE: This scene is written in lyrical stanzas. Translation by
Florence Kendrick Cooper.

*Infanta.* Thou pride of birth, which turns my love to crime,
Thy warning shall I list, or thy sweet voice
My heart, whose soft constraint compels revolt
Against that tyrant stern? In worth alone
Thou, Roderick, art mine equal; but thy blood,
Though brave and pure, flows not from royal veins.

Unhappy lot, which rudely separates
My duty and my love. Must loyalty
To valor rare condemn to misery
A loving soul? What anguish must I bear
If ne'er I learn, despite my high resolve,
Nor lover to embrace, nor love to quell!
'Twixt love and pride my reason bids me choose
Though birth's high destiny demand a throne,
Thou, Roderick, art of kings the conqueror,
And 'neath thy sway with honor shall I dwell.
The glorious name of Cid that now is thine
Points clearly to the realm where thou shalt reign.

Worthy is he, but 't is Chimene he loves.
Her father's death so slightly breaks their bonds,
That, though her duty slays him, she adores.
No hope to my long grief his crime can bring.
Alas for me! ordains a wretched fate
That love outlast the bitterness of hate.

### SCENE III. *Leonora, Infanta*

*Infanta.* What would you, Leonora?
*Leonora.*                          To rejoice

That now your spirit has found peace.

*Infanta.* Peace! Where would I find it in my sorrow?

*Leonora.* If love be fed with hope and die without it,
Roderick can no longer charm your heart.
Involved in this encounter by Chimene,
Either he dies or he becomes her husband;
And so your hope is killed, your spirit healed.

*Infanta.* Ah, still how far from that.

*Leonora.*                                 What can you hope?

*Infanta.* Say rather what hope is forbidden me?
I know too many schemes to set aside
The stern conditions under which he fights.
Love, the sweet cause of all my cruel torture,
Puts artifice into the lover's heart.

*Leonora.* What power have you to separate their hearts,
When even a father's death was powerless?
Chimene today has shown all too clearly
That she is not inspired by deadly hate.
She asked for trial by combat and she chose
To champion her the first who volunteered.
She made no effort to select a knight
Whom deeds of arms had rendered glorious.
Don Sancho satisfies her, and she chose him,
Because his sword is still untried in battle.
His inexperience is dear to her.
His lack of fame has set her heart at rest.
This easy choice must tell you that she seeks
A combat because duty drives her to it;
A combat Roderick may easily win
And yet appear to satisfy her honor.

*Infanta.* I see it all too well, and yet my heart
Rivals Chimene and loves this conqueror.
Unhappy in my love, what shall I do?

*Leonora.* Remember your high birth. The will of Heaven
Commands a king for you; you love a subject—
    *Infanta.* My heart is altered. I no longer love
This Roderick, a simple gentleman.
No, no, my love no longer calls him that,
I love the warrior of mighty deeds,
The valorous Cid, the conqueror of kings.
Yet even so I shall o'ercome my love,
Not for fear that it would bring me shame,
But lest I play this sweet devotion false.
Even if for my sake they crowned him king
I would not take again the gift I gave.
Since in this combat he is certain victor,
Let us once more assure him to Chimene.
And you who know the secrets of my heart,
Come help me finish what I have begun.

### SCENE IV. *Chimene, Elvire*

*Chimene.* Ah pity me, Elvire, my heart is torn!
Between perpetual fear and feeble hope.
No vow escapes me I would not recall;
Repentance quickly follows every wish.
Two rivals I have set to arms against me:
The happiest result will cost me tears.
Though fate has favored me, I must lament
A father unavenged, or lover dead.
    *Elvire.* In any case your comfort is assured.
Either you win your lover or your vengeance:
Whatever destiny may plan for you
You gain a husband and preserve your honor.
    *Chimene.* Yes! Him I hate or him I sought to slay,
My father's murderer or Roderick.
Whoever wins, I must accept a husband

Stained with the blood of him I most adore:
My soul recoils from either choice. I fear
The outcome of this combat more than death.
Away with both revenge and love. No more
Is either of these passions dear to me.
And you, almighty fate, from which I suffer,
Let neither win this combat. Let there be
Neither a conquered nor a conqueror!

    *Elvire.* No, that would be too cruel a destiny.
This combat will but torture you anew,
If after it you still must call for justice,
Still nurse a deep resentment in your breast,
And seek forever for your lover's death.
Better that it should crown his noble brow
With laurels new and silence your complaints.
Stifle your sighs and make the King command you
To follow the desires of your heart.

    *Chimene.* Even if he wins, can you believe that I
Shall yield my heart to him? My filial duty
Is far too strong for that, my loss too great.
This combat and the wishes of the king
Are not enough to give them satisfaction.
He can defeat Don Sancho easily,
But not with him the honor of Chimene.
That will raise up a thousand enemies,
No matter what the king has promised him.

    *Elvire.* Take care lest Heaven deny to you your vengeance
In punishment for such an impious pride.
What, will you reject the happiness
Of silence with your honor satisfied?
What does such duty mean? What can it hope?
Your lover's death, will that give you back your father?
Is one such sorrow not enough for you?

Must you heap loss on loss, and grief on grief?
By this capricious temper which you show
You make yourself unworthy of your lover,
And you shall see that Heaven in righteous wrath
Shall, by his death, present you to Don Sancho.

    *Chimene.* I have sufficient grief to bear, Elvire;
Increase it not with direful prophecy.
I would, if that could be, escape them both;
If not, my wishes are for Roderick.
'Tis not a foolish love that turns me so,
But if he loses I would be Don Sancho's
And from that fear is my desire sprung—
But what is this Elvire, 'tis over, done!

### Scene V. *Sancho. Chimene*

    *Sancho.* 'Tis mine to lay my sword here at your feet—
    *Chimene.* Still smoking with the blood of Roderick!
Traitor, dare you show yourself to me
After the murder of my dearest love?
Speak, love, you have no longer aught to fear;
My father is avenged, and you may speak.
By this one blow my honor is assured.
My love set free, my soul plunged in despair!

    *Sancho.* With calmer spirit . . .
    *Chimene.*             Still you speak to me.
Base murderer of a hero I adore!
Go! You killed him treacherously; a knight
So brave had never else been slain by you.
Hope nothing at my hand, you have not served me:
You thought to avenge me, and you took my life.

    *Sancho.* This is a strange illusion—hear me, pray. . . .
    *Chimene.* Hear you boast of how you killed him! hear

In patience with what insolence you paint
His death, my crime, and your own bravery!

### Scene VI. *Chimene, King, Diegue, Sancho*

*Chimene.* Sire, there is no need to hide from you
What all my strength was helpless to conceal.
You knew I lived but to avenge my father.
I marked for death the dearest life on earth:
Sire, your majesty himself has seen
How I made love the subject of my duty;
Now Roderick is dead and by his death
His bitter foe becomes his mourning lover.
I owed revenge to him who gave me life,
And now I owe these tears to him I loved.
Don Sancho in my own defense destroyed me.
I am the prize he wins by doing so.
In pity, Sire, if pity move a king,
Revoke a law so terrible to me:
As his reward for victory, where I
Lose all I love, let him have all my wealth.
So I be left unnoticed to retreat
Into a cloister to weep out my life
In mourning for my father and my lover.

*Diegue.* At last, Sire, she no longer thinks it wrong
To speak with her own lips her heart's desire.

*King.* Chimene, be not deceived. Your lover lives.
Your champion, defeated, spoke you false.

*Sancho.* Sire, her love it is that has betrayed her
So to mistake my message. I have come,
Sent by the noble warrior she loves
To tell her of the fight: "Fear not," he said
When I stood stripped of all defense before him,
"Sooner let victory be left in doubt

Than that the blood risked for Chimene be shed.
But since my duty calls me to the king,
Go you and tell her how our combat ended.
And in the victor's stead present your sword
An offering at her feet." Sire, I came;
This sword deceived her. Seeing me return,
She took me for the conqueror and quickly
Her wrath betrayed her love to such an outburst
That I could gain no hearing for my tale.
Defeated though I am, I am content;
Although I love her and in this encounter
I lose my love, I welcome my defeat,
Which brings to happiness their perfect love.

*King.* My child, there is no need to blush for shame
Or seek again to disavow your love.
Your duty is fulfilled, your honor saved.
Your father is avenged, and 'twas for that
Your Roderick's life so often was endangered.
You see how Heaven disposes otherwise;
And as it saves him also blesses you;
Rebel no longer against my decree,
Which puts into your arms so dear a husband.

SCENE VII. *Infanta, Roderick, King, Chimene*

*Infanta.* Dry your tears, Chimene, and take with joy
This noble warrior from your princess' hand.

*Roderick.* I crave indulgence, Sire, if in your presence
The power of love drives me to kneel to her.
I come not here to ask for my reward;
I come once more to offer you my life.
Madam, my love will not invoke for me
The law of combat or the king's desire.
If all that has been done has not avenged

Your father's death, pronounce what you require.
Whether I fight ten thousand champions,
Or carry battle to the ends of earth,
Or single-handed take a camp by storm,
Or rout an army, or surpass the fame
Of fabulous heroes of romance; if I
By any such can clear myself of crime,
I dare encounter all, and all achieve:
But if your proud, inexorable honor
Cannot be satisfied but by my death,
Arm no more champions to fight against me;
My head is at your feet, with your own hands
Exact your vengeance, to your hands alone
Belongs the right to slay the invincible.
All other vengeance is impossible.
But grant that death may end my punishment.
Banish me not from your dear memory;
And since my dying will preserve your honor,
Hold in return my memory in your heart,
And say, sometimes, in mourning for my fate,
"Had he not loved me, he were living still."
 *Chimene.* Rise, Roderick, rise—I have already, Sire,
Said far too much to you now to unsay it.
He has high virtues which I cannot hate;
And when a king commands one must obey.
But can you now, whatever your decree,
Suffer your eyes to look upon this wedding?
Though duty drive me to perform your wish,
Will justice then be satisfied in you?
Does Roderick's service to the state demand
That I be his reward against my will?
That I live ever in eternal shame,
My hands discolored with my father's blood?

*King.* Time often serves to justify a deed
Which seems at first unjustifiable.
Roderick has won you; you belong to him.
But though his valor conquered you today,
I should appear your lover's enemy
If I so soon presented him his prize.
To stay this marriage will not break the law,
Which set no time when it bestowed your hand.
Take, if you will, a year to dry your tears.
Meanwhile, let Roderick win new victories.
You have destroyed the Moors upon our shores,
Shattered their hopes, repulsed their wild assaults,
Go now and bear the war to their own land,
Command my army, pillage their domain.
At the very name of Cid they quake with fear:
They call you lord and they would make you king.
But through all mighty deeds keep faith with her:
Return if possible more worthy of her;
And make yourself so prized for your exploits
That pride will join with love to make her yours.

*Roderick.* To win Chimene and serve my Sovereign.
What feat is there too great for me to do?
Whatever absence from her sight may cost,
I am too happy, Sire, that I may hope.

*King.* Rest hope upon your courage and my word,
And since already you possess her heart,
To still that honor which cries out against you
Leave all to time, your valor, and your king.

**FINIS**

CINNA

or

THE MERCY OF AUGUSTUS

by

PIERRE CORNEILLE

# CHARACTERS

The Scene Is in Rome

# ACT I

## Scene I. *Amelia*

*Amelia.* O restless ardor for a high revenge,
Born of a father's death, oh, child of wrath,
To which my charmèd sorrow blindly clings,
You hold too strong an empire in my heart.
Grant me some moments now when I may rest
And take account in what a state I stand,
What risks I run, what ends I would accomplish.
When I behold Augustus in his glory,
And think how, murdered by that very hand,
My father was the first step to that throne
Where now I see him; when that bloody sight,
Cause of my hate and sign of Cæsar's wrath,
Presents itself to me, then utterly
I give my soul to vengeance, and I think
How, for one death, a thousand deaths he merits
Yet even in this righteous rage, I still
Love Cinna more than I abhor Augustus.
And then I feel my fury freeze within me,
Since, slaking it, I must expose my lover.
Yes, Cinna, I am angry with myself,
Seeing the dangers into which I hurl you.
Though you are fearless in my service, still
To ask his life of you, exposes yours;
When one strikes heads from such a lofty station,
He calls upon his own a thousand tempests.
Success is doubtful, and the danger sure;

One friend disloyal can betray your plan;
One order badly planned, one chance ill-taken,
Could turn the enterprise upon its author,
Bring down on you the blow that you would strike,
And in the general ruin overwhelm you.
And what your love would do for me, mischance
Might turn to your destruction. Cease, oh cease,
To risk this mortal peril; losing you
In gaining vengeance, were no gain to me.
It is too cruel a heart which can be charmed
By joys soiled by the bitterness of tears.
And one must count among the worst of evils
The death of an enemy which costs such sorrow.
But can I turn from vengeance for my father?
Is any price too dear to pay for him?
When his assassin falls beneath our hand
Should we consider what his death may cost?
Cease, vain alarms, cease, shameful tenderness,
To wring my heart to such unworthy weakness!
And you that feed them with anxiety,
Love, serve my duty, do not strive against it!
Your glory is to yield; your shame to conquer:
Show yourself noble, yielding place to duty;
The more you give, the more you shall be given,
And duty's triumph will ennoble you.

### Scene II. *Amelia and Fulvia*

*Amelia.* I swear it, Fulvia, and again I swear.
However great the love I bear for Cinna,
However I adore him in my heart,
I shall be his only if Augustus dies.
My price is Cæsar's head; and I have told him
The law my duty has imposed on me.

*Fulvia.* She has just cause to censure it. A plot
So great requires that you judge yourself
Worthy the blood of him you would avenge.
Yet grant me grace to say again, so just
A passion should be cool. Augustus seems
By daily kindnesses to make amends
For wrongs that he has done you. And you stand
So clearly in his favor; you enjoy
So much consideration at his hands,
That often his most fortunate courtiers
Press you on bended knee to speak for them.
   *Amelia.* But all his favors give not back my father.
No matter how men think of me, as rich,
Or strong in influence, I live forever
The daughter of a proscript. Kindness acts
Not always as you think; a hated hand
Renders it odious; the more we give
To one who bears us hate, the more we arm
The hand that may betray us. Daily favors
Can never change my spirit. What I was,
I am, and more than ever powerful,
For with those very gifts he showers upon me,
I buy the heart of Rome against Augustus:
And I should take the place of Livia
Only as a surer point from which
To strike his life. No contract binds a child
That would avenge her father. Cæsar buys
His own blood with the favors that he does me.
   *Fulvia.* Granted: And yet what need to seem ungrateful?
Can you not hate more covertly? There are
Enough, besides you, who have not forgotten
Upon what cruelties his throne is raised.
There are so many brave, illustrious Romans

Who, sacrificed to his ambitions, left
Their children a sufficient heritage
Of living sorrows to avenge your wrong,
In righting theirs. Many will undertake it.
A thousand more will follow them and he
Who sees hate everywhere cannot live long.
To their arms delegate your common cause
And aid their plans only with secret hopes.

    *Amelia.* What! Shall I hate him and make no attempt
To injure him? Shall I rely on chance
To strike him down? And shall I satisfy
A daughter's debt with impotent desire?
This death, which I so long for, would become
But bitterness to me if he should fall
In vengeance for another than my father.
And you should see my tears flow at the deed
Which, killing him, did not avenge my wrong.
Only a coward delegates to others
A common work which duty lays upon him.
Mine will not only be the sweet delight
Of vengeance for my father, but the glory
Of punishing a tyrant and of hearing
Throughout all Italy: "Amelia wrought
The liberty of Rome. Her soul was wrung.
Her heart was stirred with love, but she was willing
Only at such a price to grant her love."

    *Fulvia.* At such a price your love can only be
A deadly gift, bearing a certain death
To him it favors. Think, Amelia,—
Think to what dangers you expose him; think
How many have been broken on this reef.
Oh, be not blind when death is plain to see.

*Amelia.* Oh, you can strike where I am tenderest.
When I consider what he risks for me,
The fear that he may perish nearly kills me.
My troubled spirit wars against itself.—
I would and I would not. I rage and weaken;
My duty, wavering, confused, and stunned,
Yields to the urging of my mutinous heart.
Softly, passion, softly, I am weakening.
You know the risks; they are great, but what of that?
Cinna is not lost for being risked.
Whatever legions guard Augustus' safety,
Whatever care he takes, whatever pains,
He who despises life is his life's master.
The greater the danger, the more sweet the fruit.
Courage drives us on, and glory follows:
Whatever happens, whether Octavius
Or Cinna dies, I owe this sacrifice
To my paternal manes. Cinna promised
This vengeance when I pledged my faith to him,
And by this stroke alone deserves my love.
'Tis too late now to change my mind. Today
They meet together, today they set the plot,
The hour, the place, the hand, they choose today.
And after him it will be meet to die.

### Scene III. *Cinna, Amelia, Fulvia*

*Amelia.* But here he comes. Cinna, is not your hand
Disturbed by fear of danger? Can you see
In the faces of your friends that they are ready
To hold to all that they have promised you?

*Cinna.* Never did any plot against a tyrant
Hold better hope than this of happy issue.
No death was ever sworn with such a passion,

Nor any plotters better in accord:
They all display such high enthusiasm
That each one seems, like me, to serve a mistress.
And each one burns with such a powerful rage,
It seems that all, like you, avenge their fathers.

   *Amelia.* I knew that for an enterprise like this
Cinna would choose brave men; I knew that he
Never would entrust to weaklings' hands
The interests of Amelia and Rome.

   *Cinna.* Would to the gods that you, yourself, had seen
The zeal with which they enter on this plot!
At the very name of Cæsar, of Augustus,
Of Emperor, you would have seen their eyes
Flame up in fury, seen their faces blanch
With horror, and by contrary effect,
In the same moment flush with indignation.
"Comrades," I told them, "this is my happy day,
The day which consummates our glorious plan;
Heaven entrusts to us the fate of Rome,
Her welfare hangs on one man's death, if man
He may be called, who is in nothing human,
This tiger bloated with the blood of Rome.
How many factions has he formed to spill it!
How often has he changed from side to side,
Now friend of Antony, now enemy.
And never insolent and cruel by halves!"
Then by a long recital of the woes,
Which in our youth our fathers had endured,
I stirred their anger through their memory,
And doubled in their hearts the zeal for vengeance.
I drew them pictures of the piteous wars
When Rome with its own hands tore out its entrails,
When eagle attacked eagle, and our legions

On both sides fought against their liberty.
When the best soldiers and the bravest chiefs
Staked all their glory to enslave themselves;
When to assure the shame their shackles brought them
They welded to their chains the Universe;
And for the odious honor of enforcing
A master on it, made the name of traitor
Beloved by all; set Romans against Romans,
Fathers against fathers, in a conflict
Whose only glory was the choice of tyrants.
To scenes like these I joined the frightful pictures
Of their alliance, awful, impious,
Fatal to honest men, to property,
To the senate, and at last, to crown it all,
Of their triumvirate. But I could find
No colors black enough to paint their stories.
I showed them glorying in a rivalry
Of evil; Rome bathed in its children's blood:
Some slain in public places; others killed
In the very presence of their household gods;
The bad encouraged by the crime's reward;
The husband murdered by his wife abed;
The son, still bloody from his father's murder,
His head in hand, demanding to be paid,—
Still my imperfect pencil could not trace
The fearful outlines of this bloody peace.
Shall I recount the names of those great men
Whose deaths I pictured to inflame their courage,
Those noble proscripts, mortal demi-gods,
Who died as sacrifices on the altars?
But could I tell you to what hot impatience,
What shudders of disgust, what violence,
These crimes so base, even so badly pictured,

Stirred up the hearts of our conspirators?
I lost no time and, seeing their anger raised,
To the point of fearing nothing, doing all,
I added briefly, "All these cruelties,
The loss of all our goods and liberty,
The ravaging of fields, the sack of cities,
All these proscriptions, all these civil wars
Are bloody steps by which Augustus chose
To mount the throne and force his laws on us.
But we can change this deadly destiny;
Instead of three we have one tyrant only,
And by his one just act he robbed himself
Of all support, when to be king alone,
He killed two more as evil as himself.
Him dead, we have no lord, he no avenger;
Rome will be born again with liberty,
And we deserve the title of true Romans
If our hands break the yoke that bears us down.
Seize the occasion when it is propitious:
Tomorrow in the capitol he performs
The sacrifice. There let him be the victim.
And let us in that spot, before the faces
Of the gods themselves give justice to the world.
His only escort there will be our band.
My hand will give the incense and the cup
And for your signal this same hand will give him
In place of incense, a dagger in his breast.
Struck by a mortal blow, he shall discover
If I am of great Pompey's blood; then you
Make known after me that you remember
The illustrious ancestors from whom you spring."
Scarce had I finished when they each renewed
In noble words their vows of loyalty:

The occasion pleased them, but each one desired
The honor of the first blow for himself,
Which I had kept as mine. Reason prevailed
At length above the passion which enflamed them:
Maximus and half would hold the door;
The other half with me would crowd around him,
Ready for the sign when I should give it.
You see, my dear Amelia, where we stand.
Tomorrow I await men's hate or praise,
The name of murderer or liberator,
Cæsar, that of prince or of usurper.
On our success against his tyranny
Depends our glory or our infamy.
The people, always wavering towards tyrants,
If they detest the dead, adore the living.
For me, let heaven frown or smile propitious,
Raise me to glory or destroy me quite.
Let Rome itself be for us or against,
Dying for you, all will seem sweet to me.

    *Amelia.* Fear not success will soil your memory:
Good fate or bad will not affect your glory;
Failure in such conspiracy may place
Your life in peril, but not so your honor.
Think of the failure of Brutus and Cassius:
Are their names dimmed in splendor? Did they die
Eternally along with their great plan?
Do we not count them still the greatest Romans?
Their memory in Rome is precious still
As much as Cæsar's life is odious;
Although their conqueror reigns, they are regretted,
And longed for ardently by all their fellows.
Go follow in their steps where honor leads,
But be not careless to preserve your life

Remember the great love which burns within us;
Amelia is your prize as much as glory;
As you owe me your heart, my favors wait you;
My life depends on yours, as yours is dear
To me. What brings Evander here to us?

### Scene IV. *Cinna, Amelia, Evander*

*Evander.* Sir, Cæsar calls you, and with you Maximus.
*Cinna.* Maximus and me! Are you quite sure, Evander?
*Evander.* Polyclitus waits upon you even now:
He would have come himself along with me
To seek you, had I not had wit enough
To keep him from it. Fearing a surprise,
I wished to give you warning. He is urgent.
*Amelia.* Calls for the chiefs of the whole enterprise!
Both! At the same time! You have been discovered!
*Cinna.* Let us hope better!
*Amelia.*                    Cinna, I have lost you!
The gods, determined we shall have a master,
Have put a traitor 'mongst your trusted friends.
There is no room for doubt. Augustus knows!
Both summoned at the moment of decision!
*Cinna.* His order stuns me. I cannot conceal it:
And yet he often calls me to his side.
Maximus and I are both his confidants,
And at this summons needlessly alarmed.
*Amelia.* Be less ingenious in self-deception;
And do not drive my trials to the limit.
Since now you cannot work my vengeance, Cinna,
Shield at least your head from mortal peril.
Flee the implacable anger of Augustus.
I have shed enough tears for my father's death;
To all my sorrows add not the new grief

Of weeping for my lover. Flee, my Cinna.

   *Cinna*. What! On the mere semblance of danger
Shall I betray both you and the public good!
Shall I accuse myself of cowardice,
And give up all when all is to be dared?
What will our friends do, if your fears are false?

   *Amelia*. But what becomes of you, if the plot be known?

   *Cinna*. If there be some so base as to betray me,
At least my courage shall not play me false.
You shall behold it, shining on the brink
Of precipices, crown itself with glory;
In braving pain, render Augustus jealous
Of the blood he spills, and make his knees to tremble
Even as he kills he.

                  I shall be suspect
If I delay. Adieu! Strengthen my heart.
If I must bear so hard a blow from fate
At once unhappy and happy I shall die.
Happy to serve you even with my life
Unhappy that my death serves you no more.

   *Amelia*. Yes. Go. Let me no longer hold you back;
My troubles flee; reason returns to me.
Pardon, my love, a weakness so unworthy.
Your flight would be in vain. I know it, Cinna.
If all is known, Augustus has the power
To close all avenues of flight to you.
Bear, bear to him this sorrowful assurance,
Worthy of our passion and your birth.
Die, if you must, a Roman citizen,
And with a grand crime crown a grand design.
Fear not that I shall live here after you.
Your death shall bear my spirit along with yours.
And my heart too, pierced with the selfsame blows.

*Cinna.* Ah, grant that dead I yet may live in you,
And dying let me hope that you will yet
Take vengeance for your lover with your father.
There is nothing for you to fear, none of our friends
Knows of your plan or of the bond between us.
When I rehearsed to them the woes of Rome,
I said no word about the death from which
Our hatred springs, lest in my zeal I might,
Thinking of you, betray our secret love.
Only Evander knows it, and your Fulvia.

*Amelia.* I go now less afraid to Livia,
Since in your peril there remains to me
A means to use for you her strength and mine.
But if my love finds no assistance there,
Hope not that I shall live when you are dead.
Your fate shall rule my destiny, and I
Will save your life or follow you in death.

*Cinna.* Be for my sake less cruel to yourself.

*Amelia.* Go, and remember only that I love you.


## ACT II

SCENE I. *Augustus, Cinna, Maximus, troops of courtiers*

*Augustus.* Let all retire and no one enter here.
You, Cinna, stay and, Maximus, you too.
                    (*Exit Courtiers*)
This absolute power over land and sea,
This sovereign sway I hold o'er all the world,
This grandeur without limit, this high rank,
Which has already cost such suffering,—
Yes, all which in my noble eminence
Calls admiration from a flattering court,

Is but a shining bauble, dazzling first,
But losing all attraction once enjoyed.
Ambition palls when once it is accomplished;
And an opposing passion takes its place.
So now our spirit, having striven ever
To the last breath to gain some certain end,
Turns on itself, with nothing more to conquer,
And having reached the peak would fain descend.
I longed for empire, and I won to it,
But while I longed for it, I knew it not:
Possessing it, I found that all its charms
Turned into heavy cares and constant fears.
A thousand secret foes deserving death,
No pleasure without trouble, no repose.
Sulla before me held this power supreme:
Great Julius, my father, too, enjoyed it.
But with what different eyes they looked upon it.
One gave it up, the other would have held it.
One, cruel and barbarous, died well beloved,
Like any worthy citizen, at home;
The other, ever gentle, met his end
In the senate house by an assassin's hand.
These fresh examples ought to serve to teach me,
If solely by example one may learn.
One beckons me to follow, one brings fear;
Yet an example often proves to be
A mirror of deception, and the plan
Of destiny which so disturbs our thoughts
Not always written in the chosen steps.
Now one is broken and another saved,
And what destroys one man preserves another.
There, my good friends, you see what troubles me.
You, who replace Agrippa and Mæcenas,

Take o'er my soul the power which was theirs
To settle this which I discussed with them.
Think not at all of this great state of mine,
Hateful to Romans, wearying to myself;
Deal with me as a friend, not as a sovereign:
Augustus, Rome, the empire, rest on you:
You shall decide if Europe, Asia,
Or Africa be governed by a king
Or a republic. Yours to say if I
Be emperor or simple citizen.

   *Cinna.* Spite of surprise and insufficiency,
I shall obey you, Sire, without complaint:
Forget the reverence that should restrain me
From giving you advice or you from hearing.
Be gracious to a spirit so concerned
For glory you would soil with stain so black,
And keep your own soul tolerant of censure,
Even if it condemn your every act.
No one resigns legitimate eminence;
Without remorse one guards what one acquired
Without wrongdoing, and the more the prize
Which he gives up is noble, lofty, fine,
The more he who renounces it appears
To judge it badly won. Imprint not, Sire,
This mark of shame upon the noble virtues
Which made you king. You hold the honor justly,
You brought about the change in government
Without the stain of crime, and Rome is now
Under your laws by right of war, which right,
Under the laws of Rome, rules all the world.
Your arms have conquered it, and all who conquer,
Though they be called usurpers, are not tyrants.
If under their laws they enslave a province

And govern justly, they become just princes.
That is what Cæsar did, and we today
Condemn his memory when we do not so.
If absolute rule is censured by Augustus,
Cæsar was tyrant, and his death was just;
And you should pay the gods account for blood
You spilled exacting vengeance for his rank.
Fear not this mournful destiny, O Sire,
A spirit far more powerful rules your years.
Ten times your life has been attacked and he
Who sought to take it, but established it.
Enough is tried, but nothing is accomplished.
There are assassins, but there is no Brutus;
Finally, if such a stroke awaits you,
'Tis fine to die lord of the universe.
This in a few words I dare speak; I think
That Maximus agrees with what I said.

   *Maximus.* I hold with you, Augustus has the right
To hold the empire which his courage won;
That by his blood, in peril of his life,
He made just conquest of the Roman state.
But that he cannot drop without disgrace
The burden which his hand now tires of,
That he accuses Cæsar of tyranny
And marks his death approved, that I deny.
Rome is your guerdon, Sire, the empire yours;
And each is free to give away his own;
His is the choice to guard or to renounce:
Can you alone not act like common men?
Should you become, from having conquered all,
Slave to the grandeurs which your arms have won?
Possess them, Sire, but let them not possess you.
Be not their captive, make them yield to you;

And, finally, make known to everyone
That all these glories are beneath your sway.
Rome gave you birth in former years, and now
You wish to give to it omnipotence.
And Cinna charges you with mortal crime,
In giving freedom to your native land.
He calls the love of fatherland remorse.
By noble virtue glory now is withered,
Become at length a thing contemptible,
If infamy becomes its last effect.
And I would say to you, a deed so fine
Gives back to Rome more than you took from her.
But can one count a crime unpardonable
When restitution far exceeds the theft?
Give ear, Sire, to the Heaven that inspires you.
Your glory doubles when you scorn the empire;
And you will be renowned in after years
Less for its conquest than for leaving it.
Good fortune leads one to the highest glory,
But to renounce it calls for equal courage.
The sceptre won, few are so generous
As to disdain the burden of command.
Consider also that you reign in Rome,
Where, in whatever way you name your court,
The monarchy is hateful, and the name
Of emperor, concealing that of king,
Is no less horrible. They take for tyrant
Whoever makes himself their master; he,
Who serves him, for a slave; who loves him, traitor.
He who endures him has a coward's heart,
Humble and soft. They count it virtuous
To free themselves. Of this, Sire, you have proof.
Ten vain attempts against your life are known;

Perhaps the eleventh is ready to break forth,
And this design of yours may only be
A secret word that Heaven has sent to you,
Having this only way to save your life.
Expose yourself no more to great reverses.
'Tis fine to die, lord of the universe.
But the sweetest death but soils the memory
Of him who could have lived and known his glory.

    *Cinna.* If love of country be the master here,
Its welfare ought to be your sole desire;
This liberty which seems so dear to Rome
Is but imaginary, more injurious
Than useful to it, and cannot approach
The joys a good prince could afford the state:
He scatters honors with an ordered judgment,
Repays and punishes with just discernment,
Disposes all as rightly owning all,
Ungoverned by the fear of a successor.
But when the people rule, confusion reigns;
The voice of reason finds no listeners;
Honors are vended to the most ambitious,
Power delivered to the traitorous.
These little lords, who rule a single year,
Seeing how short a time their power endures,
How they may miss the fruit of their designs,
And fearful lest it fall to those who follow,
Since they have little good of what they plan,
Reap richly in the public field, assured
That everyone will freely pardon them,
Hoping in turn like opportunity.
The worst of states is where the people rule.

    *Augustus.* And yet the only kind which Romans love.
This hate of kings, which for five centuries

Our children suckled with their mothers' milk,
Is too deep rooted to be now destroyed.

    *Maximus.* Yes, Sire. Rome is stubborn in its sickness.
Its people please to shun recovery;
Custom commands them, not the light of reason.
This old mistake, which Cinna would erase,
They worship as the happiest of errors,
By which the world, serving their laws, has seen
Them tread upon a hundred kingly heads.
And fill their chests from pillaged provinces.
What better could the best of kings have done?
Not every country, Sire, it seems, receives
With equal joy all sorts of government;
Each people uses that which suits its nature,
And is not altered without injury:
Such is the law of heaven, whose wisdom just
Sows in the world such wide diversity.
The Macedonians love the monarchy.
The rest of Greece loves public liberty.
Persians and Parthians desire sovereigns.
The consulate alone is fit for Rome.

    *Cinna.* 'Tis true that Heaven's infinite providence
Has given to different peoples different spirits,
But just as truly does this heavenly order
Change with the times as with localities.
From kings Rome had its walls and its beginnings;
By your rare virtues should it now attain
The highest reaches of prosperity.
With you it is no more the prey of wars;
The gates of Janus by your hands are closed,
Which in the consuls' rule they never were,
Nor in the ages since Rome's second king.

    *Maximus.* These revolutions by the will of Heaven

Require no blood, hold nothing perilous.

    *Cinna.* It is the gods' decree, and never broken,
To sell a little dearly their best gifts:
The Tarquin's exile drowned our land in blood,
And our first consuls cost us many wars.

    *Maximus.* Then your grandfather, Pompey, must have
    flown
In heaven's face, fighting for liberty?

    *Cinna.* If heaven had wished that Rome should lose its free-
    dom
It had defended her by Pompey's hands.
It chose his death that it might worthily
Imprint on this great change a stamp eternal.
We owe the shade of such a man this glory
That with it went the liberty of Rome.
For a long time now this name has only served
To dazzle, and its very grandeur worked
Against its best enjoyment; since she sees
Herself the mistress of the world, since wealth
Has piled within her walls, and since her breast,
Fruitful of glorious exploits, has produced
Citizens more powerful than kings;
The great, well fortified by buying votes,
Hold pompously their masters to their pledges;
Who, having been enslaved by gilded swords,
Received from them the laws they thought to give.
Envious of each other they sustained
The whole by intrigue and by bloody plots.
Thus Marius stirred Sulla's jealousy;
Cæsar, my grandfather's. Mark Antony, yours.
Thus liberty may be of no more use
Than stirring up the flame of civil wars;
Then, by disorder fatal to the world,

One wants no king, the other wants no equal.
 Sire, to save herself, Rome must unite
Under a noble chief whom all obey.
If you still wish to favor it, remove
From it the chance of being more divided.
Sulla, quitting the place he had usurped,
But left the field to Cæsar and to Pompey,
Which the evil of the time had hid for us,
If he had fixed his power in his family.
What did the murder of great Cæsar do,
But raise up Antony and Lepidus
Against you? Who had started civil war,
Had Cæsar left the empire in your hands?
If you resign the empire, you will plunge it
Back in those ills whence it has just emerged;
And by a new war, sire, you will exhaust
What little blood the heart of Rome retains.
Let pity, let the love of country touch you;
Rome on her knees is pleading through my lips.
Think of the price which Rome has paid for you.
Not that she thinks that you were bought too dear,
For woes endured she has been well repaid;
But one real fear still holds her heart in terror;
If anxious and yet weary of command,
You grant to Rome a gift it cannot guard,
If she must buy another at your price,
If you hold not her good above your own,
If with this fatal gift you steal her hope,
I dare not say here what my eyes foresee.
Preserve for Rome a ruler under whom
Her happiness begins to be reborn;
And, to assure the commonweal of all,
Name a successor worthy of yourself.

*Augustus.* Speak no more: Pity has won the day.
My peace is dear, but Rome is stronger still.
However great the woe that falls to me,
I'll gladly die, if so I may save Rome.
In vain my heart sighs for tranquillity;
Cinna, on your advice I shall retain
The empire, but I shall retain it only
To share the rule with you. I see too well
Your hearts wear no disguise for me, that each,
In what advice he gave, considered only
The State and me. Your love has brought about
Between you both this combat of your spirits,
Now both shall be rewarded. Maximus,
I make you governor of Sicily;
Go, take my laws into that fertile land;
Think that you govern in my place, and I
Will be responsible for all you do.
Cinna, I grant Amelia for your wife.
You know she holds the place of Julia,
And that if sorrow and necessity
Have made me deal severely with her father
My bounty since, so open in her favor,
Should have assuaged the bitterness of loss.
I have done my part; go, you, and strive to win her.
You are not such a man as she would scorn.
Your words of love will ravish her. Adieu.
I go to bear the news to Livia.

### Scene II. *Cinna, Maximus*

*Maximus.* What is your plan after so fine a speech?
*Cinna.* The same as I have had and shall have ever.
*Maximus.* A chief of plotters flatters tyranny.
*Cinna.* A chief of plotters hopes to see it punished.

*Maximus.* I want to see Rome free.
*Cinna.*                                    And you must know
That I would free it and avenge it too.
Octavius' fury has been satisfied,
Our altars pillaged, our lives sacrificed,
Fields filled with horrors, Rome piled high with dead,
He would resign now, driven by remorse!
When Heaven has made us ready to punish him,
Shall cowardly repentance save his life?
'Twould scatter too much bait, be too inviting
For someone else to follow him if he
Were left unpunished. Vengeance for our fellows!
And let his fate be warning to whoever
After his death aspires to wear the crown.
Let Romans never suffer tyrants more.
Sulla punished, Cæsar had dared less.
    *Maximus.* But Cæsar's death, in which you see such justice,
Made possible Augustus' cruelties.
Wishing to free us, Brutus was deceived;
Cæsar unpunished, Augustus had dared less.
    *Cinna.* The fault of Cassius and his sudden fears
Reduced the State again to tyranny.
We shall not see a similar accident
When Rome shall follow leaders less imprudent.
    *Maximus.* We still have little evidence to prove
We shall conduct ourselves with greater prudence.
Certainly there is little in refusing
The happiness for which we'd risk our lives.
    *Cinna.* Still less if we imagine we can heal
So great an ill and not cut off its root.
Softness employed in such a cure is only
To pour on poison when the wound is closed.
    *Maximus.* You wish it bloody, and render it dubious.

*Cinna.* You wish it painless, and you make it shameful.

*Maximus.* One never blushes to escape from chains.

*Cinna.* Escape is base if courage does not stir us.

*Maximus.* Freedom never ceases to be sweet,
And ever was a priceless boon to Rome.

*Cinna.* That is no good which it can hold of worth,
Dropped from a hand grown weary with oppression.
Rome has too strong a heart to see with joy
A tyrant abdicate, whose prey she was.
And all true partisans of glory hate him
Too deeply to take pleasure in his gifts.

*Maximus.* For you, Amelia is a hateful thing,

*Cinna.* To take her from his hands would torture me.
But when I have avenged the wrongs of Rome,
I shall know how to brave him in his grave.
Yes. When by his death I have deserved her,
I hope to join my bloody hand with hers,
To marry her upon his tomb, and make
A tyrant's gifts the price paid for his head.

*Maximus.* But how can you delight her, comrade, stained
With blood of one whom she adores as father?
You are not one to take her violently.

*Cinna.* Here in the palace we may be overheard
And in a place so inappropriate
For confidence, we speak imprudently.
Let us go out where we may speak in safety
Of the easiest means by which we may succeed.

## ACT III

### Scene I. *Maximus and Euphorbus*

*Maximus.* He told me all himself; their love is mutual;
He loves Amelia, and is loved by her.
But vengeance for her father is her price,
And he conspires with us to win her hand.

*Euphorbus.* I do not wonder that he pressed Augustus
So vigorously to retain his throne.
If he resigns, the conspiracy dissolves,
And all conspirators will be his friends.

*Maximus.* They vie with one another to advance
The passion of one man who, though he feigns
To plot for Rome, plots only for himself;
While I, by an unequalled irony,
Would serve the good of Rome, and aid my rival.

*Euphorbus.* His rival? You?

*Maximus.* Yes. I love his mistress.
I have concealed my passion, waiting ever
Till by some mighty deed I might deserve her.
And now, when one is ready to my hand,
In doing it I but achieve my death;
And my success will speed my own disaster.
I lend my arm to him to kill myself;
To such a depth of woe does friendship plunge me.

*Euphorbus.* Escape is simple. Plot but for yourself,
Deflect the fatal blow from a design
Which means your death, and win yourself a mistress
While you betray a rival. Since, so doing,
You save Augustus' life, he cannot fail
To offer you Amelia in reward.

*Maximus.* Betray my friend?

*Euphorbus.* Love pardons any crime.

True love can never be concerned for friends,
'Tis no injustice to betray a traitor
Who for his mistress would betray his king.
Forget this friendship as he does your service.
  *Maximus.* That is an example to be shunned.
  *Euphorbus.* Against so black a plot all deeds are just;
He is no criminal who betrays a crime.
  *Maximus.* A crime by which Rome gains her liberty!
  *Euphorbus.* Beware a soul so base. His country's good
Concerns him nothing. True self-interest,
Not glory, is the mainspring of his courage.
He would love Cæsar were he not in love.
He is ungrateful, but not generous.
Think you that you can read his soul's last depths?
Beneath a public cause he hides his love,
And in like manner under that conceals
The despicable fire of his ambition.
Perhaps his hope, when Cæsar has been killed,
Is not to free Rome, but to govern it:
Perhaps he counts you now among his subjects,
Or hopes upon your death to found his power.
  *Maximus.* But how shall I accuse him and yet not
Name all the rest? Discovery were fatal
To all our fellow plotters. We should see
Unworthily betrayed those very ones
Who joined us to advance their country's good.
My spirit cannot form so base a plot;
Too many blameless lives would fall to punish
A single criminal. I dare do all
Against him, but I fear all things for them.
  *Euphorbus.* Cæsar is weary of severities,
Tired of torture, he will punish those
Who lead the plot and pardon all the rest.

So if you fear his anger for your comrades,
Speak, when you do so, in the name of all.

   *Maximus.* No more of this. 'Twere folly to imagine
By Cinna's death to win Amelia.
It is no way to please her lovely eyes
To steal the light from those she loves the best.
I would not have Augustus give her me;
Her heart is my desire, not her body.
And mere possession cannot signify,
If I have not a place in her affection.
Would I deserve her by a triple crime?
I kill her lover, I forestall her vengeance,
I save the life of him she longs to slay,
And still keep hope that she should hold me dear!

   *Euphorbus.* There is a real difficulty. Doubtless,
You will have need of craft and subtlety.
Someone must be found who can deceive her,
And, after that, all can be left to time.

   *Maximus.* But if, to clear himself, he should disclose her
As his accomplice; if Augustus wills
To punish her with him, can I demand
As my reward, that he bestow on me
The hand of one who plotted for his death?

   *Euphorbus.* You can oppose so many obstacles
That miracles were needed to surmount them.
I hope, however, and perhaps the wish—

   *Maximus.* Leave me. We shall speak of this again.
Cinna approaches; and I would draw him out,
The better to resolve what I shall do.

### SCENE II. *Cinna and Maximus*

*Maximus.* Your mien is thoughtful.
*Cinna.*                    Not without a reason.

*Maximus.* And may I know the cause of your concern?

*Cinna.* Amelia and Cæsar both disturb me,
One is too kind, the other too inhuman.
Would god that Cæsar took more pains to be
Better beloved, or that he loved me less.
That with his kindness he might move the beauty
Which charms my heart and soften her as she
Disarms my resolution. I can feel
At the bottom of my heart a thousand pangs
Of sharp remorse—which keep his many favors
Always before my eyes; his kindnesses,
So many and so badly paid, reproach me
Perpetually with deadly cruelty.
I seem to see him always as he strove
To place his royal power in our hands,
Hear our advice, approve me, and then say,
"Cinna, on your advice I shall retain
The empire, but I shall retain it only
To share the rule with you." And I can drive
A dagger in his breast! Ah, sooner would I—
Alas. I idolize Amelia.
An awful oath has bound me to her hate;
Her horror for Augustus renders him
Hateful to me as well, and my offense
Strikes equally my honor and the gods;
Perjurer or murderer I am,
Faithless to one in being true to the other.

*Maximus.* You should not be so much disturbed; you ought
At least appear more firm in your intent.
Your heart should not be troubled with reproaches.

*Cinna.* They creep upon you as the blow approaches
And crimes like these grow clearer as the hand
Draws nearer to the deed. Till then the soul,

Inspired by its own design, clings blindly
To its first purpose. Was there ever soul
That was not troubled, did not feel depressed?
I daresay even Brutus, at this point,
Wished more than once to drop the enterprise,
And that before the blow was struck, he felt
Repentance and remorse within his heart.

    *Maximus.* He was too brave to feel such qualms, he never
Charged his conscience with ingratitude
Because his hand was raised against a tyrant
Who had befriended him, and whom he loved.
Follow in his footsteps, do as he,
And base remorse on some more fitting cause,
Than timorous thoughts, which only can delay
The glorious rebirth of liberty.
'Tis you alone today who kept it back;
Brutus had taken it at Cæsar's hands
And never suffered any feeble thought
Of love or vengeance to endanger it.
Hear not the tyrant's voice although you love him,
And he would share with you his regal power.
Hear rather Rome beseeching at your side:
"Give back, O Cinna, what you took from me;
And if you hold your love more dear than me,
Hold not more dear the tyrant whom I serve."

    *Cinna.* My friend, be lenient with a wretched soul
That only in shame conceives a generous plan.
I know my crime against our citizens,
And I shall give them what I robbed them of;
But pardon this despair for our old friendship,
Which cannot die in me without a pang,
And grant that, looking forward to Amelia
I give a free course to my melancholy.

My sorrow pleads with you, and this distress
In which I stand wants only solitude.
  *Maximus.* You wish to give account to her who wounds
    you
Of Cæsar's bounty and your feebleness.
The talk of lovers calls for secrecy.
Adieu. I leave in wary confidence.

### Scene III. *Cinna*

  *Cinna.* Call by a worthier name this blessed power
Of sentiment which virtue stirs within me,
And honor sets against the head-long thrust
Of my ingratitude and shamelessness;
Yet, no!—call it rather weakness still,
Since it becomes so weak beside a mistress,
Since it respects a love it ought to stifle,
Or if it fights it, dares not conquer it.
What shall I do in this extremity?
To which side shall I lean? to which be loyal?
How painful to a noble soul to see
Whatever fruits I hope to pluck in this—
The happiness of love, the joy of vengeance,
The honor to have freed my native land—
Are not sufficient to enchant my mind
If treason be the means of winning them,
If I must wound a noble-hearted prince,
Who, little as I have deserved his favor,
Heaps me with honors, smothers me with gifts,
And takes no one's advice to rule but mine.
O treason too unworthy of a man!
Continue, Rome, forevermore enslaved!
Perish my love, perish my hope, or ever
These hands of mine take part in crime so black!

Does he not offer all that I desire,
All that my rage would purchase with his blood?
Must he be slain that I enjoy his gifts?
Must I wrest from him that which he would grant?
But I am held, bound by a reckless oath!
Amelia's hate! the memory of a father!
My faith, my heart, my arms are bound to you,
I can do nothing save by your permission:
It is for you to say what I shall do.
'Tis you, Amelia, who must grant him grace,
Your will alone controls his fate, and holds
Within my hands his life and death. O gods!
As you have rendered her adorable,
Make her, like you, amenable to prayers.
Since I have no escape from her commands
Grant me to make her yield to my desires.
But here she comes, inexorable and lovely.

SCENE IV. *Amelia, Cinna and Fulvia*

*Amelia.* The gods be praised, Cinna, my fears were **vain;**
None of your friends has played you false, and I
Was not compelled to use my power for you.
Octavius told Livia all before me,
And with this news restored to me my life.
　*Cinna.* Will you deny him and withhold from me
The happiness that hangs upon his gift?
　*Amelia.* That answer lies with you.
　*Cinna.*　　　　　　　　　But more with **you.**
　*Amelia.* I am what I have ever been, unchanged,
In giving me to Cinna, he gives nothing,
And makes him but a present of his own.
　*Cinna.* You still can—O Heaven! May I say it?
　*Amelia.* What can I do? Of what are you afraid?

*Cinna.* I tremble and I sigh, and see too well
That if our hearts burned with the same desire,
There were no need that I explain my sighs.
I am too certain of offending you.
I dare not speak, and cannot hold my peace.
   *Amelia.* You torture me! Speak out!
   *Cinna.*                 I must obey you.
I shall offend you then, and you will hate me.
I love you. Heaven's lightning strike me dead,
If in that love I find not all my joy,
Or if I love you not with all the warmth
A noble heart may feel for one so worthy!
But look you, at what price you grant your love,
To make me happy and infamous at once.
This goodness of Augustus—
   *Amelia.*             Enough. I hear you,
I see your weakness, your inconstant vows.
A tyrant's gifts erase your promises;
Your oaths give way before his blandishments;
Your credulous spirit dares to dream that Cæsar,
Being all powerful, can dispose of me.
You'd rather take me as his gift than mine,
But think not you shall ever have me so.
He may have power to shake the earth, to cast
Kings from their thrones and parcel out their states,
Redden with his proscriptions land and sea
And change at will the order of the world—
He has no power o'er Amelia's heart.
   *Cinna.* Only to you I owe my duty? I
Am ever the same. My faith is always pure;
Although I pity, I am not forsworn;
Your wishes I obey without reserve
And serve them even further than my vows.

You know that without perjury or crime
I could have let your victim save himself:
Cæsar resigning sovereign power would rob us
Of every pretext to assassinate him.
The whole conspiracy would be dissolved.
Your plot would fail, your anger would be foiled.
My words restored his weakening strength, my hand
Crowned him again, to be your sacrifice.

 *Amelia.* My victim, traitor! And you can wish that. I
Withhold your hand, and let him live and love him!
That I should be the spoil of him I spare,
The price by which he stays upon the throne!

 *Cinna.* Condemn me not that I have done you service
Without me you were powerless to kill him,
And spite of favors, I give all to love,
Wishing him dead or owing life to you.
With the first vows of my obedience,
Permit this feeble flash of gratitude,
That I may try to vanquish unjust wrath,
And stir in you the love he bears for you.
A kindly soul, and one which virtue guides
Abhors ingratitude and perfidy;
It loathes a baseness, linked with happiness,
And will have nothing at the cost of honor.

 *Amelia.* I fashion glory from this infamy:
Treason is noble against tyranny:
And breaking off the course of evil fate,
The most ungrateful show most generous.

  *Cinna.* You fashion virtues from your very hatred.
  *Amelia.* The virtues worthy of a Roman woman.
  *Cinna.* A truly Roman heart—
  *Amelia.*       Dares all to end
A hateful life which it is bound to serve.

Much more than death, it flees the shame of slavery.

    *Cinna.* 'Tis slavery with honor to be Cæsar's,
And we see often kings who at our knees
Beseech support of such poor slaves as we.
He casts at our feet the glory of his crowns,
He makes us sovereigns of their lofty grandeur,
He takes from them their tribute to enrich us,
And sets on them a yoke from which he frees us.

    *Amelia.* O base ambition which your heart proposes!
You think it something to be more than kings.
Between the ends of earth is one so vain
To think to match a Roman citizen?
Antony brought our wrath upon his head
Shaming himself even with a great queen's love.
The great king, Attila, whitened in the purple
To hear the Roman people call him free;
And though all Asia lay beneath his will,
He held his throne less dearly than that title.
Recall your name, recall your dignity;
And, with the spirit of a proper Roman,
Know that he is none, who was not born
To rule o'er kings and live without a master.

    *Cinna.* Heaven has shown in many such assaults
That it abhors assassins and repays
Ingratitude with punishment. Whatever
Is undertaken, what is carried out,
A throne once raised, it will avenge its fall;
It sides with those it gives the right to reign,
The wound by which one slays them bleeds and bleeds.
And once it has resolved to punish them,
A thunderbolt must strike them from their thrones.

    *Amelia.* Tell me. What puts you on their side and makes
    you

Depend on thunderbolts to punish tyrants?
I'll speak no more of it! Go serve your tyrant.
Forsake your love for that base soul of yours;
And soothe your wavering spirit by forgetting
Your birth and all the joy that waits for you.
Without your borrowed hand to serve my wrath
I can avenge my father and my country,
I had already won a glorious death
If love had not till now restrained my hand;
Love, holding me in slavery to your will,
Bade me for your sake to preserve my life.
Alone against a tyrant, I had died
In killing him, a victim of his guard.
I had robbed you of your captive by my death;
And since, for you alone, love bade me live,
I hoped, in vain, that I might live for you,
And give you means to become worthy of me.
Forgive me, gods, that I deceived myself
Thinking I loved the grandson of great Pompey,
And that, misled by false appearances,
I chose a slave in place of him I thought.
I love you still, whoever you may be.
And if you must betray your lord to win me,
A thousand others would accept that gauge
Gladly, if they might claim me as reward.
But think not any other shall possess me.
Live for your belovèd tyrant. I
Shall still die yours. My days shall find an end
Along with his, since by your cowardice
You show yourself unworthy of me. Come,
Look on me bathed in his blood and my own,
Behold me die in my own courage wrapped,
And hear me dying speak my spirit's peace:

"Lament me not. 'Tis you who caused my death;
The tomb I enter you condemned me to,
And glory follows me that might be yours:
I die, destroying absolute power in Rome.
But I had lived for you, if you had wished it."
 *Cinna.* So be it. 'Tis your wish, and you must have it.
Rome must be freed, your father be avenged.
Justice must be meted out to tyrants;
But know that Cæsar is less hard than you.
If he has taken our goods, our lives, our women,
He never yet has tyrannized our souls.
But the inhuman power of your beauty
Rules our spirits and controls our wills.
You make me prize that which dishonors me;
You make me hate that which my soul adores.
You make me shed the blood for which I should
Expose my own a thousand thousand times;
You wish it, I agree. My word is given;
My hand, however, will be straightway turned
Against my own breast, making of your lover
A sacrifice to such a prince's shade,
Joining to my forced crime my punishment.
And by this action mingled with the other,
I shall regain the glory which I lost.
Adieu.

### SCENE V. *Amelia, Fulvia*

 *Fulvia.* You have sunk his spirit in despair.
 *Amelia.* Let him cease to love me, or pursue his duty.
 *Fulvia.* He goes to spend his life at your command!
You weep, madam.
 *Amelia.*     Alas! Follow him, Fulvia.
And if your friendship would be kind to me,

Dissuade his heart from this design of death.
Tell him—

  *Fulvia.*     That you will let Augustus live?
  *Amelia.* Ah, that were too unjust to righteous hate.
  *Fulvia.* What then?
  *Amelia.*              That he has won, has proved his faith,
And he may choose between us, death or me!


## ACT IV.

### Scene I. *Augustus, Euphorbus, Polyclitus, Guards*

*Augustus.* Your news, Euphorbus, is incredible.
  *Euphorbus.* Sire, the tale is frightful to myself:
One scarcely can conceive of such a madness.
I quake with horror at the very thought.
  *Augustus.* My dearest friends! Cinna and Maximus!
The very two I held in highest honor,
To whom my heart was open, whom I chose
To fill the highest and the noblest posts!
After I placed my empire in their hands,
They plot together to destroy my life!
Maximus saw his fault, and sent me warning.
Showing a heart touched with sincere repentance.
But Cinna!
  *Euphorbus.* Alone retains his stubborn rage;
Your gifts but render him more mutinous.
The noble efforts, which touched with just remorse
His fellow plotters, leave him still unmoved.
In the face of terror blended with regrets
He still attempts to stir their burning souls.
  *Augustus.* He is the source and soul of their sedition!
O most disloyal man of all men born!
O treason fostered in a fury's breast!

O heartless blow to come from hand so dear!
Cinna, a traitor! Polyclitus, listen.

(*Speaks in his ear*)

*Polyclitus.* All your commands, Sire, shall be executed.

*Augustus.* And let Erastus summon Maximus,
Here to receive our pardon for his crime.

*Euphorbus.* Himself, he judged his crime too serious
To escape his punishment. And now I fear
Can scarce return even at your command;
With eyes distraught and wild bewildered look,
Broken with sighs and sobbing, he abjured
His life and all the foul conspiracy.
He spread the plot before me, as I told you,
And, having bade me speed to warn you, added
"Tell him that I shall bring myself to justice,
I am not ignorant of my deserts."
And having said that, suddenly he leaped
Into the Tiber, and the swirling waters
And darkness of the night hid from my eyes
The end of all his tragic history.

*Augustus.* He has too quickly yielded to remorse,
And placed himself beyond the reach of kindness.
There is no crime against me that repentance
Will not erase, but since he would renounce
My clemency, go grant it to the rest
And see that they have faithful witness of it.

### Scene II. *Augustus*

*Augustus.* O Heaven, to whom is it your will that I
Entrust my life, the secrets of my soul?
Take back the power with which you have endowed me,
If it but steals my friends to give me subjects,
If regal splendors must be fated ever,

Even by the greatest favors they can grant,
To foster only hate, if your stern law
Condemns a king to cherish only those
Who burn to have his blood. Nothing is certain.
Omnipotence is bought with ceaseless fear.
Look in your heart, Octavius, and cease
Your lamentations. What! Would you be spared,
Who have spared none yourself? Think of the waves
Of blood in which your arms are bathed. How much
Reddened the fields of Macedonia;
How much was shed in Antony's defeat;
How much in Sextus' fall. Then look once more
Upon Perugia drowned in its own blood,
With all its citizens. Recall again,
After all this, your murderous proscriptions
In which you were yourself the butcherer;
Sink the knife in your own tutor's breast,
And dare to cry injustice against fate,
Seeing your subjects armed for your destruction,
Taught by your own example how to kill you,
Ignoring rights, which you did not respect!
Their treason is deserved, sanctioned by heaven:
Leave your throne as you acquired it;
Shed faithless blood for infidelity;
Suffer ingratitude for having showed it.
Ah, how my reason fails me in my need!
What madness, Cinna, that I should accuse
Myself and pardon you. You, whose deceit
Convinced me to retain the sovereignty,
For which you wish to punish me, who think
Me criminal, yet make my only crime;
You who sustain a throne usurpèd solely
To strike it down and cover your intention

With shameless zeal, and set yourself against
The welfare of the State to murder me?
Should I forget this and withhold my wrath?
Let you live safely who have threatened me?
No! No! The very thought is treasonable;
Who pardons freely, but invites attack;
Punish the assassins, and proscribe the plotters!

Ah! Always blood! Always punishment!
I weary of cruelty, yet cannot stop it.
I would be feared, and yet can only anger.
Rome is a hydra bent upon my ruin,
One head struck off a thousand take its place.
And blood shed by a thousand traitors renders
My life more cursed, yet no more assured.
Octavius, wait not for the stroke of some
New Brutus. Die, and rob him of his glory;
The attempt to live were cowardly and vain
When such a host of brave men vow your death;
If every noble youth of Rome is stirred,
Time after time, to plot against your life.
Die, since it is a sore you cannot heal.
Die, since you must lose everything or die.
Life is a little thing, and what small part
Of life remains for you is not worth buying
At such a grievous cost. Die, but at least
Go grandly off, put out your spirit's torch
In this mad ingrate's blood, and, dying, offer
This traitor to yourself in sacrifice;
Fulfill his wishes, punish him for murder;
Make your own death his torture in arranging
That he shall witness it, but not enjoy it.
But let us more enjoy his punishment,

And if Rome hates us, triumph o'er its hate.
O Romans! O revenge! O sovereign power!
O awful battle of a wavering heart,
Which shrinks at once from all that it decides!
Give some command to this unhappy prince,
What counsel he should follow, what avoid,
And either let me die or let me reign.

### Scene IV.* *Amelia and Fulvia*

*Amelia.* Whence springs my joy, and how unseasonably,
In spite of all, my spirit seems at rest!
Cæsar has summoned Cinna, and I fear not!
My heart sends forth no sighs, my eyes no tears;
As if I had learned some hidden plan by which
All would be carried out as I desire!
Have I heard aright? Fulvia, do you speak true?

*Fulvia.* I have persuaded him to choose to live,
To make, more sweetly and more tactfully,
Another trial to overcome your wrath.
And I rejoiced when Polyclitus came,
The usual bearer of Augustus' will,
To find him, without following or confusion,
And led him straightway to the palace. Cæsar
Is greatly troubled, and none knows the cause;
And each suspects a different one. All think
That some great subject weighs upon his mind.
And Cinna has been called to give advice.
What worries me is what I just now learned:
That two unknowns have seized upon Evander;
Euphorbus is arrested, none knows why;
And strange, uncertain things are noised abroad

---

* Scene III is always omitted on the stage and is therefore omitted here.
—*Ed.*

About his master. He is said to be
The victim of a dark despair. Men speak
Of night, of Tiber, and the rest is silence.

   *Amelia.* Here is cause for fear and hopelessness,
And yet my sad heart scorns to speak of it.
It seems that Heaven always stirs in me
A contrary emotion; not long since
Unfounded terror overcame my spirit;
Now, when it should, fear moves me not at all.
I understand your ways, great gods, your blessings,
Which l adore, would never have me bring
Dishonor on myself, and damming up
My sighs, my sobs and tears, sustain my heart
Against such woes. It is your will that I,
Who set myself to such a noble task,
Shall die courageously; and I will gladly
Meet death as you command, and in the temper
Which you inspire.
              O liberty of Rome!
Shade of my father! I have done my part,
Such as I could; against your murderer
I leagued his friends, and for your sake I dared
More than was lawful for me; if success
Crown not my work, my glory is not less.
If I cannot avenge you, I shall join you;
So reeking still with all consuming wrath
And from a death so worthy of your fame,
You will be comforted to see in me
The blood of heroes of whose line I am.

### Scene V. *Maximus, Amelia, Fulvia*

   *Amelia.* You, Maximus, who were reported dead!
   *Maximus.* Euphorbus but deceived Octavius

With false report; seeing himself arrested,
The plot discovered, he feigned this death of mine
To save me from my doom.

    *Amelia.*               But what of Cinna?

    *Maximus.* 'Tis even now his bitterest regret
That Cæsar knows your secret. Vainly Cinna
Denied it, swore that he knew nothing of it.
Evander, hoping so to save his master
Has told Augustus all, and by his order
His messenger is here to summon you.

    *Amelia.* Whoever he is, he stays too long in coming.
I am ready to follow, weary with delay.

    *Maximus.* He waits at my house.

    *Amelia.*              Yours?

    *Maximus.*                   You are sur-
prised.
But learn how Heaven has cared for you. 'Tis one
Of our conspirators who will flee with us.
Let us be gone before we are pursued.
There is a vessel ready by the shore.

    *Amelia.* Do you know me, Maximus, know who I am?

    *Maximus.* What I can do, I do for Cinna's sake,
And seek to save from his unhappy doom
The loveliest portion of him that remains.
Let us save ourselves, Amelia, and preserve
Our lives for vengeance in a happier hour.

    *Amelia.* Cinna, in his misfortune, is one of those
Who must be followed, who dare not be avenged
For fear that we survive him. Anyone
Who after Cinna's death would save himself
Does not deserve the life he seeks to save.

    *Maximus.* What blind despair stirs you to such a madness?
O gods! What weakness in a soul so strong!

A heart so noble, so unapt for battle,
So stricken by the first reverse of fortune!
Recall, recall this marvelous strength of yours,
Open your eyes, and learn of Maximus;
Another Cinna you behold in him.
Heaven has sent in him another lover
For him you lose. Since friendship makes their hearts
To beat as one, love Cinna in his friend;
And he will love you with an equal passion.

    *Amelia.* You dare to love me, and you dare not die!
Your claims appear a trifle over high
But since you make them, show yourself at least
Worthy of that for which you sue. Refuse
To flee in cowardice from noble death
Or cease to offer me so base a heart.
Act so that I may envy your perfection:
I cannot love you, see that I regret you.
Show me a true-born Roman's last devotion,
And in the place of love, deserve my tears.
If you are so concerned for Cinna's sake,
Think you to serve him, flattering his mistress?
Learn, learn from me the duty which you owe him.
Be my example, or take me for yours.

    *Maximus.* Your natural grief is too precipitate.

    *Amelia.* And yours is too ingenious in your favor.
You speak already of a glad return,
And in your sorrow you can think of love!

    *Maximus.* This love is newly born, but all consuming:
It is your lover, my friend, I love in you,
And with the very fire that burned in him—

    *Amelia.* Stop, Maximus, you speak beyond discretion.
My loss has startled, not perplexed my mind.
My deep-set sorrow has not struck me blind.

My soul, stirred to its depths, is yet untroubled,
And I see more than I would wish to see.

   *Maximus.* Can you suspect me of some perfidy?

   *Amelia.* Yes. Since you wish that I should say the **word,**
The order of our flight is too well planned
Not to suspect you of some treachery:
The gods were prodigal of miracles
If they had raised up all these difficulties
For us without your aid. Go. Flee without me.
Your words of love are not desired here.

   *Maximus.* Oh, you are hard!

   *Amelia.*               I can be harder **still.**
Fear not that I shall break forth in abuse,
Nor hope to dazzle me with vows forsworn;
And if my harshness seems to do you wrong,
Come die with me to justify yourself.

   *Maximus.* Live, dear Amelia, but permit your slave—

   *Amelia.* I'll hear no more save in Octavius' presence.
Come, Fulvia, come.

## Scene VI. *Maximus*

   *Maximus.*         Despairing and ashamed,
Deserving, too, if that were possible,
Of still more cruel refusal, Maximus,
What can you do? What sort of punishment
Have you prepared for your vain trickery?
No dreams are left that can deceive you more.
Amelia dying will disclose all, all,
And on the very scaffold where she dies
Display her glory and your infamy.
Her death will leave for all the years to come
The shameful memory of your faithlessness.
One day has seen you in one treacherous speech

Betray your king, your friend, and her you love.
Besides so many laws in one day broken,
Besides two lovers basely sacrificed
To tyranny, nothing remains for you
But shame and anger and a vain remorse.
This is your work, Euphorbus, your base counsel;
But what can one expect from such a man?
A freed-man never can be aught but slave;
His rank may alter but his spirit never.
And yours, still servile, took with liberty
No glimmer of nobility; through you
I stirred within myself an evil power,
Denied the very honor of my birth—
My heart resisted you, you fought it back
Until your villainy befouled its virtue.
Your baseness cost my life, my fame, and I
Deserve it all for that I trusted you.
Yet in return the gods will grant me leave
To sacrifice you in these lovers' sight,
And I dare hope, in spite of my offense,
My blood will later serve them with a victim
Pure enough, if in your blood my arms
May wash away the stain of having heard you.


## ACT V

### Scene I. *Augustus, Cinna*

*Augustus.* Be seated, Cinna, and on every point
Follow the orders which I lay upon you;
In silence lend your ear to what I say;
Neither by word nor cry break in upon me;
Hold your tongue captive, and if silence stir

Some violence in your feelings, afterwards
You shall be able to reply at leisure.
Only on this point grant me my desire.

   *Cinna.* I shall obey you, Sire.

   *Augustus.*                Remember then
To keep your word, and I shall hold to mine.
You live, Cinna, but those who gave you life
Were enemies to my father and to me.
Your birthplace was their very camp and when,
After their death, you came within my power,
Their hate, deep rooted in your breast, had armed
Your hand against me. You were my enemy
Before your birth, and when you came to know me
Were still my enemy, and our attachment
Could never overcome the heritage
Which placed you on the other side; as much
As you were able you remained my foe.
My only vengeance was to give you life;
My prisoner, I loaded you with favors;
Your prison was my court, my gifts your bonds;
First I restored to you your patrimony,
And afterwards enriched you with the spoils
Of Antony, and ever since, you know,
My favors fell upon you in profusion;
Every distinction which you asked of me
I granted you at once without reluctance;
I gave you preference even over those
Whose fathers formerly within my camp
Had held the highest ranks, o'er those whose blood
Had bought my empire for me, even those
Who had preserved the life which now I breathe.
Finally, I have so lived with you,
The conquerors are jealous of the conquered.

When Heaven willed that I recall Mæcenas,
And after many favors show some anger,
In that sad time, I gave his place to you
And you became my dearest confidant.
Even today when my irresolute heart
Urged me to retire from sovereign power
I sought my sole advice from Maximus
And you, and spite of him, I followed yours.
Still more, on this same day I gave to you
Amelia, worthy of the adoration
Of all of Italy, who occupies
So high a place in my concern and love
That had I crowned you king, I had given you less.
You must remember, Cinna; so much fortune
Cannot so soon have faded from your mind.
Yet something more incredible has happened,
You do remember, Cinna, and yet would kill me.
   *Cinna.* I, Sire! Have I a soul so traitorous,
So base a plan—
   *Augustus.*      You keep your promise ill:
Sit down, I have not spoken all I would.
Afterwards clear yourself, if possible.
Meanwhile, give ear to me, and keep your word.
You planned to kill me in the Capitol
Tomorrow during the sacrifice, your hand
From which I should have taken the incense
Was to have struck the fatal blow as signal;
Half of your people were to hold the door,
The other half to follow you and help.
Are these true words, or simply base suspicion?
Shall I recite for you the murderers' names?
Proculus, Glabrius, Virginius,
Rutilus, Plantus, Lenas, Pomponius,

Marcellus, Albinus, Icilius,
Maximus, whom next yourself I loved;
'Twere too much honor even to name the rest;
A mob of men sunk deep in debt and crime,
On whom my just decrees rest heavily,
And who, despairing of escape, knew well
They could not live if all were not o'erthrown.
You are silent now, and you preserve your silence
More from confusion than obedience.
What was your plan, what did you mean to do
When I lay in the temple at your feet?
To free your country from a monarch's sway?
If I interpreted your words aright,
Her future welfare hung upon a sovereign
Who, to preserve all, holds all as his own;
And if her liberty was your desire,
No force was needed to make me give it back.
In the name of all the State you might have had it
Without the trouble of assassination.
What was your plan? To reign here in my place?
It were a strangely evil destiny
If in your mounting to the royal throne
You found in Rome no obstacle but me.
If she be sunk to such a state that you
Are, after me, her greatest, that the weight
Of the Roman Empire, after I am dead,
Could fall into no better hands than yours.
Know yourself, Cinna, look into your heart:
They honor you in Rome. They court you, love you,
Tremble before you, offer you their homage;
Your star is high. What you would do, you can:
But none would be too mean to pity you
If I abandoned you to your deserts.

Deny it if you dare, tell me your worth,
Recount your virtues and your glorious deeds,
Those rare accomplishments with which you pleased me
And all that raised you up above the herd.
My favor makes your glory, out of that
Your power grows; that only raised you up,
And held you there, 'tis that the Romans honor,
Not yourself. You have no rank or power
Except I give it you, and for your fall
There needs but the withdrawal of my hand,
Which is your sole support. But I prefer
To yield to your desire. Reign, if you will,
Even if it cost my life. But dare you think
That Cassius, Servilius, Metellus,
Paulus and Fabius and all the rest
For whom the noble heroes of their blood
Are living images, will sink the pride
Of such an old nobility as theirs
Only that you may rule them in my stead?
Now speak, I give you leave.

 *Cinna.*      I am struck dumb—
Not by your anger or the fear of death—
I am betrayed and I am wondering
Who was the traitor, and I cannot find him.
But that is not all that occupies my thoughts.
Sire, I am a Roman citizen,
Of Pompey's blood. A father and two sons
Done cruelly to death were all too weakly
Avenged by Cæsar's death. There is the cause,
The only cause of all our grand design.
Though treachery expose me to your wrath
Expect no cringing penitence from me,
No vain regrets, nor weak, disgraceful sighs:

The die was cast, the fortune fell to you.
I know what I have done, what you must do.
Posterity must have a precedent
And for your safety, that must be my death.

*Augustus.* You brave me, Cinna, far from asking pardon,
You glory in your treason. Let us see
If constancy will serve you to the end.
You know what you deserve, that I know all,
Pass your own sentence, choose your punishment.

SCENE II. *Livia, Augustus, Cinna, Amelia, Fulvia*

*Livia.* You know not yet all the accomplices.
Sire, your Amelia is one of them.
*Cinna.* She, here, O gods!
*Augustus.* And you, my daughter, too!
*Amelia.* All that he did, he did but for my sake,
I was the cause of all, Sire, and the payment.
*Augustus.* What! Has the love which but today I sought
To stir within your heart led you so soon
So near to death for him! It seems you love
With far too much abandon, 'tis too soon
To love this lover whom I give to you.
*Amelia.* 'Tis love that has exposed me to your wrath
Not my too prompt obedience to your will.
These flames were kindled in our hearts and burned
For four years secretly, without your orders:
But though I love and though he burns for me,
A hate more strong than love commands us both,
Never would I permit him hope of me
Till he assured me vengeance for my father:
I made him swear it; he sought out his friends;
Heaven withheld the prize that I was promised,
And now I come to offer you a victim

Not in the hope to save his life by taking
Upon myself the burden of his crime.
Death is just punishment for his attempt,
And all excuse is vain against high treason:
Only to die with him, to join my father,
That is my whole desire, my every hope.

*Augustus.* How long, O Heaven, and for what cause have
you
Aimed shafts against me in my very house?
I banished Julia from it for her lewdness;
My love picked out Amelia in her place,
And now I see she too has proved unworthy.
One shamed my name, one thirsted for my blood;
Both took their passions for their guide, and one
Was shameless, one a murderess.
O my daughter! Is this my love's reward?

*Amelia.* My father's love received the same from you.

*Augustus.* Think with what care I watched o'er you in
youth.

*Amelia.* With the same care my father fostered you;
He was your tutor, you were his assassin;
You pointed out to me the road to crime.
In one point only mine is different.
'Twas your ambition sacrificed my father,
And this just wrath with which I am consumed,
Would sacrifice you to his innocent blood.

*Livia.* This is too much, Amelia. Stop. Consider.
He has done all for you a father could:
This death of which the memory stirs your fury,
That was Octavius', not the emperor's crime.
These crimes of state, committed for the crown,
Heaven absolves when once the crown is given,
And in the sacred rank which Heaven favors

The past is justified, the future free.
He who attains it is not culpable;
Whatever he did or does, he is inviolate:
We owe our happiness to him; our lives
Are in his hand. The king is not in ours.

*Amelia.* In all that you have heard me say, I spoke
To stir his anger, not defend myself.
Then punish, Sire, these felonious charms
That make your favorites such illustrious ingrates.
Cut off my weary life to save your own.
As I won over Cinna, I shall others,
And I am more to fear, you more in danger
If love be joined to blood to cry for vengeance.

*Cinna.* You my seducer! Must I suffer still
To be dishonored by her whom I adore!
Sire, this moment calls for all the truth:
I made this plot before I came to love her;
Finding her cold to all my eager prayers,
I thought to win her by another plan.
I spoke of her father, of your severity,
And with my heart I offered her my arms.
Revenge is sweet to any woman's spirit!
There I attacked her, there I found her heart.
Heedless of my small merit, she could not
Be heedless, too, of arms that would avenge her;
My cunning won her to conspiracy.
I, the creator, she but the accomplice.

*Amelia.* Cinna, dare you speak so? Is this true love
To rob me of honor when I have to die?

*Cinna.* Die, but in dying do not stain my glory.

*Amelia.* If Cæsar will believe you, mine is withered.

*Cinna.* And mine is dead if you take to yourself
All that results from such a noble plan.

*Amelia.* Be it so. Take then your part, and leave me mine;
'Twould weaken mine, were I to weaken yours:
The glory and the joy, the shame and torture
All should be common to those who truly love.
Our spirits, Sire, both are Roman, both,
United in desire, are one in hate.
A quick desire to avenge our fathers' death
Taught us together where our duty lay;
Our hearts were joined in this conspiracy;
Together we conceived it, and together
We seek the honor of a glorious death.
You wish to join us; do not part us now.

*Augustus.* Yes. I shall join you, traitors that you are,
Ungrateful couple, and more my enemies
Than even Antony or Lepidus:
Yes. I shall join you, since you wish it so;
The fire that burns within you must be quenched,
And all the world, knowing what is in my heart,
Be stunned by punishment as well as crime.

SCENE III. *Augustus, Livia, Cinna, Maximus, Amelia, Fulvia*

*Augustus.* Heaven at last is kind to me in saving
Maximus from the fury of the waves.
Approach, my only friend, who proved his faith.

*Maximus.* Oh, be less gracious to a traitor's heart.

*Augustus.* Speak no more of crime after repentance,
After the danger which you saved me from:
To you I owe my empire and my life.

*Maximus.* Let me lay bare the worst of all your foes:
If you still reign, if you are living, Sire,
You owe it only to my jealous rage.
No dutiful remorse disturbed my heart;

To kill my rival, I exposed his plot:
Euphorbus lied in saying I was drowned,
Fearing that you would send for me. I wanted
Time to deceive Amelia, to dismay her,
And carry her from Italy. I hoped
To win her to this plan by holding out
Hope of returning to avenge her lover.
Instead of nibbling at my clumsy bait,
Her courage doubled in the face of danger;
She read my very heart; you know the rest.
And my retelling were superfluous.
You see the outcome of my shameful craft:
If any grace is owing my confession,
Condemn Euphorbus to a thousand tortures,
And let me die before these lovers' eyes.
By his advice I have betrayed my friend,
My love, my king, my honor and my country;
Yet might I still be happy, if I could
Punish myself, once I had punished him.

   *Augustus*. Enough, O Heaven! Has fortune, for my ruin,
Someone of mine it still would turn against me?
Let him be aided by the powers of hell;
I am master of myself as of the world,
I am the master and I will to be so.
O rolling years, O memory of man,
Preserve forever my last victory;
Today I triumph o'er the justest wrath
That yet was stirred within a human breast.
Let us be friends, Cinna. 'Tis I who ask it:
As to my enemy I gave you life,
And spite of fury at your base design,
I give it you, even as my assassin.
Let us begin a battle, which of us

Shall have the better, giver or receiver.
You have betrayed my gifts, I double them.
I have heaped them on you, I shall smother you;
And with this grace that I have granted you,
Take, too, the consulate for the coming year.
My child, love Cinna in this noble station,
Prefer its crimson to my blood's, and learn
From me to conquer wrath. I give you back
A husband, and in him, more than a father.

   *Amelia.* And I surrender, Sire, to your great kindness.
With clear brilliance I regain my sight.
I recognize my crime, which I thought justice,
And—what no fear of punishment could do—
I feel a strong repentance born within me
And acquiescence in my secret heart.
Heaven has set its seal upon your grandeur
And for the proof, Sire, I am satisfied.
And this I dare declare with pride, since heaven
Has changed my heart, may it too change the State.
My hate is dying, that I believed immortal;
Is dead, and in its place, a loyal heart.
Henceforward, in stark horror of this hate,
Ardor of service shall replace its fury.

   *Cinna.* What can I say, Sire, after our offenses
Receive rewards instead of punishment?
This rare nobility, this mercy shows
Your power more just, my crime more infamous.

   *Augustus.* Do not retard a kind forgetfulness;
And join me in forgiving Maximus:
He has deceived us all, but what he did
Preserves you guiltless, gives me back my friends.
   (*To Maximus*)
Take your accustomed place with me again:

Resume your reputation and your fame.
But grant Euphorbus grace, too, in his turn,
And let tomorrow, Hymen crown their love.
If you still love her, that is your punishment.

    *Maximus.* I cannot murmur. I have more than justice.
And I am more confounded by your kindness
Than jealous of the joy you rob me of.

    *Cinna.* Let but my duty, reborn in my heart,
Pledge you a faith already basely broken,
But now so firm, so far from wavering,
The very fall of heaven could not shake it.
May the great author of fair destinies
Prolong your life, cut short our years, and grant
To me the happiness supreme of losing
For you a hundred times what by your grace I hold.

    *Livia.* This is not all, Sire: a celestial flame,
A light prophetic bursts upon my soul.
Hear what the gods would say to you through me:
The certain law of your high destiny.
After this action you have naught to fear;
Your yoke will be endured without complaint
And those most violent, by change of heart,
Will count it glorious to die your subjects;
No shameful plots and no ungrateful envy
Will strike henceforth at such a life as yours:
No more assassins or conspirators:
You have achieved the mastery of their hearts.
Rome, with a deep and heart-felt joy, will place
Within your hands the empire of the world.
Your royal virtues will convince the State
Its happiness depends upon your reign:
Its ancient error finally shaken off,
It will be faithful to the monarchy.

Temples and altars it prepares for you
As heaven makes a place with the immortals.
And future years in every land will hold you
A bright example to their noblest kings.
  *Augustus.* I bow before your prophecy, I dare
To hope for its fulfillment; thus the gods
Have ever been accustomed to inspire you.
Tomorrow let our joyous sacrifice
Be doubled, that the auspices may be
Most favorable and your conspirators
Hear published through the city how Augustus
Discovered all and willed all be forgotten.

FINIS

# ANDROMACHE

by

## JEAN RACINE

## CHARACTERS

ANDROMACHE....... *Widow of Hector, captive of Pyrrhus*
PYRRHUS........... *Son of Achilles, King of Epirus*
ORESTES........... *Son of Agamemnon, lover of Hermione*
HERMIONE......... *Daughter of Helen*
PYLADES........... *Friend of Orestes*
CLEONE............*Confidante of Hermione*
CEPHISSA..........*Confidante of Andromache*
PHŒNIX...........*Tutor of Achilles, follower of Pyrrhus*
FOLLOWERS OF ORESTES

The scene is at Buthrotum, city of Epirus, in a room in the palace of Pyrrhus.

# ACT I

*(Enter Orestes and Pylades)*

*Orestes.* Yes, since I find again my truest friend
My fortune takes herself a newer face.
Her wrath already seems to have been soothed,
Since she has let us meet each other here.
Who would have thought that this ill-omened coast
Would bring you first before Orestes' eyes,
And, lost six months and more, that I should find you
Here in Epirus, at the court of Pyrrhus?

*Pylades.* I thank the gods, who often slowed my steps
And seemed intent to shut me out of Greece,
Since that most fatal day, when all our vessels
Were tossed and scattered by the wind and waves
Close on Epirus. How I've feared for you!
How many tears I've wept for your misfortunes,
Always for you, fearing a new mischance,
Some sorrow which my friendship could not share.
And most of all I feared that brooding gloom
Which I have seen clouding your soul so long.
I feared lest Heaven, for a cruel boon
Might offer you the death which you were seeking.
I see you here, my lord, and I dare say
A fate more happy brings you to Epirus.
The splendor which attends your footsteps here
Is not the train of one who seeks for death!

*Orestes.* Alas, who knows what fate is guiding me?
Love sends me here, to seek a cruel mistress,

But I can never know what Fate has ordered,
Whether I come to find my life—or death.

   *Pylades.* Then is your soul so bound in slavery
That you would live because of love, alone?
What spell has sent you to those flames again,
Forgetting all the tortures you have suffered?
Will she, who would not hear you pray in Sparta
Prove kinder, now she finds you in Epirus?
You should despise her; you should blush with shame
For vows so futile. Speak no more of her,
Your words deceived me.

   *Orestes.*            I deceived myself.
Oh, do not crush a wretch who loves you well.
What yearning have I ever hidden from you?
You knew my flame new-born, and my first sigh.
You saw how I despaired, when Menelaus
Made promise of his daughter's hand to Pyrrhus,—
He who avenged his race; and you have seen
How I have dragged my chains from sea to sea.
I saw you, full of pity for my state
Ready to follow where I chanced to go.
Day after day you saved me from myself,
And checked my madness in its wild career.
But when I was distracted, when I thought
Of how Hermione was lavishing
Her charms on Pyrrhus, well you know I tried,
Filled with my anger, to repay her scorn
With my forgetfulness. Then you believed
And I, myself, believed the fight was won.
I thought my passion had been turned to hatred,
I mocked her charms, and thought that I abhorred her,
I loathed her coldness. I defied her eyes
To bring again the love that I had crushed.

It was in that false calm I came to Greece,
And found the kings in arms against a danger,—
No little peril,—which had newly risen,
Heavy with troubles. Then, most eagerly
I joined them, for, indeed, I hoped to find
Freedom from other cares, in this new work,
I hoped that, if my strength came back to me
My heart would lose remembrance of its love.
But look you how my persecuting fates
Snared me the sooner in the trap I shunned.
I heard the threats and murmurs everywhere
Raised against Pyrrhus by the whole of Greece,
Which cried that Pyrrhus had forgot his promise
And his own blood, that at his court he harbors
The enemy of Greece, Astyanax,—
The young and most unhappy son of Hector,
The child of many buried kings who lie
Beneath the walls of Troy. As I have heard,
Andromache deceived the great Ulysses
To save her baby,—for another child
Torn from her arms, was killed in place of him.
They tell me that Hermione has failed.
She has not won my rival; he has offered
To give his heart and kingdom to another.
Though Menelaus will not trust the rumor,
The long delay has tried his patience sorely.
To me, the very reason for his anger
Is my own secret triumph, though at first
I thought it but a feeling of revenge,
A flattery of pride. But soon enough
I found my lovely persecutor taking
Her old place in my heart; the old fire burned,
I felt my hatred melt and quickly vanish,—

Or rather, knew I'd never ceased to love her.
I begged the aid of all the Greeks; they sent me
Here, where I am, to Pyrrhus, and the mission
Which brings me here is but to seize this child.
Many there are to fear him while he lives,
I come to snatch him out of Pyrrhus' arms,
Yet I should be most happy, could I capture
Not Hector's son indeed, but my own princess.
No, do not think this flame, which has been fanned
By being smothered long, can be extinguished
By any sort of peril. I've resisted
And proved resistance vain, and so I yield me
Blindly to passion; loving Hermione,
I come to win her, fly with her, or die.
You know this Pyrrhus. What will Pyrrhus do?
Tell me what happens in his court, and what
Passes within his heart. Is he still bound
To my Hermione; will he restore her,
And give me back the treasure he has stolen?

    *Pylades.* If I should promise that, I should deceive you,
She never will be yours, with his consent.
And yet he does not seem too greatly pleased
That he has won her, since his heart is burning
For Hector's widow with a warmer passion.
So far, Andromache has been unkind,
And always she has paid his love with hatred;
Each day he tries, by every sort of means
To break her will, or to arouse her fears.
He hides her child, and threatens it with death,
Then seeks to dry the tears which he has caused.
A hundred times Hermione has seen him,
Chastened, go seeking for her love again
And humbly make his promises once more

With troubled sighs, half loving, half in anger.
And so you must not think that I could tell you
What moves within a heart so poorly managed.
In such a turmoil, he may choose to marry
Her whom he scorns, and lose the one he loves.

    *Orestes.* But tell me how Hermione looks on it—
When he neglects her charms, delays her marriage.

    *Pylades.* Why, it would seem, my lord, that she is angered
Since he who is her suitor proves so fickle.
She thinks that he is far from wanting her,
That he'd be glad, should she take back her heart.
Indeed, she has revealed her grief to me.
And she laments his carelessness in secret,
Ready to leave,—and yet she always stays
And sometimes calls Orestes to her aid.

    *Orestes.* Oh, if I thought so, Pylades, why, then
I would go quickly, throw myself—

    *Pylades.*                   Yet wait—
Look to your task, and go before the king.
Tell him the whole of Greece is now united
Against the son of Hector. He will never
Surrender them the child of her he loves;
Rather their hate will only make him fonder.
All that is done to part them draws them closer,—
Then press your mission, and its end must fail,—
He comes.

    *Orestes.*    Go, make her ready, then, to see
A lover, come here only for her sake.

        *(Exit Pylades. Enter Pyrrhus and Phœnix)*
Before all Greece addresses you, through me,
I'll say that I am glad to be her choice,
And I am glad to see here, face to face,
Achilles' son, the conqueror of Troy.

Yes, we admire your deeds as we do his;
Before him, Hector fell; Troy before you;
You dare and you succeed—and both have shown
Only Achilles' son can fill his place.
And yet, with pain, we see you do what he
Never would so; you give unhappy Troy
New strength to injure; you let pity move you
With a fatal touch; and you prolong a feud
Already fought too long. Have you forgotten
The might of Hector? We can still remember
The blood his strength has cost us; at his name
Our orphans and our widows well may tremble.
There's not a home that does not call for vengeance
Upon this son of his, because of fathers
Or husbands lost through him; who knows what evil
This child may bring upon us in his time?
He will come down, as we have seen his father,
Upon our harbors, he will burn our ships
And, bearing fire, chase them across the waves.
Sir, shall I dare to tell you what I think?
I think you fear how he will pay your kindness
And that this serpent, cherished in your bosom,
Will some day strike you down for caring for him.
Why then, let Greece's wish be satisfied,—
Make your life safe by working her revenge.
Destroy an enemy so full of danger,
One who will practice first, upon yourself,
That sword which he will later turn on her.

   *Pyrrhus.* Greece is too much alarmed on my behalf.
I thought her moved by cares of greater moment.
I had supposed that such an envoy brought
Some greater mission than the one you tell me.
Who would have thought the son of Agamemnon

Would stoop to have a part in this affair,
Or that the whole of Greece, after her triumph,
Would make a plot upon a baby's life?
To whom am I to make this sacrifice?
Greece may no longer claim his life as hers;
Or is it that, of all the Greeks, I only
May not treat captives, fallen to my lot
As I may please to treat them. Under the walls
Of smoking Troy, the conquerors, all bloody,
Divided spoils, and to me fell this child,
The son of Hector and Andromache;
Ulysses made the cup of misery
To overflow for Hecuba, Cassandra
Was taken off to Argos by your father.
And have I sought to rule them, or their captives?
Or dared to claim the harvest of their courage?
They fear the day when Hector lives again,—
They say his son may take my life from me
If I should spare him his. It is a caution
Which shows too great a care. 'Tis too remote,
And such misfortunes are beyond my thinking.
Why, I can see proud Troy, as once she was,
Mother of heroes, queen of the whole of Asia,
Crowned with high towers; after that I see
How she fell, headlong,—how she lies outstretched,
With only heaps of ashes for her walls,
A river, running blood, and fields forsaken,
A child in chains; and I can little think
That Troy, so fallen, dreams upon revenge.
If we have sworn that Hector's son should die,
Why did we let a year pass over him?
Why not have killed him in the arms of Priam?

Troy would have served him for a tomb as well
As it has served the others. Age and youth
Both plead their weakness vainly then. War's frenzy
And darkness of the night were worse than we.
They left no choice for our destroying swords.
My own rage was as fierce against the conquered
As that of any there. But now I ask,
Should cruelty remain, outliving fury?
And can I, when my blood is cool again
Throw pity by, and slaughter one poor child?
Not so! And Greece may hunt some other prey,
And seek elsewhere to blot out Troy's last traces.
My hatred's done, and what the war has spared
Shall be preserved in safety, in Epirus.

   *Orestes.* My lord, you know quite well the cunning trick
Which brought a false Astyanax to death
In place of Hector's son. It is not Troy
Nor Trojans,—it is Hector whom they seek.
Greece tracks the father's footsteps to the son.
The wrath that bloodshed kindled must be quenched
Only in blood, and in no blood but Hector's.
And they will seek it even in Epirus.
Prevent them—
   *Pyrrhus.*      No, I will accept the challenge,
And that with joy, and let them come to find
A second Troy before them, in Epirus,
Since, in their hate, they look upon the friend
Who brought them triumphs, as their enemy.
It will not be the first time Greece repays
All of Achilles' service with injustice;
Once that was Hector's gain; the day may come
When Hector's son may profit in his turn.

*Orestes.* So Greece will find you a rebellious son?

*Pyrrhus.* And do you think that I have made my conquests
Only to lean on Greece?

*Orestes.* Hermione
Will stop you in your foolish course, her eyes
Will come between her father and yourself.

*Pyrrhus.* Hermione may be most dear to me,
And yet I need not be her father's slave
Because I love her. It may be that time
Will bring back honor to the claims of love.
You may see Helen's daughter, in the meanwhile,
I know what ties of blood link you together,—
And after that I will no longer keep you.
Say to them I refused what Greece demanded.

(*Exit Orestes*)

*Phœnix.* And so you send him to his mistress' feet!

*Pyrrhus.* They say his passion has been burning long.

*Phœnix.* And what if it should burn in him again?
If he should give his heart, and she give hers?

*Pyrrhus.* Why, Phœnix, let them love. I shall consent,
And she may take her leave. If these two love,
Let them go back to Sparta. Not a port
Shall bar their going hence. I shall be spared
From having more of her constraints.

*Phœnix.* My lord!

*Pyrrhus.* I'll lay my soul bare at a better time.
Andromache is coming.

(*Enter Andromache and Cephissa*)

*Pyrrhus.* Is it I
Whom you are seeking? Lady, may I hope
For anything so pleasant?

*Andromache.* I was going,
To find my son, since I have leave to see him

Once in a day; to see the only being
That still is left to me of Troy and Hector.
I have not wept with him, as yet, nor held him
A moment in my arms.

    *Pyrrhus.*             If rumor's true,
Greece will soon give you reason for more tears.

    *Andromache.* What is this terror in the heart of Greece?
Is it that some one Trojan has escaped?

    *Pyrrhus.* The hatred that they one time felt for Hector
Is not yet vanished, and they dread his son.

    *Andromache.* They find a worthy object for their fear!
He does not know that Hector was his father,
He does not even know that you're his master.

    *Pyrrhus.* No matter—for the Greeks demand his blood
And Agamemnon's son has come from them
To ask for his destruction.

    *Andromache.*           Will you give it?
Will you pronounce a sentence quite so cruel?
His only crime is that I love him dearly.
They do not fear he will avenge his father;
They tremble lest he dry his mother's tears.
He would have filled the place of husband, father,
But I must lose them both, and at your hand.

    *Pyrrhus.* Nay, do not weep. I have refused their wishes,
Although they threaten war. And if, again,
They set their sails with twice five hundred ships,
Seeking to force your son away from you,—
If all the blood that flowed because of Helen
Must be the price of it; if I must see
Ten years of war, and at the end my palace
Sinking in flames, why, still I would not falter,
And still I will defend his life with mine.
But if I meet such perils for your sake,

Will you refuse to grant one kinder look?
When I am pressed about, when all Greece hates me,
Must I still struggle with your cruelty?
My arm is here to serve you; might I hope
That you will take my heart's devotion, too?
Do not let him who would defend you, find you
Ranked in the number of his enemies.

    *Andromache.* Think what you do, my lord, what Greece
    will say
Can any soul so great as yours show weakness?
You would not have your goodness seem to be
Only the madness of a lovesick youth.
How should you wish the love of any captive
Sad as I am, who cannot bear myself?
Can eyes, haunted with grief, have charms for you,
When you have doomed them to eternal tears?
Oh, no; respect a captive's misery,
And if you would make wretchedness more light,
Restore a son into his mother's arms,
Stand out against the cruelty of Greece,
And do not make my heart the price of it.
Protect him, in his need, against my will,—
That were the conduct of Achilles' son.

    *Pyrrhus.* So? Is your anger still so hot? Shall hatred
And all its punishments be never done with?
Doubtless I caused much anguish. Troy has seen
This hand, stained crimson, with her own red blood,
A hundred times; but since I have been struck
By shafts from Beauty's eyes, have I not paid,
And dearly paid for all the tears they shed?
And have I not long since been taught repentance?
I suffer all the hurt I gave to Troy,
For I am vanquished, taken prisoner,

And burdened with regrets, consumed with fires
More fierce than those I lit. Such tears are mine,
Such restless longings, such anxieties!
When was I ever harsh, as you are now?
Oh, have you still not punished me enough?
Why, let our common enemies unite us!
If you will only tell me I may hope,
Then I will give your son to you again,
I'll be a father to him. I will teach him
To be the avenger to his country's wrongs.
I'll punish Greece myself, for your misfortunes,
And for my own. One look will give me strength
For all that I will do. Troy shall spring up
Even from ashes, and her walls shall rise
Sooner than once they fell before the siege.
Your son shall wear the crown, and be her king—

    *Andromache.* I do not care for such a glory now.
These thoughts had pleased me while his father lived.
Troy's sacred walls, that Hector could not save,
May never hope to see us there again.
My lord, the wretched are content with less.
These tears are only asking you for exile.
Oh, let me hide my son and mourn my loss
Far from the Greeks, and far away from you.
Your love can only make them hate us more.
Go back,—return once more to Helen's daughter!

    *Pyrrhus.* I cannot do that. Why distress me longer?
How can I give to her a heart that's yours?
I know that I have promised she should rule it,
I know she came here to become a queen;
Fate brought you both alike into Epirus,—
It brought her here to fasten chains of bondage,
It brought you here to wear them. For myself,

I took no pains to please her. It might seem
Since your charms conquer me, and hers are scorned,
That she is captive here, and you are queen.
Oh, how one sigh, of all I breathe for you,
Would bring her joy, if it were given her!

*Andromache.* Why should it not be welcome? Can she ever
Forget the services that you have done?
Hector and Troy, for her, are not such names
As make her shudder; all her tenderness
Is not devoted only to the dead.
Oh, what a loss was mine, bitter to think on!
Your father slew him, and became immortal,
'Twas thus he gained the crown of all his glory,
And now my tears have made you both renowned.

*Pyrrhus.* Then it must be that I obey you, madam;
That I forget,—nay, even that I hate you.
My love has been too violent a thing
To change itself to mere indifference.
I tell you that the heart that can no longer
Love passionately, must with fury hate.
And in my righteous anger, I'll spare nothing.
The son shall answer for his mother's scorn.
Greece asks his life; why do I bend to save
Ungrateful ones? No, I'll no longer do it!

*Andromache.* Alas, he'll die then,—for his mother's tears
And his own innocence are all that save him.
And yet, perhaps, because my life is wretched,
His death may lift this weight of misery.
I bear my woes, my life, for his sake only;
And going after him, I'll find his father.
And when we are united, by your grace,
We three shall—

*Pyrrhus.* Lady, go and see your son.
The sight of him may teach your heart to shun
That path which beckons to you, in your anger.
I'll take another time to learn my fortune;—
And while you clasp him, think how you might save him.

(*Exeunt*)


## ACT II

(*Enter Hermione and Cleone*)

*Hermione.* Yes, he may see me, since you wish it so.
I'll grant him that one pleasure, once again.
Soon Pylades will bring him, but, indeed
Were I to use my judgment, I'd not see him.

*Cleone.* What evil is there in the sight of him?
Is he not still the very same Orestes
For whose return you sighed a hundred times;
Whose love and constancy have been the burden
Of your regrets?

*Hermione.* Paid with ingratitude!
It is that love which makes me loathe his presence.
For him it is a triumph,—shame for me,
That he should see my grief, so like his own!
He'll say, Is this the proud Hermione?
Look! She who scorned me,—she herself is scorned!
This wretch who set her heart at such a price,
Is learning, now, the pain of outraged love!
Just Heavens!—

*Cleone.* Leave these most unworthy fears.
For he has felt the power of your charms
Only too deeply, and he comes to love,
Not to insult your state. He brings a heart

From which he cannot ever blot your image.
You have not told me what your father writes.

*Hermione.* If Pyrrhus still continues his delays,
And if he will not let the Trojan die,
I am to leave this place—go with the Greeks.

*Cleone.* That's well. Then hear Orestes, and at least
It will be you who'll end what Pyrrhus started.
But if you would succeed, you must forestall him.
Have you not told me that you hated him?

*Hermione.* Hate him, Cleone? Could my pride do less,
When he neglects my favor, given freely?
The heart I learned to love was treacherous.
He was too dear not to be hated now!

*Cleone.* Why, leave him, then; and since you're truly
        loved—

*Hermione.* But give my anger time; it will grow stronger.
Leave me to guard myself against my foe.
Oh, it is terrible to part, Cleone,
And he will force that parting, much too well,
This faithless one!

*Cleone.*            You'll wait for newer wrongs?
He loves his slave, and that before your eyes!
What would you have to make him odious?
What greater insult can he give you now?
If he had known how to displease you further
He would have done it.

*Hermione.*            Why will you torture me?
For I should wish to hide the truth, and try
To think that what your eyes have seen is false;
To think my love is vanished. Give me joy
That I have conquered so, and that my heart
Is steeled against its weakness. Make me think it!
If you would have me fly, why, there's no hindrance.

Then let us go. We'll leave him to take pleasure
In a most shameful conquest, being the subject
Of his own slave. We'll go! And yet suppose
That faith and duty should win back his heart?
That he should beg for pardon, at my feet,
That love should have the strength to make him mine?
No, for he only seeks to make me humble!
Let us stay longer, spoiling their happiness,
And take our own joy in destroying theirs;
Or forcing him to break his solemn promise,
We'll show him guilty in the eyes of Greece.
I have brought down their anger on the son,
And now I'll have them ask him for the mother,
And so I shall repay the agonies
Which she has made me suffer. Let her lose him!
Nay, let him cause her death—

    *Cleone.*               And do you think
That she whose eyes are over-filled with tears
Can find much joy in seeking for your place?
That she who bends beneath this weight of sorrow
Can wish to gain the love of her tormentor?
Has there been any sign that she takes comfort,
Or finds her sorrows eased, because he loves her?
Why is her soul so plunged in misery?
Why is she harsh with such a favored lover?

    *Hermione.* Ah, I have lent an ear all too believing
To vows unfaithful; spoken what I felt.
I saw no danger in sincerity,
My eyes were careless, and they told their secret,
And my own heart defended him too well.
What woman would not thus have told her love
Even as I did, trusting in his oaths?
And did his eyes look scornfully upon me

As now they do? You must remember well
How everything combined to aid his suit;
My family avenged; the joy of Greece;
And all our vessels filled with the spoils of Troy;
His father's deeds made little by his own;
And his high passion, seeming more than mine;
My heart—why, even you were dazzled by him!
Before he had betrayed me, all of you
Conspired to that same end. It is enough.
I have not ceased to feel, though Pyrrhus has.
Orestes' heart is noble as his deeds,
And he can love when there's no love for him;
Yes, and perhaps can make himself beloved.
I'll see Orestes.

    *Cleone.*      He is coming here.

    *Hermione.*  Ah, but I had not thought he was so near!

              (*Enter Orestes*)

Am I to think that there are still remaining
Some traces of old love, that bring you here,
And urge that you should see me in my sorrow?
Or is it duty's voice, and that alone
Which sends you to me?

    *Orestes.*         Very well you know
That there is such a fatal blindness in me
That I am destined still to come to you
Again and yet again, to worship you,
Even when I have sworn to come no more.
I know that seeing you will only open
Wounds that were closed. Each step that brings me near you
Makes me forsworn: I know it, and I blush.
Yet Heaven saw how our last parting hurt me,
And how it wrung my heart, and that same Heaven
Can witness how I tried to free myself

From oaths so hard to keep, and from my torture
By a sure death. I offered up my life
To savage tribes whose gods are satisfied
Only with human blood; They would not have
A sacrifice so anxious for his doom;
They shut their temple doors. And now at last
I come to you, and from your eyes must take
That death which always shuns me; let them end
All my despair with their indifference.
They only need to cut hope's last fond thread,
And they will bring the fatal time I long for;
They need but say what they have said before,
And always said! Through all this long year past,
This was my only aim; it is for you
To shed the blood that Scythians might have spilt
If only I had found them so relentless.

   *Hermione.* Be done, Orestes, with these hopeless words,
For you are charged with things of greater moment.
Why talk of Scythia, or my cruelty?
Think of the many kings who sent you here.
Must their just vengeance wait upon these transports?
Is it Orestes' blood that they are asking?
Fulfill the duty they have given you.

   *Orestes.* Pyrrhus refuses, and my work is done.
He sends me back, my lady. Some strange power
Moves Pyrrhus to defend the son of Hector.

   *Hermione.* False and forsworn!

   *Orestes.*                And now that I must go,
I come to learn my own fate from your lips.
I think I hear your words before they're spoken,—
They say that in your inmost heart, you hate me.

   *Hermione.* Always unjust? Why will this grief of yours
Complain forever of my hatred for you?

How have I shown this cruelty to you
For which you blame me so repeatedly?
Obedience to my father brought me here,
But who can know that I have not been heart-sick.
Or that I have not shared your fears with you?
Indeed, I may have shed some bitter tears
Here in Epirus. There is none can say
I have not sometimes wished that you were here,
In spite of duty.

    *Orestes.*        You have wished me here?
But can it be that you are saying this—
These happy words—to me? Open your eyes,
And let them see Orestes, on whose presence
They frowned so long!

    *Hermione.* Yes, you,—who taught them first to know their
      power,
Whose love for them grew stronger, with their charms,
Whose worth I could not help but value highly,
Who would have had my fondest sighs, and whom
I truly wished to love.

    *Orestes.*        Ah, well I know
How hopeless is my lot. I know you've given
Your heart to Pyrrhus, and to me, vain wishes.

    *Hermione.* Ah, but you need not envy him, Orestes,
Unless you crave that I should hate you!

    *Orestes.*                Yes!
For love might spring from such a strange beginning.
I whom you wish to love,—I cannot please you,
But if you wished to hate me, only love
Would be obeyed, and I should have your heart.
O gods! Such worship, such a tender love,—
Do they not speak for me, if you could hear them?
Only your voice is urging Pyrrhus' claim,—

Speaking, perhaps, against your own desire,
Against his, surely, for within his soul
He only hates you, and he loves another.

 *Hermione.* Who was it dared to tell you that he scorns me?
Have his own looks and words betrayed it to you?
Think you my eyes can light no lasting fire,
But only rouse contempt? Then it may be
That somewhere else I'll find another judge
To look upon them with a kinder favor!

 *Orestes.* You taunt me well! Am I the one who scorns you?
And have you not yet tried my faith enough?
Am I to witness that your eyes lack charm?
Shall I despise them? Ah, they would be happy
To see my rival hate them, as I hate!

 *Hermione.* What do I care whether he loves or hates me?
Go you, and arm all Greece against this rebel.
Pay him the price of one who disobeys.
Go! Let them make this land another Troy!
Now will you say I've given him my heart?

 *Orestes.* Do more, my lady. Come to Greece yourself.
Will you stay here, a hostage? Come with me.
And let your lovely eyes touch every heart,
Till, in a common hate, we all attack him.

 *Hermione.* And meanwhile, if he weds Andromache?
 *Orestes.* Lady!
 *Hermione.*   How deep a shame 'twould be for me,
To see this Phrygian woman hold my place.

 *Orestes.* And yet you hate him! Why, confess the truth!
We cannot shut the fires of love within us;
Our very eyes betray us,—silence, speech;
And flames, hidden in vain, burst out more fiercely.

 *Hermione.* Your mind is set; yes, I can see it well.
It spreads a deadly venom on my words.

It finds deceit in everything I say,
And thinks my hate is prompted by my love.
I must explain. You'll act accordingly.
You know that it was duty led me here,
That it is duty still that keeps me, waiting;
I cannot go, till Pyrrhus or my father
Order me hence. Go, make my father see
How Greece's enemy will form no marriage;
Make Pyrrhus choose the Trojan or myself,
Say which of us he'll keep, and which put by.
Farewell, I only wait his word to follow.

*(Exit Hermione and Cleone)*

*Orestes.* Yes, you will follow me; I do not doubt it.
Your father will consent; that's certain now,
Nor do I need to fear lest Pyrrhus keep you,
Because indeed, he has no eyes at all
Save only for his dear Andromache.
All other things are irksome. He is seeking
Some pretext that can part himself and you.
Only a word, and all is done! What joy
To rob Epirus of so rare a treasure!
Why, she may save Troy's relics,—she may keep
Brave Hector's widow and his son, unharmed,—
And a thousand others! 'Tis enough for me,
That, never to see thee or thy prince again,
Hermione is going! Here's good fortune
Bringing him here. And while we talk, O Love,
Shut fast his eyes; let him not see her charms.

*(Enter Pyrrhus and Phœnix)*

*Pyrrhus.* I've come to find you, sir, and to confess
That it was in a fit of violence
I fought against your reasons. Since I went,
Their justice and their force are clearer to me.

I feel, like you, that I have thwarted Greece,
And all my father's efforts and my own
In aiding Troy; that I am making futile
All that Achilles and myself had done.
I do not now condemn a just resentment.
It was well founded. You shall have your victim
At your disposal soon.

    *Orestes.*                A firm resolve,
And wise as it is firm. By this decision
You buy us peace with blood of those we hate.

    *Pyrrhus.* And I consent, to give you more assurance,
To wed Hermione, and let our marriage
Pledge peace forever. Such a happy sight
Can have no better witness than yourself,
The envoy of the Greeks, and most of all,
The envoy of her father, for in you
His brother lives again. Go to her, now.
And you may say to her that, in the morning,
I will receive her from your hands, with peace.

    *Orestes* (*aside*). Oh, you great gods!
                  (*Exit Orestes*)

    *Pyrrhus.*                     Well, Phœnix, has
    love won?
Say, do your eyes refuse to know me still?

    *Phœnix.* I see you as you were; that righteous anger
Restores you to the Greeks and to yourself,
No more the plaything of a servile flame.
'Tis Pyrrhus, 'tis Achilles' son—his rival,
Bowing at last before the laws of honor,
Winning a second triumph over Troy.

    *Pyrrhus.* Say, rather, that my other victory
Begins today, when I can feel its joy,
And that my heart, lifted from low estate,

Seems to have won against a thousand foes
In crushing love. Think what a host of troubles,
Following close on passion, I've escaped!
Think how I was content to sacrifice
All duty and all friendship, scorning danger,
Courting destruction from the arms of Greece,
Only to win a single look of love.

   *Phœnix.* My lord, I bless the kind severity
Which gives you back—

   *Pyrrhus.*         See how she treated me!
I thought that, when the mother's fears were wakened,
She would have yielded for her baby's sake,
Disarmed by tenderness, and yet I found
No sign of weakness mingled with her tears.
Embittered by her grief, she seemed more fierce
Each time the name of Hector passed her lips.
And when I promised to protect her son,
Then she would say, " 'Tis Hector," holding him
Close in her arms, "His eyes and mouth; his heart,
Bold even now; and I embrace my husband
In this, his image." Can she truly think
That I shall let her keep him, in this fashion,
To feed her love for Hector?

   *Phœnix.*         That, no doubt,
Would be her gratitude. But leave her now.

   *Pyrrhus.* I see how consciousness of her own beauty
Flatters her still, and makes her proudly wait
Despite my wrath, to see me at her knees.
Rather I'll see her crouch in vain at mine!
It is a lasting hate that's parting us,

                    Widow of Hector and
   Achilles' son!

   *Phœnix.* Then speak of her no more to me, my lord.

Go to Hermione, and at her feet
Think only of her pleasure, and forget
All that is past, and you, yourself prepare her
For the wedding rites, and do not leave that task
To one who loves her all too well himself,—
To a rival—

    *Pyrrhus.*    Do you think she will be jealous
If I should marry with Hermione?

    *Phœnix.* Still harping on the Trojan woman? Still?
What do you care if she be vexed or happy?
What spell is this that draws you always to her
In spite of your own will?

    *Pyrrhus.*            I have not told her
All that I meant to say. I have not showed
But half the fury that I feel for her.
She does not know the bitter enemy
She has in me. Let us return to her.
We'll flout her vengeance, give my hate full scope,
We'll see her pride and beauty in the dust.
Come, let us go.

    *Phœnix.*    Go cast yourself before her;
Go swear that in your heart you love her still,
And urge her thus to scorn you more than ever.

    *Pyrrhus.* And so you think my heart is always ready
To find excuses for her, yearns for her,
And seeks to make atonement.

    *Phœnix.*             Yes, you love her,
And that's enough.

    *Pyrrhus.*    Love her, forsooth,—I love her,
Who hates me more, the more I flatter her?
She has no friends, no hope but what I give her!
She is a stranger, and she is a slave.
I can destroy her son; perhaps I ought.

I give that son, myself, my throne to her,
And I can gain no place within her heart
But that of one who persecutes her! No!
No, I have sworn it, my revenge is certain
And now, for once, shall give her cause for hatred.
Now I'll desert her infant. She may weep
Whatever tears she wishes, call upon me
With any name her misery can prompt!
Ah, what a sight her eyes will see today!
Phoenix, 'twill be her death; and I shall cause it;
And I shall hold the dagger at her breast!

  *Phœnix.* Why shout it out? A little time ago
You were too certain of your strength.

  *Pyrrhus.*                 Your pardon!
It is an old wound, and it still is tender.
You need not fear. It's equal to my anger.
It is the final spark of love extinct!
I'll take your counsel. And you say I must
Give up her son, and I must see the princess?

  *Phœnix.* Yes, Sire, and with your humble vows assure
    her—

  *Pyrrhus.* I promised it. I'll do what I have promised.

             (*Exeunt*)

# ACT III

### (*Enter Orestes and Pylades*)

  *Pylades.* Restrain this rage, my friend. 'Tis most imprudent,
And you are not yourself, I do not know you,
Let me—

  *Orestes.*   Oh, no! Your good advice is late.
The voice of reason only wearies me.

I must cut short the torture of my life.
I'll carry her away, or I will perish.
I've taken my resolve, and I will do it,
Indeed, I will!

   *Pylades.* Why then, by all means do it.
I'll sanction that. And yet, think where you are
To show your hand will only bring defeat.
Disguise your feelings. Learn to calm your rage,
These guards, these walls, and every breath of air
Are serving Pyrrhus and Hermione.
Take greatest care to hide your wrath from her.
Why, in the name of Heaven, did you seek her
In such a state?

   *Orestes.*      I did not know nor care.
I was enraged, I may have gone too far,
I may have made plain threats on both of them.

   *Pylades.* What fruit did that fit bring you?

   *Orestes.*                     Was the blow
Not quite enough to make the coolest frantic?—
Drive reason from her seat? Yes, in the morning
He'll wed Hermione, and as a mark
Of honor, he'll receive her from my hand!
Ah, may it sooner with his blood—

   *Pylades.*               You blame him
For what he does only in desperation,
I think that you should rather pity him
As I do you. He suffers quite as much.

   *Orestes.* But I know well he laughs at my despair.
He always scorned her, till he knew I loved her,
And but for that, her charms were lost upon him.
He'll have her but to tear her from my arms.
O gods! When I had thought her won already,
Willing to leave the sight of him forever!

Her heart was torn between her love and hate,
She only waited for his last refusal
To be my own. Her eyes were opened to me,
Her ears had listened to my pleas with pity;
One other word, and then I had succeeded.

   *Pylades.* You think so?

   *Orestes.*                   Yes, for indeed her wrath was hot
Against the wretch.

   *Pylades.*           She never loved him more!
Do you suppose, had Pyrrhus passed her by,
No other pretext would have held her here?
Oh, do not let her charms deceive you longer.
Fly far away from her, and stay forever,
Rather than try to carry off a fury
Who hates your love, who'd make your whole life bitter
With vain regrets for having nearly won
What she held dearest.

   *Orestes.*           But that very thought
Urges me on. All things are smiling on her,
While I have nothing but a fruitless rage,
And while I try to find oblivion
Far, far from her, and exile once again.
Oh, no; for she must share those torments with me
Which I have borne for her, too long alone.
I'll not be pitied! She shall have her turn
At feeling what it is to fear my anger,
To weep in sorrow and to call me cruel,
Even as I did her!

   *Pylades.*         And thus Orestes
Ends his high mission—as ravisher!

   *Orestes.* What matter, Pylades? Greece shall not work
Her vengeance at Orestes' cost, nor shall
This most ungrateful princess mock my tears.

What profit will my country's praises do me
When here they jeer at me, and call me fool?
What would you have? In very truth I think
My innocence weighs heavily upon me!
When have the gods been so perverse before,
Hunting the guiltless down, with crime unpunished?
I turn my eyes, and everywhere I see
Troubles and sorrows that condemn their justice.
Then let me earn their wrath, deserve their hate.
If I must pay the penalties of crime,
I'll eat the fruits of it. But why should you
Draw down their anger? It is aimed at me.
My friendship's brought you harm enough already.
Leave me alone in guilt and misery.
Dear Pylades, your pity spoils your wit.
Escape the dangers that surround me here.
Take to the Greeks the child that Pyrrhus gives us.
And now begone!

   *Pylades*          We'll take his bride with us!
A heart that's brave has little fear for danger.
Where love goes, friendship follows. It can act
As boldly too. We'll rouse your followers.
Our fleet is ready, and the breeze invites us.
I know each dark and twisted passageway.
The sea washes against the palace walls,
And so, this very night, by secret ways,
Your treasure shall be taken to your ship.

   *Orestes.* My friend, I think I trespass on your love.
Those griefs of mine, which you alone could pity,
Beg you to pardon one who loses all,—
All that he sets his heart on. Being hated
By the whole world, he hates himself; and yet
Under more happy stars, I in my turn—

*Pylades.* Be careful lest you should betray yourself,
But hide the purpose, till the blow is struck.
I ask no more. And now, forget your wrongs,
Forget your love. But see, she's coming.
    *Orestes.* Go,
               Answer for her as I will for myself.
       (*Exit Pylades, enter Hermione and Cleone*)
My lady, you have won, thanks to my care.
I have seen Pyrrhus, so that now your marriage
Soon will take place.
    *Hermione.*        I know, and I am told
That you were seeking me to make me ready.
    *Orestes.* You'll not refuse these vows that come so late?
    *Hermione.* Who would have thought that Pyrrhus still
       was faithful?
That any passion could have been withheld
And kept so long from bursting into flame,
That it should linger till I almost left him?
Like you, I'll think that it is Greece he dreads.
It is not love, but it is prudence moves him.
My eyes had greater power over you.
    *Orestes.* No, no; it is his love. I cannot doubt it.
Your eyes have done what they have wished to do,
They would not now displease him.
    *Hermione.*              But, Orestes,
What can I do, when I have pledged my faith?
Rob him of what I had not given him?
The star that rules a princess is not love.
She must obey; there is no other glory
For such a one. And yet I would have gone.
You saw how I made duty yield to you.
    *Orestes.* Ah, cruel one, you knew! But every heart
Is free to follow in the course it wishes,

And your own heart was for your own disposal.
Had it been given me, I had no right
To claim it as my own. And yet, I hoped.
I blame my fortune more than you, and why
Should I wear out your patience with complaining?
Act as your duty bids you act; for me,
I'll only spare you words of sad reproach.

(*Exit Orestes*)

*Hermione.* Had you supposed his anger was so mild?
*Cleone.* Sorrow is not less fatal, when it's silent.
I pity him the more since he himself
Causes his grief; 'tis his own blow that kills him.
When were the wedding preparations started?
Orestes spoke; Pyrrhus declared himself.

*Hermione.* You think that it is fear? Fear! And of whom?
Fear of those men, who during twice five years
Fled before Hector, with Achilles lost,—
Crouched in their dread within their burning ships,
Who, but for Pyrrhus, would have gone from Troy,
Left her unpunished, stopped in their useless quest!
And now, why should he fight against himself?
Whatever Pyrrhus does is what he wishes,
And if he marries me, why then, he loves me.
So let Orestes blame me for his sorrows.
A better cheer awaits me, than his sighs!
Pyrrhus returns to me! Ah, dear Cleone,
There's rapture in the thought! Know you his exploits?
You've heard them told? They are beyond all number!
And he himself, so brave, so great a charm,
So faithful too, as we have seen at last!
There's nothing lacking in his glory. Think—

*Cleone.* But hide your feelings, now. Your rival comes,
No doubt to lay her troubles at your feet.

*Hermione.* Ah, it is much too soon to check my joy!
Let us begone. What should I say to her?
(*Enter Andromache and Cephissa*)
*Andromache.* Why will you fly? Is it not pleasing to you
'To see great Hector's widow here before you,
And weeping at your knees? I do not come
With jealous tears, nor do I envy you
The heart that has surrendered to your charms.
A cruel hand has robbed me of that one
Whom I admired alone. The flame of love
Was lit for me by Hector, long ago,
With him, it was extinguished in the tomb.
But he has left a son. A day will come
When you will know how closely to your heart
A son can cling; but you will never know,
Nor do I wish you should, how keen the pain
When danger threatens, and when they would take him
Away from you; take all that's left to soothe you,
And ease your blighted heart. When Troy was weary
With ten long years of woe, and when the Trojans
Cried for your mother's life, 'twas I moved Hector
To give her aid. You've power over Pyrrhus
As I had over Hector. Can they fear
The child he left with me? Oh, let me hide him
In some far distant island, and be sure
My fears will keep him there. I'll only teach him
To weep with me.
*Hermione.*          I feel for you, but duty
Keeps my tongue silent, when my father speaks.
It is by him that Pyrrhus has been stirred.
Who can move Pyrrhus better than yourself?
His soul has long been subject to your eyes.

You make him speak the word, and I'll consent.

    (*Exit Hermione and Cleone*)

 *Andromache.* What scorn she had when she refused **my** prayer!

 *Cephissa.* Take her advice, and see him, as she says.

One look from you may thwart the Greeks and her.

But look, he seeks you of his own accord.

    (*Enter Pyrrhus and Phœnix*)

 *Pyrrhus* (*to Phœnix*). Where is the princess? Was she here, you say?

 *Phœnix.* I thought so.

 *Andromache* (*to Cephissa*). Now you can see how great a power

My eyes have over him.

 *Pyrrhus.* What does she say?

 *Andromache.* Then all is lost!

 *Phœnix.* Hermione is gone,

And we will follow.

 *Cephissa.* Speak, Andromache!

Why obstinate and silent?

 *Andromache.* Has he not

Promised my child to them?

 *Cephissa.* Promised, perhaps,

Not given up.

 *Andromache.* Vain are the tears I shed.

His death is sure.

 *Pyrrhus.* And how her pride disdains

Even to look at me!

 *Andromache.* Let us go hence.

I should but anger him the more.

 *Pyrrhus.* Come, Phœnix.

I'll yield the son of Hector to the Greeks.

*Andromache* (*throwing herself at his feet*).
Oh stop, my lord! What is it you will do?
Give up my son? Why not his mother, then?
Where is the kindness that you swore to me
So short a time ago? Is there no chord
Even of pity, that my pleas can touch?
Is there no hope of pardon in your sentence?

   *Pyrrhus.* Phœnix will tell you that my word is pledged.

   *Andromache.* No danger was too great for you to face
Because of me!

   *Pyrrhus.*        Then I was blind, but now
I see more clearly. Once there was a time
Your wishes might have won his pardon for him.
But then you never asked it. Now you come
A little late.

   *Andromache.* You understood full well
The sighs which feared lest they should be disdained.
My lord, forgive the little trace of pride
That did not leave me with my royal rank
And made me shrink from begging ceaselessly.
My lord, you know that, were it not for you,
Andromache would never stoop to clasp
The knees of one her master.

   *Pyrrhus.*              No, in your soul
You hate me, and you scorn to be my debtor.
This son of yours, the only thing you care for,—
You would have loved him less, had he been saved
Through what I did. You hate me bitterly,
And more than all the other Greeks together.
Enjoy a rage so noble at your ease!
Come, Phœnix.

   *Andromache.* I will go where Hector is.

   *Cephissa.* Madam—

 *Andromache.*   Ah, what more can I say to him?
He knows my woes. He is the author of them.
(*to Pyrrhus*) See what a state you've brought me to, my lord!
I've seen my father slain, I've seen our walls
Flame wrapped, I've seen my kindred all cut down,
My husband's corpse dragged, bloody, through the dust,
And his one son is kept for chains, with me.
It is for his sake that I am a slave.
And this thought, too, has sometimes brought me solace,—
That Fate has fixed my place of exile here.
He is the son of many kings. I thought
That, even as a slave, under your rule,
He might be happier than if he were
In other places. I had thought his prison
Might be his place of refuge. Priam found
Achilles could respect his fallen state;
I thought his son was yet more generous.
Hector, forgive that trust I put in him,
When I supposed thine enemy so noble,
And thought he would not do so vile a thing!
Ah, had he only let us make our dwelling
Where I had raised a tomb above thine ashes,
And ended there his hatred and our woes,
Not parting us from what remained of thee!
 *Pyrrhus.* Go, Phœnix. Wait for me.
     *(Exit Phœnix)*
   A moment, madam.
Your tears may still win back your son for you.
Yes; I regret that I have made you weep,
And gave you, thus, a sword to turn on me.
I thought I could have brought more hatred here,
At least you could consent to look at me!
Are these the eyes of justice, in its anger,

Taking its pleasure in your misery?
Why will you make me faithless to yourself?
Think of your son, and let us cease to hate.
Now it is I who urge it; save your son!
Must my own sighs beg that you spare his life?
And must I clasp your knees to plead for him?
Only this once! Save him and save yourself!
I know what solemn vows I break for you,
And how much hate I bring upon myself.
Hermione shall go, and on her brow
For crown, I'll set a burning brand of shame.
And in the temple, ready for her marriage
Andromache shall wear the diadem.
Lady, I offer this, and you will dare
No longer to disdain it. Rule or die!
A year of scorn has made me desperate,
And I am done with living still in doubt,
Torn by my fears, now making threats, now **groaning.**
I lose you, and I die,—and waiting longer
Is also death. I leave you to consider,
And soon I'll come to bring you to the temple,
And there my fury shall destroy this child,
Or else, in love, I'll crown you as my queen!

        (*Exit Pyrrhus*)

  *Cephissa.* Even as I foretold! In spite of Greece
You're still the mistress of your destiny.
  *Andromache.* Yes, and I grieve much that it should be so!
I have no choice; I must condemn my son.
  *Cephissa.* That would be stretching faith a little far.
There may be guilt when there is too much virtue.
Hector himself would urge a milder course.
  *Andromache.* Pyrrhus to be as Hector was? I loathe it!
  *Cephissa.* Yet think how they will tear his son from you;

How, most of all, his ghost would blush at that!
It would not shame him if your conqueror
Should give your royal rank to you again,
Should trample down your enemies, in anger,
Forget that fierce Achilles was his father,
And so undo his deeds.

  *Andromache.*    But can I cease
Remembrance of those deeds, though he forgets them?
Forget dead Hector's body, all unburied,
Dragged in dishonor round the walls of Troy?
Forget his father slain before mine eyes,
Grasping the altar, stained with his own blood?
Forget that cruel night, and all its horrors
Which brought an everlasting night to Troy?
Remember how this Pyrrhus looked upon us,
Crossing our burning threshold, how his eyes
Glared in its light, and how my fallen brothers
Were trampled by his feet. He urged the slaughter;
And he was dyed from head to foot with blood!
Ah, can you hear the shouts of victory,
And can you hear the groans of dying lips
As fire and sword rush on? And can you see
Andromache, in her despair, and Pyrrhus
Doing, before her eyes, these frightful things
That won his glory for him? There you see
The husband you would give me! No, my friend,
I will not share his bloody crimes with him.
Let him make me the latest of his victims
And I will yield to him without a word.

  *Cephissa.* Then let us go. We'll watch your baby die.
They only wait for you—but how you shudder!

  *Andromache.* Yes, memory sends pain that pierces deep!
So I must see my baby perish, too?—

'The only joy I have, my Hector's image,
The one last token of the joy I lost!
I think of how he went to find Achilles,—
A fatal day for him—he pressed his boy
Close to his heart, and dried my tears, and said,
"Dear wife, I do not know how Fate may settle
The issue of the fight to which I go.
I leave my son to you, a pledge of faith,
And if he lose his father, you must be
A father and a mother both, to him.
If you hold dear the happiness we've shared
Then show him how you loved me while I lived."
And shall that precious blood be spilt before me,
And all his line become extinct with him?
Oh, cruel king, must my offense be his?
He has not hated thee; he has not charged thee
With all his kinsmen's death; this little child
Cannot resent the ills he cannot feel.
Yet you must die, my son, unless your mother
Turns from your head the sword that hangs above it.
I have my choice. Then shall I let it fall?
Oh no, I cannot ever let you die!
Let us find Pyrrhus! No, Cephissa, you—
Go find him for me.

   *Cephissa.*        What shall I say to him?

   *Andromache.* Tell him a mother loves her son enough—
But has he truly sworn to kill the child?
Can passion make this man so merciless?

   *Cephissa.* Madam, he will be back, and in his fury—

   *Andromache.* Then go to him. Assure him—

   *Cephissa.*               Of your faith?

   *Andromache.* And must I still give such a promise to him?
Oh, ashes of my husband and my father!

How dear a price I pay for thee, my son!
Come then, we'll go.
   *Cephissa.*         Where? And with what intentions?
   *Andromache.* To Hector's tomb; and there we'll ask his
   will.

(Exeunt)

ACT IV

(Enter Andromache and Cephissa)

   *Cephissa.* It is your husband, lady, do not doubt.
Hector has worked this miracle for you!
Surely he wishes Troy to rise again
Under that son whose life he bids you guard.
Pyrrhus has sworn to give the boy to you.
Why, even now, you heard him say he waits
Only a word from you to make him yours,
And you may trust his love. He'll be content,
Having your heart. Father, friends, the sceptre—
He little cares for them, if you will reign
Over himself, and over all his people.
Then can you say that he deserves your hate?
His anger braves the Greeks, and, too, he pities
No less than you, this child of yours. He guards him,
Keeps him from danger, stands against their rage,
And risks his own life, while he shelters him.
But everything is ready, and you promised—
   *Andromache.* Yes, I will be there. Let me see my son.
   *Cephissa.* Why such a haste? Now you may visit him
With none forbidding it. Be satisfied,
And soon your love for him may take its freedom
In many fond caresses, unrestrained.

And will you not be happy, since you rear him
No longer now to live his life in bondage,—
But to bring back the glories of his line.

    *Andromache.* It is the last time I shall see my child.
    *Cephissa.* Why, what is this you say?
    *Andromache.*                   Oh, my dear friend,

With you my soul should never wear a mask.
You have been faithful to me in my trouble.
I hoped you knew me better than to think
That I should ever have so little faith.
And better than to think I could betray
My husband, living still within my heart,
Or that I care not how I vex the dead;
Or that I only think of my own peace.
And would that be the keeping of the promise
That I have often made to Hector's ashes?
And yet, I know that I must save his son.
Pyrrhus has vowed that if he marries me
He will protect him. I may trust his word.
I know him well: he's violent, but true.
He will do more, Cephissa, than his promise.
And also I depend on Greece's anger.
It is her hatred will bestow a father
On Hector's son. But since a victim's needed,
I'll promise Pyrrhus all that's left of life,
And I will bind him to my boy with words
Unspeakable and sacred. After that,
This hand shall, straightway, with a fatal blow,
Cut through the cord of life that's true no longer,
And so I'll keep me free from any stain,
And still give Pyrrhus what is due to him,
Nor fail in paying what I owe my husband
And owe my son, and owe, indeed, myself!

This is the harmless plot my love has made,
Or rather, 'tis the plan of Hector's spirit.
And so, alone, I'll join him and my fathers.
Close you mine eyes.
    *Cephissa.*        Ah, lady, if you die,
Then do not think that I'll live after you!
    *Andromache.* But I forbid that you should follow me.
I trust my only treasure to your care.
You lived for me; now live for Hector's son.
He is the only keeper of our hopes.
The royal line of Troy will need your care.
Look you to Pyrrhus. See that he keeps faith,
If there be need, then speak to him of me.
Tell him again how I, before I died,
Yielded to him; teach him to prize that bond,
And so to blot his anger from his soul.
Show him, that, since I left my son to him,
I thought him worthy. You must tell my son
Of all his race's heroes; yes, and guide him
To follow in their steps. Tell him their fame;
Not what they were, but rather what they did.
Recount, each day, his father's virtues to him,
And whisper, sometimes, of a mother's love.
But he must never dream that he'll avenge me.
Let him still seek to win his master's friendship.
He'll look upon his birth with modesty,
Though Hector's blood is his; yet he'll remember
Troy lives in him alone. Now, in one day,
I lay down life for him, and hate, and love!
    *Cephissa.* Alas!
    *Andromache.* You must not come, unless your heart
Is brave enough to stop your tears from flowing.
Cephissa, dry your eyes. I hear a step.

Remember always what a trust you have.
It is Hermione. We'll shun her anger.

(*Exit Andromache and Cephissa*)
(*Enter Hermione and Cleone*)

*Cleone.* Madam, this silence quite surprises me.
You do not say a word. This cruel slight
Seems not to ruffle your tranquillity!
You suffer such a rude rebuff quite tamely,—
You, who would shudder at your rival's name!—
You who could scarcely see, without despair,
A glance that Pyrrhus might have given her!
And now he weds her, brings her to his throne,
And swears the vows he lately gave to you,
And still your lips are silent, and your tongue
Scorns the reproaches that the traitor earns!
I fear what such a fatal calm may mean!
It would be better far—

    *Hermione.* You sent for him?
Is it not so?

    *Cleone.* Orestes will be here,
And as you know, he'll place himself quite wholly
At your disposal, hoping for no reward.
Your eyes are always certain to bewitch him.
See, he is coming.

(*Enter Orestes*)

    *Orestes.* Can it be, this once,
That when I seek you, it is at your bidding?
Or am I flattered still with a false hope?
Is it, then, true that you have wished to see me?
Shall I believe your eyes have been disarmed,
And now, at last, will look—

    *Hermione.* I wish to know, sir,
If you do love me.

*Orestes.*            Love you! Oh, you gods!
All of my vows, that are too hard to keep,
My going, coming back, my reverence
That stopped reproaches, and my eyes, tear-drowned,
My dark despair,—what witness will you ask,
If these cannot be trusted?

*Hermione.*                Yes, I trust them.
Avenge me, then!

*Orestes.*            Oh, let us go, my lady,
And let us set all Greece on fire again.
This is the arm will make your fame for you.
You'll rival Helen; I, the king of men!
We'll make Troy's misery to live again
Here in Epirus, and our deeds shall darken
The fame that was our fathers! I am ready.
Come, let us go!

*Hermione.*        No, let us stay a time.
We must not carry these affronts so far.
You'd have me crown the insults of my foes,
And go away, and wait for slow revenge;
To be content with what a war might do,
And yet a war might fail to right my wrongs!
I'll have Epirus weeping, when I go!
Work my revenge this hour, or not at all.
Delay, and you refuse me. Go to the temple,
For there it is that you must kill—

    *Orestes.*                Ay, whom?
    *Hermione.* Pyrrhus!
    *Orestes.*            The king?
    *Hermione.*                So! Does your hatred
    falter?
Run there. Go quickly, lest I call you back.
Speak not of duties. I would fain forget them!

Go! I will hear no words in his defense,
And least of all from you!
   *Orestes.* Hear them from me?
Your tenderness has stamped his crime too deeply!
Let us have vengeance,—but some other way.
We'll be his foes, but not his murderers;
Taking arms justly, we will ruin him.
Shall I bring back his head, to answer Greece?
And have I taken on myself this mission
That I might turn assassin? No! By Heaven,
Let Greece accept the challenge, let her crush him,
Under the weight of hatred, till he dies.
The name of king is sacred, and that brow—
   *Hermione.* Then is my sentence not enough for you,
That my offended honor now demands
That there should be some victim offered me?
And that if you, yourself, destroy this tyrant,
You'll have me for reward? And that I hate him,
Whom once I loved? Oh yes, I must confess it—
For he could win my heart; it does not matter
Whether it was my father's will that moved me.
Act on that knowledge! Though his vows are broken,
Though I must look upon his crime with horror,
Yet fear that, while he lives, I may forgive him,
And do not trust my anger's wavering
Till death removes this monster; for unless
He dies today, tomorrow I may love him!
   *Orestes.* Death must prevent his pardon, then. But how?
Can I avenge your injuries so soon?
Where is the path to lead him to his doom?
I've newly set my feet upon this soil,
And you would have me overthrow the State,
Murder the king—and you will only give me

A day to punish him! No, not an hour.
It must be done before his people's eyes;
My victims shall be brought before the altar.
I'll hesitate no longer. I will go,
Only to see the place of sacrifice.
At night I'll do your bidding, and he dies!
     *Hermione.* While, in the day, he weds Andromache!
His throne is set already in the temple,
His crime is done, and my disgrace is certain!
Why should you wait? He offers you his life!
He is not guarded, at the festival;
His men are all surrounding Hector's son.
He gives himself to my avenger's arm!
Will you take greater care of this man's life
Than he does? Arm my followers,—your Greeks,
Stir up your friends; you may rely on mine.
Why, he betrays me, tricks you, scorns us all!
And they must hate him quite as much as I.
They would not spare the husband of the Trojan!
You need but speak; my foe cannot escape you,
And if he does, they'll cut him down themselves.
Lead or be led by them, in their just rage!
Return to me, dyed with his faithless blood,—
For only thus you'll win my heart. Now go!
     *Orestes.* But, madam, think of how—
     *Hermione.*                         This passes
          bounds!
Your scruples grate upon me in my anger!
I've shown the way to win Hermione,
To make Orestes glad,—but now I see
Orestes will do nothing to deserve her;
He'll only whine forever. Go away!
Boast elsewhere of your constant heart, and leave me,

For I'll avenge myself. My soul is filled
With shame for these weak promises I made.
One day of these refusals is too much!
When all is ready for the marriage rites,
Then I will go, and I will go alone
There where you dare not venture,—I will find
Some way to bring me close beside my foe,
To stab the heart I could not reach with love.
And then my bloody hands, turned on myself
Will join our destinies, in spite of him.
And though he is a traitor, it will be
More sweet to die with him than live with you!

   *Orestes.* No, I will rob you of that dismal pleasure.
He shall not die but by Orestes' hand.
Your enemy shall fall before my arm,
And then you shall reward me if you will.

   *Hermione.* Then go; and leave your future in my keeping
Have all your ships made ready for our flight.

(Exit Orestes)

   *Cleone.* Oh, lady, think before you call down ruin—
   *Hermione.* Ruin or not, I mean to have my vengeance!
No matter what he promises, I doubt
The trust I give to any but myself.
The guilt of Pyrrhus does not scorch his eyes
As it does mine; my stroke would be more certain.
It would be sweet to be my own avenger,
To stain this white arm with a traitor's blood,
And then, for my more pleasure, and his pain,
To hide my rival from his dying sight!
What if Orestes should not tell his victim
How he is dying, sacrificed to me!
Go find him, and be sure he tells this wretch
He owes his death to me, and not to Greece.

Run, good Cleone, my revenge is thwarted
If he should die, not knowing that his doom
Was sent by me.

 *Cleone.*   I will obey you— Wait!
What do I see? Who would have looked for this?
It is the king himself!

 *Hermione.*   Go find Orestes.
He must do nothing now, until he sees me.

     *(Exit Cleone)*
   *(Enter Pyrrhus and Phœnix)*

 *Pyrrhus.* You think it strange that I should seek you out,
My coming has disturbed you, talking here.
I do not come with wiles that are unworthy;
No false excuse can hide the wrong I do.
My heart accuses me. Its voice is strong.
I cannot make a plea I know is false.
I wed a Trojan woman. Yes, I own
The faith I promise her was given you.
I could remind you that our fathers made
These ties at Troy; that we were never asked,
Nor were we ever bound by any choice
Or love, that was our own. But I submitted.
It is enough for me. I sent my envoys,
And they made promise of my heart and hand.
I was so far from wishing to retract it,
That I confirmed it gladly, and with them
You came here. Even though another's eyes
Had conquered me already, and outdone you,
That passion did not make me hesitate,
And I resolved that I'd be true to you.
I welcomed you as queen; until this day
I thought my oath would hold in place of love.
Yet love has won, and by a fatal turn,

Andromache has gained a heart she hates.
We draw each other on, unwillingly.
We hurry to the altar, and we'll pledge
Eternal union there. And much you blame me,
And call me traitor; I'm a willing one,
And yet I grieve that I have proven false.
I would not think to check your proper anger.
It is as much relief to me as you.
Then say that I'm forsworn; I fear your silence
Much more than I should ever fear reproaches.
My heart is wrung; it holds a secret witness.
The less you speak, the more I know my guilt.

   *Hermione.* You make confession, bare of all deceit.
It shows that to yourself, at least, you're just.
And though you still will break this solemn bond,
Your crime has made you see how you are guilty.
But why, indeed, should one who conquers stoop
To common honesty that keeps its word?
No, faithlessness has secret charms for you.
You seek me but to revel in your shame!
You are not hampered by your oath or duty.
A maid of Greece, and then a Trojan woman
Have caught your fancy; first it flies away,
Then it returns, then leaves me, once again.
It crowns, in turn, the princess and the slave.
Troy bows to Greece; then Greece must bow to Troy!
Thus goes a heart that's master of itself;
It is heroic,—not a slave to promise!
Your bride might well be angered, if I stint
Such honeyed names as rogue and perjurer!
Perhaps you came to see if I were pale,
And, in her arms, you would have mocked my sorrow.
If I should follow after her, in tears,

You would be glad of it. And yet, one day
Has brought you joy enough; you need not seek
To add to your renown. You have enough.
It should be quite sufficient for your greed,—
There's Hector's aged father, struck to earth,
Dying before the eyes of all his kindred,
While your good sword, deep in his feeble heart,
Seeks the last frozen drops that linger there;
There's flaming Troy, swallowed in seas of blood;
'Twas your hand cut Polyxena's white throat—
A sight so cruel even Greece condemned it.—
Such glory needs its due acknowledgment!

   *Pyrrhus.* I know quite well it was too great a rage
To which revenge for Helen carried me.
You are her child, and I might charge to you
The blood I've shed; but let the past be done.
And now I thank high Heaven that your coldness
Has stirred a bitter passion in my breast.
My heart, too quick at making its own torture,
Should know you better, and forgive itself!
I wronged you, madam, when I felt remorse;
For how can one who is not loved, be faithless?
You have not tried to keep me bound to you.
I fear to injure you, and yet it may be
I serve you well. We have no love to hold us.
Why, it was only duty that I followed,
And so did you. You never truly loved me.

   *Hermione.* I never loved! What was it that I did?
For you I scorned the princes of my country;
Myself, I sought you in your farthest realms;
Still I am here, though you've been false to me,
And all my Greeks have seen me in disgrace.
I ordered them to hide the wrongs you've done me,

And secretly I've waited till your duty
Should call you back,—believed that, soon or late,
You'd bring to me once more the heart I claimed.
I loved you, though you were not ever constant.
Could I have loved you more, if you'd been true?
And even while your cruel lips, quite calmly,
Are telling of the death of all my hopes,
I think I have not ceased to love you yet!
Well, if it must be so, if Heaven's anger
Has kept for other eyes the strength to charm you,
Why then, complete this marriage; I but ask
You will not make me watch my own disgrace.
Hear me—for this may be my last request—
Let one day pass, and you shall wed tomorrow.
You do not answer? Oh, you faithless one,
You count these moments lost; they're spent with me!
Go, then! Profane the majesty of Heaven,
And the just gods, who never will forget
How these same oaths bound you, one time, to me!
Hurry to bring that perjured heart before them,
And fear lest there you meet Hermione!

(*Exit Hermione*)

   *Phœnix.* My lord, you heard these words. Guard yourself
    well.
Beware the vengeance of a love that's thwarted.
It burns, inflamed with fury. It is armed,
For Greece will aid her, and support her cause;
Orestes loves her still; for such a prize—

   *Pyrrhus.* Andromache is waiting. Guard her son!

(*Exeunt*)

## ACT V

### (*Enter Hermione*)

*Hermione.* Where am I? What is this that I have done?
And now,—do what? What frenzies clutch at me?
I wander through these halls, I know not whither.
I am destroyed with grief! I do not know
If I do love or hate him! When he left me,
His eyes,—they seemed to freeze my very soul.
He would not even look as if he pitied.
No, not a moment's tenderness or sorrow!
His heart would never grant one cry to me.
He could not hear my sighing. He was calm
Through all my agony, and all my tears
Could wake no sympathy. And yet I mourn!
To crown its sorrow, this poor heart still throbs
Only for him. The blow will soon be struck.
I tremble at it; I forget revenge.
Indeed I think I almost might forgive him!
No, I shall not call my sentence back.
The traitor dies, since he is dead to me!
He laughs in triumph, and he scorns my anger,
Thinks it a storm that will be spent in tears,
That I am always weak, that I will waver,
That my own hand will shield him from my blows!
I have been kind; he thinks it has no bounds!
And there are other thoughts to fill his mind.
The traitor, in his triumph, does not care
Whether the absent wish him life or death,
And leaves this great perplexity to me!
But one stroke ends it! By Orestes' hand
He meets the death that he might well have looked for,
Which I desire, because he made me wish it!

Then is it I who must pronounce his doom?
He dies because Hermione has loved him?—
He whose great deeds were told and told again,
To give me new delight whene'er I heard them?—
To whom I'd bound my fate, all secretly,
Before they tied us, by that fatal bond?
And have I crossed so many lands and seas,
Coming so far only to dig his grave,
To be his murderer? Before he dies—

     *(Enter Cleone)*

 *Hermione.* What have I done, Cleone? Have you news?
What can you tell me? Where is Pyrrhus now?

 *Cleone.* He's at the peak of love and happiness,
Proudest of men. I saw him lead his bride
Into the temple,—the latest of his conquests,—
And in his eyes great joy and hope were shining.
He gazed on her; it seemed that he was drinking
Intoxicating draughts! Andromache,
In all the shouting and the glad acclaim,
Was bearing in her heart sad thoughts of Troy.
She could not love nor hate; she bowed, submissive;
She did not murmur; she did not rejoice.

 *Hermione.* But Pyrrhus? Did he go so boldly on
Quite to the last? His face—you saw it well?
He tasted pleasure calmly, all untainted?
He did not cast a single glance this way?
Tell me, Cleone, did you meet his eye?
And when he saw you there, did he not blush?
Did he not show his guilt with troubled brow?
Or did his pride carry him to the end?

 *Cleone.* No, he saw nothing, and it seemed his safety
And honor's voice, and you, were all forgotten.
He heeds not whether friends or foes will follow,

He hurries to the goal of love he seeks.
He's thrown his guards around the son of Hector;
He thinks that danger threatens only him.
He is in Phœnix' care, taken away.
They keep him from the temple and the palace.
The child would seem to be the only care
That Pyrrhus has, today.
 *Hermione.*    The traitor dies!
What did Orestes say?
 *Cleone.*    He and his men
Are in the temple now.
 *Hermione.*   Ready for vengeance?
 *Cleone.* I do not know.
 *Hermione.*   Not know? And will Orestes
Also be false?
 *Cleone.*  Orestes worships you,
But he has many scruples, much remorse.
They struggle. Now he listens to his honor,
And now to love. He has respect for Pyrrhus,—
The throne, Achilles, and Achilles' son.
He fears the wrath of Greece and of the world,
And yet he says that, most, he fears himself.
He'd come as victor, bringing Pyrrhus' head,
But not as one who must be called assassin!
But he went in, at last, and still not knowing
If he should leave with blood-guilt on his head,
Or having only watched.
 *Hermione.*   No, he will watch.
He'll see their triumph, and he will not wish
To break upon it. Well I know the scruple
That makes his courage shrink: he is a coward,
He fears to die, and fears no other thing!
My mother never stooped to make a prayer,

Yet all of Greece took arms because of her.
She saw ten years of war, saw twenty kings
Whose very names she knew not, die for her.
I only ask one perjured man should die;
I send a lover to avenge my wrongs,
And thus to win me, at a little risk,—
I give myself,—and yet I am refused!
Well, then my own arm strikes the blow for justice!
And cries of pain shall ring through all the temple.
Their marriage day shall have its end in slaughter.
They shall be man and wife but one small moment!
Yes, and my fury need not choose its prey.
Pyrrhus,—Orestes—they're the same to me!
And if I buy revenge by my own death,
I'll gladly die in such good company!

*(Enter Orestes)*

  *Orestes.* It is all over. What you wished is done.
Yes, for the traitor yields his life before the altar.
  *Hermione.* Is Pyrrhus dead?
  *Orestes.*               He's drawing his last breath.
Our Greeks have blotted out his guilt in blood.
Although this plot seemed horrible to me,
I gave my promise, and with hasty steps
I went into the temple. There I found
That all our men had crept, amid the crowd,
And quite unseen, up to the very altar.
Pyrrhus received me with a face unchanged.
The sight seemed even to have warmed his courage:
In me, he braved the Greeks. It gave fresh glory
Unto his marriage rites. Then, very proudly,
He raised the royal diadem, and placed it
Upon the Trojan's brow, with his own hand.
He said, "I give my crown to you—my faith.

Reign o'er my realms, and over me, myself!
Your son shall find I am a loving father;
May Heaven witness this, the vow I make
To you, his mother. Let his foes be mine.
Behold, I hail him as the king of Troy!"
And as he said these words, the cheers resounded,
Answered by cries of rage from Grecian throats.
They closed about the traitor where he stood,
So I myself could find no place to strike him.
Each struggled with the other for the slaying.
He sought escape in vain from countless blows,
And, drenched with his own blood, fell at the altar.
I have come here through terror-stricken throngs.
I've come to bring my princess to the harbor.
Our friends will join us there quite soon, their hands
Red with this slaughter. I have kept my promise.

    *Hermione.* What have they done?

      *Orestes.*                If they have spoiled
      your vengeance
By too much zeal, then you must pardon them.
You wished that I should be the first to strike,
That he might know he died because of you.
But it was I who stirred them up to act.
I brought them to the temple for your sake—
Only for that, and you may justly claim
The life they took as your own sacrifice.
They acted in the vengeance you had planned.

    *Hermione.* Be still, you traitor! Do not lay this deed—
This crime which brands you coward, at my feet!
Go! Let the Greeks applaud so vile an act!
Go! I disown your cruelty and you,
Who have destroyed the noblest man alive,
On this most fatal day! Was there no pity

To visit your black hearts, to stop such murder?
Who made you judge, to sentence him to death?
What was his crime? What right had you to kill him?
Yes, tell me that! Who bade you do it?

   *Orestes.*                      Gods!
Why, it was you, just now, upon this spot!
                             You gave the order!

   *Hermione.* You should not heed a love bereft of reason.
You should have read more deeply in my thoughts!
Did you not see that, while I raved, distracted,
My heart belied whatever words I spoke?
Why, had I meant them, you should have refused
A wish like that, if made a hundred times!
You should have asked again, before you struck,
And still again, or rather, shunned my sight.
You should have let me take my own revenge.
What lured you here? You're hateful to my eyes!
See now what bitter fruit your love has borne!
You bring the ills that follow you, to me.
Your embassy was fatal to us both.
It made his thoughts incline to her—my rival,
For otherwise he might have let me share
His heart again,—at least have played at love!
You go, for I will stay in this Epirus.
Here I renounce my Spartan home and Greece,
Yes, all my kindred! 'Tis enough for me
That they have bred a monster, such as you!
           (*Exit Hermione and Cleone*)

   *Orestes.* Is this Hermione I see and hear?
She for whom all the blood I've shed has flowed?
Was it not traitor, murderer, she called me?
Am I Orestes? And is Pyrrhus dead?
Oh, was the light of reason dark within me,

That I should kill a king, one I revere,—
In one day violate a ruler's rights,
An envoy's duty, all good human ties,
Profane the altars where he stood against me,
Making myself a lawless regicide?
And all for one who knows not gratitude,
For one who made me promise I should slay him,
Or she would never see me more! And now,
When I have done the task her fury set me,
She taunts me with the spilling of his blood!
She loves him!—Looks on me as on a monster!
She takes herself forever far from me,
And, going thanklessly, leaves for my hire
Reproaches I have earned to please her fury!
              (*Enter Pylades and Soldiers of Orestes*)
    *Pylades.* We must depart, sir; we must leave this palace,
Or be content, and never leave at all!
Our Greeks can hold the gate one moment more,
Before their forces grow too strong for us.
They all obey Andromache's commands,
They look on her as queen; we are their foes;
And she herself, unmoved while Pyrrhus lived,
Takes all the duties of a faithful widow,
And presses on to vengeance, all the more
Since Hector's ghost demands the blood of Greece.
Let us not stay until they hem us in.
Our men will join us. While the silly rabble
Still gapes and gazes at Hermione,
We may go through in safety. Here's the way.
    *Orestes.* Oh, no, my friends; it is Hermione
Whom I would follow, for I cannot live
After her final sentence. Go. I'll stay—
In penance for my crime.

*Pylades.*        Hermione!
Forget her. Are you still her tool, the object
Of all her rage? Would you seek newer insults
Even among the dead? And, since she dies,
Must you, then, die with her?

     *Orestes.*            She dies! O gods!
What do I hear you say?

     *Pylades.*          Did you not know?
We met her as we came; she sought the temple,
With hurried steps, and frenzy in her eyes,
And there found Pyrrhus, carried by the soldiers,
All of them roused to vengeance by his blood.
No doubt that sight drove her to madness, too,
For, as we stood above the gate, we saw her
Bend above Pyrrhus, dagger in her hand—
Lift up her eyes, then plunge it in her breast,
Then fall!

     *Orestes.* Oh, Heaven has been pleased to bring us
More sorrows than I looked for, and the gods
Turn not one moment from relentless justice.
Now they have sent my greatest agony.
They find delight in planning miseries,
That I may stand, a proper monument
To wrath celestial, born to wretchedness!
Well, I have drunk the cup. I die content.
Where are these lovers? Now, to top my joy,
I will be drowned in blood,—their blood and mine.
Let me behold them, now they both are dying,
And let three hearts, that were too long discordant,
Be one, at last— But what thick, murky blackness,
What sudden night is this, that comes to shroud me?
What horror is it thrills through all my body,
With no escape? I see a little light.

'Tis blood—red blood, that streams all round about me!
    *Pylades.* My lord!
    *Orestes.*              So, Pyrrhus! Must I always meet thee?
How has the one I hate escaped his wounds?
Wait—I have yet a blow I've kept for thee!
What now? Hermione! Her arms embrace him!
They snatch him from the blow that threatens him!
O gods! What fearful looks she casts at me!
Serpents, faces of fiends come after her!
Why do you reach and stretch your hands, O Furies?
These snakes that hiss and writhe above your heads—
Whom would they sting? What do these horrors mean?
You come to bear me to eternal darkness?
Ah, be it so! Orestes yields to you.
No, leave your vengeance to Hermione!
'Twere better she should tear me, limb from limb,
Yes, and devour that heart I offered her!
    *Pylades.* Friends, he has lost his mind. While there is time,
Let's take advantage of it; save the prince.
It will be vain to try it, should his madness
Turn once again, and give him back his senses.
                    (*Exeunt*)

**FINIS**

# BRITANNICUS

*A Tragedy*

by

JEAN RACINE

## CHARACTERS

NERO .......*Emperor of Rome, Son of Agrippina*
BRITANNICUS .*Son of Messalina and the Emperor Claudius*
AGRIPPINA ...*Widow of Domitius Enobarbus, father of Nero, and widow, by a second marriage, of the Emperor Claudius*
JUNIA .......*Loved by Britannicus*
BURRUS .....*Tutor of Nero*
NARCISSUS ...*Tutor of Britannicus*
ALBINA ......*Confidante of Agrippina*
GUARDS

The scene is in Rome, in a chamber in Nero's palace.

# ACT I

*(Enter Agrippina and Albina)*

*Albina.* Why should you come here, waiting till he wakes,
While Nero seeks to sleep? Shall Cæsar's mother
Walk unattended through these halls, and watch
Beside his door alone? Madam, go back.

*Agrippina.* I must not leave him for a single moment.
I shall wait here for him, thinking upon the cares
He causes me, however long he sleeps.
What I foretold seems to be all too certain.
Nero has doomed the prince Britannicus,
Nero has fled the reins of his impatience.
Now he would terrorize, since he is weary
Of being always loved. Britannicus
Torments him much, and I myself, each day
Know I become more irksome.

*Albina.* You to whom
He owes the very breath of life,—who called him
From his low station up to the very throne?
Who took from Claudius' son his heritage,
So that Domitius bears the name of Cæsar?
All this speaks for you; all this claims his love.

*Agrippina.* Indeed, his love is due to me, Albina.
What I have done would win a gracious heart,
But to ingratitude all things are hateful.

*Albina.* Ingratitude? But all his doings show
A soul that's learned to know the voice of duty.
In three long years what is there he has said,

What has he done but things which give to Rome
The promise of a reign of perfect justice?
Beneath so mild a rule Rome must believe
The days when consuls held authority
Have come once more. A reign so fatherly
Shows this young Nero is as good a man
As was Augustus in his later years.

   *Agrippina.* No, but my interest cannot make me blind.
Though it is true that Nero has begun
Quite as Augustus ended, yet the future
May make the past forgotten, and I fear
As one began, so will the other finish!
There's no disguise; I read upon his brow
The savage nature of Domitius,
And see it mixed there with the pride of Nero—
His gift from me. The face of tyranny
Is always mild at first: why, even Caius
One time delighted Rome, yet his feigned mercy
Turned into madness soon and Rome's delight
Became the thing she hated. But indeed,
Why should I care so much for Nero's virtue?
Did I commit him to the helm of State
That he might please the senate and the people?
Why, let him be the father of his country,
If that's what he desires, but let him not
Forget his mother's claims! What can we call it,
This crime which daylight has revealed to us?
For well he knows Britannicus loves Junia;
And yet this Nero, he of model goodness,
Screened by the night will have her carried off!
What moves him? Is it hatred? Or desire?
Is it his only joy to injure them?
Or does he, in his malice, visit them

With spite he feels for me because I helped them?
  *Albina.* How have you helped them?
  *Agrippina.* Quiet, dear Albina.
I know they owe their fall to me alone:
And that Britannicus was hurled by me
Down from the throne that was his rightful place:
That Junia's brother threw his life away
Because I stopped his marriage with Octavia.
Nero has all, and for my just reward
I hold the balance evenly between them
In order that, some day, Britannicus
May do the same between my son and me!
  *Albina.* What is your plan?
  *Agrippina.* I'll make myself a harbor
Against the coming storm. I cannot check him
But only with these reins.
  *Albina.* Against a son
Surely such care is needless.
  *Agrippina.* I should fear him
Only the more if he feared me no longer.
  *Albina.* Perhaps this fright is groundless; and if Nero
Is failing in his duty, if he's changed
We have not seen him show it. These are secrets
Between your son and you, for each new honor
That Rome bestows upon him goes to you.
His love is lavish, keeping nothing from you.
Your name is sacred as his own in Rome,
And poor Octavia is little heeded.
Augustus honored Livia much less.
Think how the fasces, decked with bay, are carried
In front of Nero's mother. Never before
Has any woman had such honor paid her!
How would you have him show his gratitude?

*Agrippina.* With less respect and greater confidence!
I scorn these honors, since my hold on him
Grows less as these increase. The time is gone
When Nero, still a boy, responded quickly
To all the wishes of my loving heart;
When he would lean on me in every strait;
When my command would bring the senate here,
And, hidden by a screen, but always there,
I moved them with my animating touch.
He was not sure of Rome's capricious will,
And so his greatness had not turned his head.
I think with pain upon the day I found him
First dazzled with the brightness of his glory.
It was the day when many kings had sent
Envoys to greet him, from earth's farthest realms.
I went to take my proper place beside him
There on the throne. I do not know whose counsel
Made him disgrace me so, but when he saw me,
His face looked on me with so much displeasure
That in my heart I knew it boded evil.
And then, with false respect to mask the insult,
He rose up quickly, running to embrace me,
And so he turned my footsteps from the throne.
And Agrippina's power, since that blow,
Has hurried fast and faster to its fall,
All but its shadow gone! They seek my favor
Less than a word from Seneca or Burrus!

*Albina.* But if your heart is filled with these suspicions,
Why do you keep such poison in your breast?
Go, and let Cæsar's lips answer your doubts.

*Agrippina.* Others are always there when Nero sees me.
He sets a time and talks with me in public,
And speaks or holds his peace, as he is prompted.

We have two masters; one is always there
To mark the interview and watch it closely.
But I'll pursue him more the more he shuns me.
I'll turn his own confusion to my profit.
I hear his door unlocked. We'll go to him
And ask him what he means by this abduction.
Perhaps he may reveal the truth, not thinking.
So! Burrus! He has been with him already!

*(Enter Burrus)*

   *Burrus.* Madam, I come to you in Cæsar's name,
To tell you that the order which alarmed you
Was only given as a wise precaution.
The emperor has wished that you be told.
   *Agrippina.* Then let us enter, since he wishes it,
And learn his purpose better.
   *Burrus.* But of late
Cæsar has sought to be alone. The consuls
Both came before you, by a secret gate.
I will go back—
   *Agrippina.* No, I will not disturb him.
But let us two be frank, for once, and talk;
Exchange our thoughts with somewhat less restraint.
   *Burrus.* The tongue of Burrus always scorns to lie.
   *Agrippina.* How long, then, do you mean to hide him
     from me?
And must I always be intruding on him
When I would see him? Have I raised you up
So high as this, to have you place a bar
Between my son and me? Do you not dare
To trust him but a moment out of sight?
Do you and Seneca dispute the glory
Of blotting out the image of his mother
From his remembrance? Has my trusting you

Fed your ingratitude until you rule
Supreme beneath the shadow of his name?
I cannot think you'd make a tool of me—
Of me who might have left you quite obscure,
Me, whose great ancestors have filled the throne,
The daughter and the sister—wife and mother
Of your imperial masters. What do you mean?
Think you my voice has made an emperor,
Only to set two others over me?
Nero's no more a child; is it not time
He ceased to fear you, and began to rule?
For how long must he see all things through you?
His ancestors are models he may follow,
Choosing between Tiberius and Augustus,
Or, if he can, Germanicus, my father.
I do not dare to rank myself with these,
Yet there are lessons he might learn from me.
Perhaps he might be taught at least that caution
Which sets the proper limits on a prince
And on his confidence.

    *Burrus.* I have been charged
To make excuses for one act of Cæsar's.
But since you do not wish for this defense,
And lay the blame for all his deeds on me,
I'll answer, as a soldier should, with candor,
As one who knows not how to gloss the truth.
You trusted Cæsar, in his youth, to me;
I own this, and I could not well forget it.
But have I ever promised I would cheat him,
Or make him always bow before your will?
My duty is no longer paid to you,
But to imperial Rome, which sees its safety
Or ruin in my hands. He was your son,

But now he is the master of the world.
If you had sought for men to pamper him,
Could only Seneca and I do this?
Why did you not have flatterers to guide him?
Were we called back from exile to corrupt him?
Could not the servile court of Claudius give you
A thousand men more fit for this than we?
And all of them most eager to be raised
By Cæsar's degradation, until he
Should have grown old, in a protracted childhood?
What would you have? Are you not well respected?
Is your name not held sacred, linked to Cæsar's?
Indeed, the emperor no longer comes
And lays his sceptre at your feet each day,
Paying you humble service; gratitude
Need not be shown by such a base dependence.
Must Nero always be a timid child,
Not daring, but in name, to be Augustus?
But I can tell you Rome upholds his conduct.
She has been long in bondage, been a slave
To three low-born usurpers. Now this yoke
Which chafed her so has been removed, and Rome
Sees her recovered freedom spring from Nero!
And more! Why, Virtue's very person seems reborn!
To be a master does not mean to plunder:
The people freely choose their magistrates;
Those in command are those the soldiers trust;
Corbulo and Thrasea still are faithful
In army and in senate, though in fame
They are the foremost. Now those desert islands
Which senators have peopled well with exiles
Keep the informers. What if Nero trusts us,
So long as our good counsel helps his glory,

And Rome has freedom which will be as lasting
As Cæsar's power, through a happy reign?
But Nero, madam, does not need our guidance.
Our part is to obey him, not direct him.
He has the models of his ancestors,
And by those models rightly guides his steps.
He shall be happy if his later virtues
Be linked in one long chain with those of youth!

   *Agrippina.* And so you will not dare to face the future.
You think your prince would go astray without you.
Then tell me, since your work so far contents you,
And since you've come to witness me his virtues—
Tell me why Nero has become a robber,
And carried off the sister of Silanus?
Is it because he wishes by such insults
To cast a stain upon my ancestors
Whose blood fills Junia's veins? Or by what crime
Has she become so dangerous today?
What is his charge? Of what does he accuse her,
She who, till now, bore grandeur modestly;
Who never would have seen him but for this,
Who would have counted it a mark of favor
Had she been kept forever from his sight?

   *Burrus.* Why, she is not suspected of a crime,
Nor has the emperor condemned her yet.
There is no object here to wound her eyes,
For she's at home among her ancestors.
Her title to the throne is strong enough
To make her husband stir rebellion up.
'Tis well that Cæsar's blood should be allied
Only to those that Cæsar well may trust.
And, you must own, without his due consent
No one should wed the offspring of Augustus.

*Agrippina.* I understand you. Nero, by your lips,
Tells me Britannicus relies quite vainly
Upon my choice for him, and I have tried
Without success to turn his eyes away
From his own sorrows, with a bait so tempting.
It seems the emperor has wished to show
That Agrippina makes more promises
Than she can keep. Rome puts too high a rating
Upon a mother's influence, he thinks,
And by this insult he will undeceive her,
And teach the world that it must not confuse
An emperor with a son. He may do this,
Yet I am bold to tell him he should make
His sceptre strong before he strikes at me.
He forces me to match my feeble arm
Against him, and in doing this betrays
How weak his own is, and it well may be
That when they're tested in the balances,
My name will weigh more heavy than he thinks.
    *Burrus.* Then will you always doubt your son's devotion?
Can he not take one step, but you distrust it?
How can he think that you would side with Junia
Or make your peace with young Britannicus?
Do you support your foes, that you may find
Excuses to complain against your son?
Must you be ready to divide the empire
For every little rumor that you hear?
Shall you let such a constant dread possess you
That you must ask these questions as you kiss him?
You need not take such care to find out blame.
Rather indulge him fondly as a mother.
Suffer a slight, but do not make it known,
For fear the court should learn to disregard you.

*Agrippina.* But who would seek the help of Agrippina,
When Nero thus proclaims my fall, himself—
When Nero keeps me banished from his presence,
And Burrus dares to hold me on his threshold?

*Burrus.* I see that it is time I kept my silence.
My frankness only makes for your displeasure.
Pain is unjust, and all the arguments
That cannot soothe it only rouse suspicion.
Britannicus is coming. I will go,
And you shall hear of his disgrace with pity.
Perhaps you'll lay the blame for it on those
Whose counsel Cæsar has not deigned to follow.

(*Exit Burrus. Enter Britannicus and Narcissus*)

*Agrippina.* Whither so fast? What restless zeal, my lord,
Brings you among your enemies so blindly?
Whom do you come to seek?

*Britannicus.* Whom do I seek?
By Heaven, madam, all I've lost is here!
Hemmed in by multitudes of savage soldiers,
Junia has been dragged hither most ignobly.
Ah, what a horror must her timid heart
Have felt at seeing such a spectacle!
Yes, they have taken her away from me.
It is a cruel order that would part
Two lovers who are one in misery!
No doubt they grudged that we should share our sorrows,
And so help one another to endure them!

*Agrippina.* Enough. I feel your wrongs as much as you,
And my complaint was made before your murmurs.
And yet I know quite well that helpless anger
Does not release me from my solemn promise.
You do not understand. If you would do so,
Follow my steps to Pallas. There I'll wait.

(*Exit Agrippina and Albina*)

*Britannicus.* Narcissus, can I trust her? Shall I make her
The one to judge my quarrel with her son?
What think you? Is she not that Agrippina
Whom once my father married, to my ruin,
And who, you say, cut short his ebbing life
Because she found it was too long for her?

*Narcissus.* No matter. She feels outraged, like yourself.
Has she not promised you the hand of Junia?
Unite your griefs, and both your interests.
This palace vainly echoes your regrets,
And if you're seen here, with a pleading voice
Spreading complaints about rather than terror,
Losing the fierceness of your rage in words,
No doubt you'll be complaining here forever!

*Britannicus.* Narcissus, well you know if I am willing
To come at last to tameness, to submit,
Or if I was so frightened by my fall
That I renounced my rightful throne forever.
But I am still alone. My father's friends
Have grown so strange that now they chill my heart
Those in the court who yet are true to me
Still hold themselves apart from such a youth.
And after one brief year has passed to teach me,
To make me know what wretched fortune's mine,
What do I see about me? Friends that are false,
All hired to watch my steps with eyes unsleeping!
Chosen by Nero for so base a duty,
They sell the secrets of my soul to him,
And out of me they take their daily profits!
He sees my plans beforehand, hears what I say;
He knows what's in my heart as well as you!
What do you think, Narcissus?

*Narcissus.* You are foolish!
Choose only friends whom you can truly trust,
And do not be so lavish of your secrets.
　　*Britannicus.* Quite right, Narcissus, but a noble heart
Too long deceived, is always slow to learn
Suspicions such as these. But I trust you,
Or rather, I have sworn to trust no other.
My father often told me of your zeal.
Of all his freedmen, only you are faithful,
And you alone are watchful of my welfare,
Saving me still from countless hidden rocks.
Then go and see if this new-stirring storm
Has fanned the failing courage of my friends.
Watch their eyes well, and listen how they speak.
See if, indeed, I may expect their help.
But chiefly look within the palace here,
And see how closely Nero guards the princess.
Learn if her precious life is safe from peril,
And if I still may see her. In the meanwhile
I'll go to Nero's mother. She's with Pallas,
One whom my father freed, as he did you.
I'll stir her anger up, and it may be
She'll promise more than she had thought to do.
　　　　　　　　　　　*(Exeunt)*


## ACT II

*(Enter Nero, Burrus, Narcissus, Guards)*

　　*Nero.* Burrus, remember this; she is not just,
But she's my mother, and I'll take no heed
Of all her whims, yet I will never spare
The underling who dares to urge them on.

Pallas has poured his poison in her ears,
And every day corrupts Britannicus.
They hear his voice alone. If we should follow,
Perhaps we'd find that they were with him now.
It is too much. He must be kept from them.
This last time I command it; let him go.
Now I have spoken; ere this day is over
My court and Rome had best be rid of them.
See to it for the safety of the State.
Come here, Narcissus.

                    (*To Guards*) Let my guards retire.
                (*Exit Burrus and Guards*)
  *Narcissus.* Thank Heaven, Sire, that you have taken Junia,
And so today the peace of Rome is safe.
Your enemies' vain hopes have fallen down.
They've gone to Pallas to bewail their weakness.
But what is this? I see you vexed and worried,
And more dismayed than is Britannicus!
What do they mean, this frowning and this gloom?
These startled looks that shift uneasily?
All things are smiling. Fortune crowns your wishes.
  *Nero.* The die is cast, Narcissus. Nero loves!
  *Narcissus.* You, Sire?
  *Nero.* A moment past—and yet, forever!
Love? Said I love? Why, Junia is my idol!
  *Narcissus.* You love? Love *her?*
  *Nero.* I was most curious.
I went tonight to see her when she came.
So sad! She raised her tear-stained eyes to Heaven.
They shone amid the flash of swords and spears—
A beauty unadorned, in simple dress,
As when they seized her, sleeping; and I know not
Whether that turmoil, and the torch-lit darkness,

The cries breaking the silence, and the faces,
The savage looks of those who took her captive,
Made sweeter still those sweet and timid eyes:
But quite bewitched by such a lovely sight,
I tried to speak, and found my tongue was tied.
I was amazed. I could not even move.
And so I let her go to her apartments.
I sought my chamber. There in solitude
I tried in vain to turn my thoughts from her,
But she was always present to my eyes.
And so it seemed I talked with her. I loved
The very tears that I had caused to flow.
And sometimes, yet too late, I asked forgiveness,
And often found my sighs would end in threats.
And thus I have been nursing this new passion.
I have not closed these eyes, watching for daylight.
Perhaps I conjure up too fair an image
Of her whom I first saw at such a time.
What says Narcissus?

 *Narcissus.* Who'd believe, my lord,
That she had lived so long unseen by you?

 *Nero.* You know it well, Narcissus. Moved by a wrath
That thought me guilty of her brother's death,
Or guarding still her pride with jealous care
That would not let me see her dawning charms,
True to her grief, and wanting dim seclusion,
She stole away. She shunned all admiration.
And it is this, a virtue new to the court,
That, persevering so, has piqued my love.
Is there another maiden here in Rome
Who would not grow more vain at such an honor
If I should love her? Is there one but tries
Her loving looks upon great Cæsar's heart,

Soon as she knows their strength? But she alone,
The modest Junia, scorns the prize they covet.
It may be that she would not even deign
To try to learn if Cæsar merits love,
Or if he knows its rapture. But, Narcissus,
Tell me, is young Britannicus her lover?
   *Narcissus.* Her lover, do you ask?
   *Nero.* He is too young.
He does not know himself, nor love's sweet poison.
   *Narcissus.* Ah, but my lord, love never waits for reason.
He loves; you need not doubt it. He is taught
By charms of such great power that his eyes
Have quickly learned to melt with tenderness.
He knows how best to do her slightest wish.
It may be he has conquered her already.
   *Nero.* What! Can this boy have won her heart and faith?
   *Narcissus.* I do not know. I'll tell you what I can.
Sometimes I've seen him tear himself away
Full of an anger which he hides from you,
Vexed when he's shunned by the ungrateful court,
Fretting against your power and his weakness,
Fear and impatience ruling him in turn.
He goes to Junia and comes back content.
   *Nero.* He is the more unhappy that he knows
How he can please her. He should wish her anger.
If Nero's jealous, he will have revenge.
   *Narcissus.* You, Sire? But why should you be ill at ease?
Junia has pitied him and shared his sorrows,
For she has seen no other tears but his.
But now, my lord, her eyes have been unsealed,
And she shall see your royal splendor near her,
And kings uncrowned, who wait upon your person;
Her lover, too, unknown amid the crowd,

All hanging on your look, and honored by it,
If you, my prince, may chance to glance upon them.
When she shall see you coming down to her
From that high glory, owning her victory,
You will be master of her heart already.
You'll only need command, and she will love you.

    *Nero.* I must prepare to meet so much chagrin!
Such wearisome entreaties!

    *Narcissus.* Who will hinder
My lord's good pleasure?

    *Nero.* All—Octavia, Burrus,
Seneca, Agrippina, Rome herself!
Three years unstained! But not one tender relic
Remains to me of all the bonds that bound me
Once to Octavia. Long since I tired of her.
Mine eyes can seldom look upon her tears.
I shall be happy if I soon divorce her,
And free me of a yoke imposed by force!
The gods themselves have secretly condemned her.
For four years, now, her prayers have all been vain.
The gods are little moved by all her virtue;
They honor not her couch with any pledge,
And, still in vain, the State demands an heir.

    *Narcissus.* My lord, why hesitate to cast her off?
Your sceptre and your heart have both condemned her.
Did not Augustus sigh for Livia,
And did he not, by means of two divorces,
Unite her to him? To those broken ties
You owe the crown. Tiberius, whom his marriage
Had linked with him and you, made bold to scorn
The daughter right before the father's eyes.
And only you refuse this welcome course,
And thwart your own desires.

*Nero.* Do you not know
The rage of Agrippina? 'Tis as if
I see her bringing me Octavia,
And with an eye of fury, bidding me
To honor this most sacred bond she tied,
And charging me with long ingratitude
In no soft terms. What shall I say to her?
How shall I face attacks so violent?

*Narcissus.* Be your own master, and be hers as well.
Will you submit to being taught forever?
Reign for yourself; you've reigned for her too long.
You fear to do so? No, you do not fear her!
Just now did you not banish haughty Pallas,
Knowing that she supports his insolence?

*Nero.* Out of her sight, I threaten, I command.
I listen to your counsels, dare approve them;
My anger grows; I think that I can brave her.
But I will lay my feelings bare for you;
So soon as ill luck brings me to her presence,
I either dare not disregard the spell
Of eyes in which I long have read my duty,
Or else remembrance of her kindness gives her
The power over all she's given me,
And all that I would do does not avail me.
My spirit trembles; it is awed by hers!
It is to free myself of this submission
That I avoid her always, and offend her,
And sometimes I have even stirred her anger,
That she should fly from me, as I from her!
I keep you here too long. Go now, Narcissus,
For fear Britannicus should think you false.

*Narcissus.* Oh no, he puts a perfect trust in me.
Why, Sire, he thinks I'm here at his command,

To hear what you may say concerning him,
And thinks he'll learn your secrets from my lips.
He's anxious to behold his love again,
And so he wants the help my care can bring him.

   *Nero.* I give consent to that. Yes, he shall see her.
Give him this pleasing news.

   *Narcissus.* No, keep him from her.

   *Nero.* But I have reasons. Trust me, good Narcissus;
Although he sees her, he shall dearly pay!
Now boast to him of how your scheme succeeds;
Tell him that I myself have been deceived,
That he is seeing her against my will.
She comes. Go, find your master. Bring him here.

           (*Exit Narcissus. Enter Junia*)

   *Nero.* Your cheek is pale. You seem so troubled, lady!
Is it you see ill omens in my eyes?

   *Junia.* I cannot hide my error from you, Sire.
I thought to see Octavia, not Cæsar.

   *Nero.* I know this, and Octavia's good fortune
In winning favor makes me envious.

   *Junia.* You, Sire?

   *Nero.* Then do you think Octavia
And only she, of all within these walls,
Has eyes to see your virtues?

   *Junia.* Ah, whom else
Can I implore to pity me, and tell me
What crime I have committed unawares?
So I beseech you, let me learn my fault.

   *Nero.* But, lady, is it then a light offense
That you have hid your beauty for so long?
Has Heaven given you its choicest gifts
That you might bury what was made to shine?
Is not Britannicus afraid to hide

Your charms from us—yes, and his growing love?
Why have you been so cruel till today
As to have kept us here, within our court,
Exiled from eyes so bright? 'Tis even said
That you've allowed his overtures of love!
I'll not believe that you have favored them
Without consulting us, nor been so heedless
Of proper conduct as to plight your faith,
And let us gain our only news of it
Through common rumor's voice.
    *Junia.* I must confess
His sighs, sometimes. tell me his heart's desires.
His eyes are ever fixed upon a maid,
The sole survivor of a famous line,
Thinking, perhaps, of how, in better days
His father meant that she should be his bride.
He loves me, for he heeds his royal father,
He heeds your mother's wish—I think your own—
For your desires are always one with hers—
    *Nero.* My mother has her wishes; I have mine.
We'll speak no more of her and Claudius,
For it is not their choice that fixes mine.
I, and I only, must decide for you.
I'll have you choose a husband as I wish.
    *Junia.* But think, my lord, how any other union
Would bring disgrace upon my ancestors.
    *Nero.* It is not so, my lady, for the husband
Of whom I speak will need to feel no shame
To place his parentage along with yours.
I think you may consent to hear his suit
And spare your blushes.
    *Junia.* Then who is he, Sire?
    *Nero.* It is myself.

*Junia.* You?

*Nero.* I would name some other
If I knew any name more high than Nero's.
I've searched the court—nay, Rome, and all the world,
To choose you such a partner as you'd wish.
And still the more I seek for proper hands
To which to trust this treasure, all the more
I see that Cæsar can alone deserve
To hold it; only he is worth your love.
He should entrust you to no other hands
But those which hold the empire of the world.
Do you, yourself, remember long ago,
How Claudius betrothed you to his son?
'Twas at a time when he had thought to name
That son, one day, as heir of all his empire.
The gods declared for me. Do not oppose them,
But follow where they point your way to power.
They have bestowed this honor on me vainly,
Unless your heart should be united with it:
If my great cares may not be soothed by smiles—
If, while I give to watching and alarms
These days which others envy, and I grudge,
I may not spend some while before your feet.
Let not Octavia's image cloud your sight.
Rome is like me, and gives to you her suffrage,
Rejects Octavia, and would have me break
A tie that even Heaven must disown.
Consider what I say. Think of it well.
It is a choice that's worthy of a prince—
A prince who loves you! Yes, and it is worthy
Of those bright eyes, kept hidden far too long,—
And of the world, to which you owe your charms.

*Junia.* My lord, I have good cause to stand amazed!

For in the course of one short day I find
That I am brought here as a criminal,
And when I come before your eyes, all trembling,
Hardly confiding in my innocence,
At once you offer me Octavia's place!
Yet I am bold to say I've not deserved
Either so great an honor, or such insult!
Then can you wish, my lord, that a poor girl,
Whose earliest remembrance is the sight
Of her own home destroyed,—who nursed her sorrow,
Learned to be patient in obscurity,—
You wish that she, with but a single step,
Should pass from darkness into that great brilliance
That once, afar, she shrank from, there to sit
Where all the world may gaze on her and see her
Usurping majesty that is not hers?

    *Nero.* Have I not said but now that I renounce her?
Be rid of all these fears, these timid scruples,
Nor do not think my choice is blind and rash.
I know you're worthy. Give me your consent.
Remember what a line it is you spring from.
Then do not choose the glory of refusal
Of all those honors Cæsar offers you.
It would be followed but by vain regrets.

    *Junia.* But Heaven knows the secrets of my thoughts.
I am not proud of boasting and vain-glory.
I know the value of the prize you offer,
But when my fortune shone more brightly on me,
The more I'd be ashamed to face the guilt
Of having robbed the one whose right it is.

    *Nero.* You think too carefully upon her interests.
The claims of friendship scarcely reach so far!
Come, let us leave pretense. Let us be plain.

The sister does not move you. 'Tis the brother,—
And for Britannicus—
   *Junia.* Yes, he has learned
To touch my heart, and I confess it freely.
Perhaps my frankness may not be discreet,
But never have my lips belied my heart.
Since I was not at courts, I had not thought
That I had need to learn dissimulation!
I love Britannicus. I was to wed him
When marriage would have led me to the throne.
But evil fate, denying him the crown,—
His vanished honors, and his empty palace,
The courtiers whom his fall has banished from him,—
These only serve as ties to Junia's faith.
Here all things work to serve your least desire.
Your days pass calmly, and in endless pleasures
Which have their constant source in your great power;
Or if some trouble mars their placid course,
The universe is anxious you be pleased,
And quickly blots it from your memory.
The lot of poor Britannicus is lonely.
In all his sorrows he has only me,
My tears the only solace he can take
To lead him, sometimes, to forget his grief.
   *Nero.* It is that solace and those tears I envy.
Another one should buy them with his life.
And yet, I keep a milder course for him;—
Fair lady, he shall soon appear before you.
   *Junia.* My lord, your kindness ever reassures me.
   *Nero.* I might forbid his coming to your presence,
And yet I would anticipate the danger
To which resentment soon might carry him.
I do not wish his death. It is far better

That he be sentenced by the lips he loves.
His life is dear to you; then part him from you,
And never let him think that I am jealous.
Take on yourself the blame for banishment,
And, either by your words or by your silence,—
At least by looking coldly, you'll persuade him
To take his wishes and his hopes away!

*Junia.* I? Shall I, then, pronounce so hard a sentence?
My tongue will swear I mean the opposite!
Even if I were traitor to myself,
My eyes must still forbid him to obey me.

*Nero.* I shall be near, behind a curtain, lady.
Shut up your love within your inmost heart,
For I shall miss no secret words you say.
Looks that you think are silent, I will hear,
And he shall have his death for a reward
If any little move or sigh betray you.

*Junia.* Ah, if I dare to make a wish, my lord,
Then only grant that I may never see him!

(*Enter Narcissus*)

*Narcissus.* My lord, Britannicus would see the princess.
He is close by.

*Nero.* Then let him enter.

*Junia.* Sire!

*Nero.* I leave you, and his fate depends on you
More than on me. Remember, I am watching.

(*Exit Nero*)

*Junia.* Run, dear Narcissus,—run to meet your master.
Tell him—Oh, it is useless! He is coming.

(*Enter Britannicus*)

*Britannicus.* Dear girl, what happiness has brought me
   near you,
And lets me come to such a sweet encounter?

But even in this pleasure grief consumes me
Because I may not see you more than this.
Now I must steal, by means of greatest craft,
A boon that once you gave me every day.
Ah, what a night I've passed! How many wakings!
Your tears have not disarmed our enemies!
What was your lover doing? Did some god
Grudge me the right of dying at your feet?
Alas, have you in secret, struck with terror,
Made your complaint to me? Have you, my princess,
Happened to breathe a wish that I were with you?
But did you think what grief that wish would cost me?
What! Say you nothing? Are you cold as ice?
Is this the way you solace my disgrace?
Speak. We're alone. Our enemy's deceived.
He's busy elsewhere, while we stay together,
And take what joy we may from his good absence.

   *Junia.* His power fills each corner of this palace.
Its very walls may well have eyes to see us.
Cæsar is never absent from this place.

   *Britannicus.* How long have you been timid in this
     fashion?
What! Does your love yield to its bonds already?
What is it can have changed the heart that swore
Nero himself should envy us our love?
But, lady,—rid yourself of needless fear.
All hearts have not yet lost their loyalty.
I see no eye but it approves my anger.
Why, Cæsar's mother is upon our side,
And Rome herself, offended at his doings—

   *Junia.* Surely your words must contradict your thoughts.
For you yourself have said a thousand times
That all Rome lauds him with a common voice

You always were respectful of his virtues.
Grief has upset you, giving you such words!

    *Britannicus.* Your words surprise me much, I must confess.
I had not thought to hear you praising him!
I scarcely find one favorable moment
To share with you this grief that overcomes me,
And you will take these precious moments up
In praises of the foe who crushes us!
How much unlike yourself one day has made you!
Even your looks have learned a strange restraint.
What's this? You seem afraid to meet my eyes!
Then am I hateful? Can it be that Nero
Has won your favor? If I ever thought so—
Oh, by great Heaven, drive away this darkness
Which you have cast about me! Will you speak?
Then have you quite forgot Britannicus?

    *Junia.* Please go away. The emperor is coming.

    *Britannicus.* This blow has cut my one last hope, Narcissus
        *(Exit Britannicus. Enter Nero)*

    *Nero.* Madam—

    *Junia.* No, Sire, I cannot hear your words.
I have obeyed you. Let my tears, at least,
Flow freely, now that he no longer sees them.
        *(Exit Junia)*

    *Nero.* Well, my Narcissus, you have seen the passion
With which they love. It's silent, yet quite plain!
I know quite well my rival has her heart.
I'll have my joy in making him despair!
How pleasant is his anguish to my fancy,—
And I have seen him doubting if she loves him!
I'll follow her. My rival waits for you,
And he will vent his fury. Go, torment him
With new suspicions. Make him pay most dearly

For boons that he despises. I will witness
The tears she sheds for him!

(*Exit Nero*)

*Narcissus* (*alone*). And yet again
Fortune invites me. Shall I scorn her offer?
No! To the end I'll follow her commands,
Dooming the wretched, to secure myself!

(*Exit*)

## ACT III

(*Enter Nero and Burrus*)

*Burrus.* Pallas obeys you, Sire.

*Nero.* But Agrippina,—

How does she think, now that her pride is fallen?

*Burrus.* Why, do not doubt but that the blow strikes home.
And soon a storm of loud reproach will burst.
Her wrath began to show itself long since.
It will not ever stop at useless clamor.

*Nero.* What is it that you think she may be planning?

*Burrus.* Well, Agrippina's always to be dreaded.
Your army,—all of Rome revere her line.
They'll not forget Germanicus, her father.
This much she knows, and you well know her courage.
And that which makes me dread her all the more
Is that her fury's fed by you, yourself,
And that you give her arms to fight against you.

*Nero.* I, Burrus?

*Burrus.* Yes, my lord. That love which holds you—

*Nero.* I see your meaning. But it must be so.
My own heart tells me more than you can say,
And yet I cannot choose but love.

*Burrus.* A fancy!
And, since you're satisfied with slight resistance,
You fear an evil, feeble at its birth.
But if your heart, made strong to do its duty,
Will make no truce with any foe of yours;—
If you recall the glory of your past;
If you bring back to your remembrance, Sire,
The virtues of Octavia, not worthy
Of such a recompense,—think of her love
Which still remains through all the scorn you give it.
If, more than all, you shun the sight of Junia,
And doom your eyes to some short absence from her—
My lord, no matter how this passion charms you,
Trust me—none love, but they who wish to love!

   *Nero.* Burrus, I'll trust you when we are at war,
And when we need your aid, for martial glory;
Or when, in peace, and in the senate's meeting,
The welfare of the State has need of you,—
Then I will heed the counsel that you give me.
But in a matter close to my own heart,
It is not so, and I should have some care,
Nor bring your grave mind to consider trifles!
Farewell. I'm not at ease, away from Junia.

             (*Exit Nero*)

   *Burrus* (*alone*). Well, Nero shows his own true self at last!
Burrus, the fierceness you had thought to tame
Is almost ripe to burst your feeble bonds,
Spreading destruction, like a swollen river!
What can I do in this unhappy hour?
Seneca can't ease my cares with counsel.
He's far from Rome; he does not know this danger.
If I could only touch his mother's feelings
Of tenderness and love. She comes! Good fortune!

(*Enter Agrippina and Albina*)

*Agrippina.* Well, Burrus, tell me,—was I wrong to fear?
Yes, you have taught fine lessons to your pupil!
Pallas is banished, for the crime, no doubt,
Of having raised your master to the throne!
Quite well you know that never, but for him,
Would Claudius, ruled by him, have fathered Nero.
You thrust a rival in Octavia's place,
And you would break the marriage of my son,—
A proper task for one who has been chosen
To curb the wild career of youth, indeed!
See how the enemy of flatterers
Has turned himself to flattery, and teaches
How one may heap contempt on wives and mothers!

   *Burrus.* As yet you have no reason to accuse me.
There is some justice in this act of Cæsar's.
Pallas has richly earned his banishment,—
Due payment for the pride he's always shown.
Cæsar has only, and with much regret,
Done what the court has secretly desired.
The other evil can be cured, I think.
Octavia's tears may dry before they spring.
But calm your anger. There's a milder way
Will call him back the sooner to her arms,
While threats and angry words will make him worse.

   *Agrippina.* Oh, you may try in vain to stop my mouth!
I see my silence only brings your scorn.
What I have done has had too much respect!
No, all my strength has not been lost with Pallas.
The gods leave some who will avenge my fall.
For now the son of Claudius begins
To feel his wrongs. Not only I am guilty!
Nay, do not doubt I'll show him to the army,

Complain to them of how his youth is blasted,
And make them, like myself, repair their wrong!
Here they shall see the son of royal fathers
Claiming a faith sworn to his family,
And hear the daughter of Germanicus;—
While over there, the son of Enobarbus,
With those who aid him, Seneca and Burrus,—
By me called back from exile, both of them,—
Sharing their sovereign's rights before my eyes!
And I shall see they know the crimes we've done,
And they shall know the paths in which I've led him.
Yes, I shall swear the vilest rumor's true,
To make his rule, and yours, detested by them.
I'll tell them all,—all exiles and all murders,—
Poison itself—
    *Burrus.* They'll not believe you, madam.
They'll not be tricked by all of this deceit.
They'll know that anger prompts self-accusation!
As for myself—I first advanced your plots.
I made the troops swear fealty to Nero,
And I do not repent this zeal of mine.
A son succeeded to his father, madam,
For, in adopting Nero, Claudius chose
To give his son, and yours, an equal right.
Rome's choice has been for Nero. So she took
Tiberius, adopted by Augustus,
Not wronging young Agrippa, his own grandson,
Who sought in vain to hold the royal sceptre.
His power safely rests on such foundations,
And so, today, you cannot weaken it.
And if he'll heed me still, why, then his bounty
Will soon remove the wish to injure him.

I have begun the work. I will complete it.

    (*Exit Burrus*)

 *Albina.* In what a sea of passion grief has plunged you!
And can it be that Cæsar does not know it?

  *Agrippina.* Ah, should he dare but once come in my sight—

  *Albina.* In Heaven's name, my lady, hide your anger.
Let not your zeal for sister or for brother
Destroy your peace forever! Must you thus
Be checking him, even because he loves?

  *Agrippina.* Can you not see how they would humble me?
It is to me that they will give a rival.
And if I break not this ill-fated tie,
My place will soon be taken. I'll be nothing.
Thus far Octavia has only held
An empty title, one which all the court
Sees as quite useless,—but the eyes of all
Have ever looked to me for gain and power.
And now another love has cast out mine.
And she, whether she's his wife or mistress,
Will reign alone, and in her pomp and glory,
Reap all the harvest of my work, as payment
For one kind look she gives. I'm lost already!
I cannot bear to think of it, Albina.
And even if I hasten the dire sentence
Of Heaven, thankless Nero— See! His rival!

    (*Enter Britannicus and Narcissus*)

 *Britannicus.* Our common foes are not invincible.
There are some hearts that feel for our misfortunes.
Your friends and mine, that have been still so long,
Are fired with anger, kindled by injustice.
They've brought their grievances to good Narcissus.
Nero has not quite gained the full possession
Of her whose conquest brings my sister shame.

And if her wrongs still move you, though he's faithless,
He may be brought again to duty's path.
Why, we have half the senate in our cause;—
Sylla and Piso, Plautus—
   *Agrippina.* What do you say?
You name the highest nobles of the State!
   *Britannicus.* I see my words have wounded you, my lady,
And that your anger trembles, half-resolved,
And is afraid to take what it had wished for.
No. My disgrace has taken root too firmly.
You need not fear what friends of mine may do,
For I have lost them all. Your own good prudence
Long since has scattered them, or won them from me.
   *Agrippina.* Trust your suspicions less. Our safety, sir,
Demands that we should understand each other.
Depend on me. Despite your enemies
I will be true to all that I have promised.
Nero is guilty, and he shuns me vainly.
Sooner or later he must hear his mother.
I'll try persuasion; I will turn to force;
And if I fail, I'll take your sister with me
And spread abroad my fears and her alarms.
I'll make all hearts respond, when she shall weep.
Farewell. I'll press the battle on all sides.
And I advise that you avoid his presence.
      (*Exit Agrippina and Albina*)
   *Britannicus.* Have you not flattered me with feeble hopes?
Can I be sure that what you say is true?
   *Narcissus.* You may, my prince. But this is not the place
Where I can tell you of this mystery.
Let us go out. What is it you await?
   *Britannicus.* I? Wait? Alas!
   *Narcissus.* But tell me what you mean.

*Britannicus.* If any scheme of yours could let me see her
But one time more—
    *Narcissus.* See whom, my lord?
    *Britannicus.* I blush
For such a weakness. Yet I think that then
I'd meet my fortune better.
    *Narcissus.* Still you think
That she is true, in spite of all I tell you?
    *Britannicus.* Why, no, I think her false, and most deserving
Of hot reproaches, yet despite myself,
I do believe it less than that I ought!
My heart still pardons all her fickleness,—
Finds out excuses, for it still adores her.
I would that I could crush this disbelief!
Would I could hate her with an easy mind!
Yet who would think a heart that seemed so noble,—
Foe of the faithless court through all her life,
Could so forget its honor all at once,
And turn to perfidy too base for courtiers?
    *Narcissus.* Who knows if, when she hid herself so long,
The wretch had not been looking for this conquest?
She knew her beauty could not be concealed;
Perhaps she fled that she might then be followed,
Thus urging Nero to the hard-won glory
Of taming one who never had been conquered.
    *Britannicus.* May I not see her, then?
    *Narcissus.* Why, at this moment
She listens to the words of her new lover.
    *Britannicus.* Well, let us go. But who is this I see?
Look, it is she!
    *Narcissus* (*aside*). Cæsar must know of this!
          (*Exit Narcissus. Enter Junia*)
    *Junia.* Oh fly! Face not the wrath that burns against you!

Nero is angered by my firm resolve.
I have just now escaped, while Agrippina
Is trying to detain him. So farewell.
And do not wrong my love, but look to see
The happy day when I shall be absolved
Of all this blame. Your image lives within me.
There's nothing that shall ever banish it.

   *Britannicus.* I know your purpose, madam; yes, I know
That you would have me fly and leave you free
To take your pleasure in your new desire.
No doubt while I am here a secret shame
Disturbs, somewhat, the flavor of that pleasure.
Yes, I must go!

   *Junia.* But do not think that I—

   *Britannicus.* You might have held the field a little longer
I do not murmur that your love is fickle,
Or that you join the side which Fortune favors;
Or that you're dazzled with imperial splendor,
And would enjoy it, at my sister's cost:—
But rather that, beguiled like others, now,
You should have seemed untouched so long a time
By these deceits. I own I am despairing.
This was the only evil I'd not thought
That I must fight. I've seen injustice flourish
Upon my fall; why, yes, I have seen Heaven
In league with my oppressors. Yet these horrors
Have not been all my cup. There still remained
To be forgot by you.

   *Junia.* More happy moments
Might make me more impatient with distrust.
But Nero threatens you, and danger presses,
And I have other thoughts than to distress you.
Go, now. Assure your heart, and cease complaining.

Nero, who heard us, forced me to pretend.

　*Britannicus.* Ah, cruel one—

　*Junia.* He watched us as we talked.
He watched my face with a most careful eye,
Ready to let his vengeance burst on you
If any gesture should betray the secret.

　*Britannicus.* So Nero listened? But I think your eyes
Might have looked cold, and not deceived me so.
They might have told me who had made them cruel!
Love is not dumb. The heart speaks many ways.
One glance had saved me from a bitter sorrow.
There needed only—

　*Junia.* There was need of silence
To save you, then. How many times my heart
Came near to telling how perplexed it was!
How many sighs I stopped before they rose;
And how I feared to meet the eyes I longed for!
Silence is torture, when a loved one grieves,
When we must only make him weep the more,
Yet know we might console him by a look!
But such a look had caused more bitter tears!
And when I thought of that, I was most fearful.
I thought that my pretense seemed hardly real.
I feared the pallor of my trembling cheek,—
My eyes that showed too plainly their distress.
Each moment I was fearing Nero's anger
Might come upon me for my lack of rigor,
Because it seemed so vain to try to quell
The love I almost wished I'd never known.
Alas, he's read your heart and mine too clearly
For his own peace of mind, and ours. Once more
I say farewell. Go, hide you from his sight.
I'll tell you more at some more likely time,

For I can tell a thousand other secrets.

    *Britannicus.* Too much already! More than I can bear!
How guilty I have been! And you,—how kind!
Do you know all that you forsake for me?

              *(Throwing himself at Junia's feet)*

When may I come, repentant, to your feet?

    *Junia.* What are you doing? See, your rival comes!

                  *(Enter Nero)*

    *Nero.* Prince, do not pause in these delightful raptures.
His thanks, my lady, show you very kind.
I have surprised him at your knees, and surely
Some gratitude is rightly due to me.
He finds the place I keep you most convenient,
And ready for such sweet and charming meetings!

    *Britannicus.* I'll lay my joy or sorrow down before her
Wherever she is kind enough to see me.
Nor can this place, where you think fit to keep her
Show anything that awes Britannicus.

    *Nero.* So you see nothing here to warn a subject
To bow before my power and obey me?

    *Britannicus.* This palace did not see us raised together,
Me to obey, and you to taunt my weakness.
The fortune of my birth made it unlikely
That I should own Domitius for a master.

    *Nero.* Our wishes have been altered by our fates.
Once I obeyed, and now you take your turn.
If you have not yet learned so hard a lesson,
Why, then, you're still a boy; you must be taught it!

    *Britannicus.* And who will teach me?

    *Nero.* Rome and all her empire!

    *Britannicus.* Does Rome allow you, with your other rights,
Much cruelty and violent injustice,
Unfair imprisonment, divorce and rape?

*Nero.* Rome does not pry with such a careful eye
Into the secrets that I choose to hide.
Copy her prudence.

*Britannicus.* We know what she thinks.

*Nero.* Well, but she holds her tongue, and so should you.

*Britannicus.* So Nero thus has ceased to curb his passions!

*Nero.* Nero has ceased to care to hear you longer.

*Britannicus.* All hearts should bless him. 'Tis a happy
  reign!

*Nero.* Happy or not, they fear me. 'Tis enough.

*Britannicus.* I know not Junia, or such words as these
Would scarcely win much praise from her, I think.

*Nero.* If I am little able to content her,
At least I'll punish any cock-sure rival!

*Britannicus.* Whatever danger seems to overwhelm me,
I fear to lose her love,—and only that!

*Nero.* 'Twere better wished for. I shall say no more.

*Britannicus.* My only hope is to enjoy her love.

*Nero.* And she has pledged that love to you forever.

*Britannicus.* At least I have not learned to play the spy
Upon her words. I let her praise or blame me
Without my watching, hidden, o'er her silence!

*Nero.* I see. Guards!

*Junia.* But what is it you will do?
Pardon the jealous love of one so near me.
He suffers from a thousand miseries.
Can his least happiness arouse your envy?
Oh, my lord, let me knit your hearts together,
And hide me from the eyes of both of you!
If I'm away, your fatal strife will cease,
And I will join me to the Vestal Virgins.
Oh, let my vows not be the cause of quarrels
Between you; let them only trouble Heaven!

*Nero.* This plan is strange indeed, and it is sudden.
Guards, let her now be taken to her chamber.
And let Britannicus stay with his sister.

*Britannicus.* This is the way that Nero wins a woman!

*Junia.* Do not provoke him. Bend before the storm.

*Nero.* Guards, do my bidding, and delay no longer.

(*Exit Britannicus and Junia, guarded. Enter Burrus*)

*Burrus.* You gods! What do I see?

*Nero* (*not seeing him*). Their flame burns fiercer.
I know what hand it was arranged their meeting!
It was for this that Agrippina sought me,
And all her long and tiresome talk was meant
Only to further this vile scheme of hers.

(*Sees Burrus*)

Discover if my mother still is here,
For I would hold her, Burrus, in this palace,
And let my bodyguard relieve her own.

*Burrus.* Your mother, Sire? You will not hear her, then?

*Nero.* Stop! Now I do not know what you are plotting,
But for some days all wishes I have made
Have found in you an over-eager censor.
Answer for her,—or else, if you refuse,
Others shall answer for her,—and for Burrus!

(*Exeunt*)


# ACT IV

### Scene I. *Agrippina and Burrus*

*Burrus.* Here, madam, you may clear yourself at leisure,
Cæsar consents to give you audience.
If his command restricts you to the palace,
Perhaps his purpose is to speak with you;

In any case, if I may speak, forget
He has offended you, and show yourself
Ready to take him back with open arms;
Defend yourself, but do not censure him.
See how the court obeys his word alone.
Although he is your son and owes you all,
He is your emperor, and you, like us,
Are subject to the power that you gave.
Upon his favor or disfavor hangs
Your favor or disfavor with the court.
'Tis his support they seek in seeking yours.
But look, the emperor comes.

   *Agrippina.*        Leave us together.


## Scene II. *Agrippina and Nero*

   *Agrippina* (*seating herself*). Come, Nero, sit beside me.
   'Tis my wish
To clear your mind of every false suspicion.
I know not with what crime I have been slandered,
But all that I have done can be explained.
You hold Earth's sceptre now; and yet you know
How far below such eminence you were born.
My fathers, whom Rome placed among the gods,
Had not exalted you without my help.
When Messalina's execution left
The couch of Claudius an open prize,
I sought to triumph over the fair field
Of women who employed his freedmen's aid
Only because I hoped in after years
To give the throne where I should sit to you.
I choked my pride to garner Pallas' favor;

His master, daily cherished in my arms,
By slow degrees drew from his niece's eyes
The love to which I sought to lead his heart.
But kindred blood between us barred our union
As impious incest, nor did Claudius dare
To wed his brother's daughter till the senate,
Subservient to his wish, relaxed the law,
And placed him in my arms, Rome at my feet.
So much for me; for you still nothing gained.

Hard on my steps I made a place for you
Within his household, made you his son-in-law,
Gave you his daughter, whom Silanus loved,
And he, forsaken, marked the fatal day
With his own blood. Still nothing was accomplished.
Could you have guessed that Claudius one day
Had held his son-in-law above his son?
Again I went to Pallas for his help.
On his advice Claudius adopted you;
He called you Nero, and before 'twas time
Wished you to share the power with himself.
Thus it was that thinking on the past,
Men saw my plan already far advanced;
And seeing Britannicus threatened with disgrace,
His father's friends began to murmur. Some
I blinded with fair promises, and exile
Delivered me from those most treacherous;
Claudius himself, grown weary of my plaints,
Sent from his son all those whose constant zeal,
Long loyal to his destiny, could still
Place him upon the pathway to the throne.
I went still further, choosing for my suite
Those only whom I wished to guide his course.

Yet I was careful to appoint for you
Such guardians as Rome held most in honor;
Deaf to intrigues, I trusted only fame;
Recalled from exile and withdrew from war
That very Seneca, that very Burrus,
Who later— Rome then held them honorable.
Tapping the wealth of Claudius meanwhile,
In your own name I gave you lavish gifts.
Presents and shows, invincible attractions,
Won you the people's hearts; the soldiery,
Recalling all their former loyalty,
Favored in you Germanicus, my father.

Claudius, meanwhile, weakened towards his death;
His eyes, long closed, were opened at the end;
He saw his error. Stricken with his fear,
He dropped some words of pity for his son,
And wished, too late, to call his friends together.
But I controlled his bed, his guards, his palace,
And let him vainly waste his tenderness.
I watched him to his latest breath. My care,
Which seemed to minister to his distress,
But hid his son's tears from the dying king.
He died. A thousand shameful rumors spread.
I quickly stopped the news that he had died,
And while in secret Burrus was dispatched
To swear the army to your cause, and you
Were marching to the camp, at my command
The altars smoked through Rome with sacrifices.
Tricked by my deception, all the people
Prayed for the health of a king already dead.
At last, with all the legions sworn to you,
Your power o'er the empire firmly fixed,

I showed them Claudius' body, and the people,
To their astonishment, learned all at once
That Claudius was dead and you were king.

This was what I wanted to confess;
These were my crimes, and this is my reward.
Now that you reap the fruit of all my pains,
In six short months your gratitude is spent;
You feel the burden of respect too heavy,
And scarcely seem to recognize me more.
I have seen how Seneca and Burrus
Stirred you to treachery, and set you lessons,
Till you excelled your teachers in deception;
I have seen young rakes like Senecio
And Otho favored with your confidence
Because they pandered to your every wish;
And when in desperation at your treatment,
I asked some explanation of your acts,
You fled to the sole refuge of an ingrate,
And answered my complaints with fresh affronts.
Today I promised Junia to your brother,
And both were flattered at your mother's choice.
But you—as soon as she was brought to court,
Made her at once the mistress of your heart.
I see your heart has turned against Octavia;
I see you ready, too, to turn her out
From the bed in which I placed her; I see Pallas,
An exile, and Britannicus, a captive.
Finally you destroy my liberty:
Burrus dares to lay his hands upon me,
And you, too conscious of your perfidy,
You dare not come to me and beg forgiveness,
You order me to justify myself.

*Nero.* Never can I forget that 'tis to you
I owe the empire, and there is no need
For you to take the trouble to repeat it.
Madam, you may repose your happiness
With perfect trust on my fidelity.
But these suspicions, these persistent plaints,
Have led all those who heard them to believe
That formerly—I say this privately—
You worked in my name for your own advantage.
"Such honors," so they say, "such deference—
Are these such mean reward for what she did?
What is the crime for which she blames her son?
Is it to do her will that she has crowned him?
Did she but deputize him with the power?"

And, madam, if I could, I would have pleased you;
I had been glad to give you back the power,
Whose restitution you so loudly claim,
But Rome would have a master, not a mistress.
You hear the rumors which my weakness stirs:
How daily senators and populace
Complain at hearing my voice speak your will,
Saying that Claudius dying, with his power,
Bequeathed me also his subservience.
A hundred times you have seen our soldiers bear,
With angry mutterings, their eagles past you,
Ashamed to put to such a use the heroes
Whose effigies are stamped upon them still.
Any other woman would have yielded,
But if you do not rule, you must complain.
Leagued with Britannicus against my cause,
You strengthened him by mating him with Junia;
And Pallas was the hatcher of your plots.

And when against my will, I take such measures
As will assure my peace, I stir your hatred.
You plan to show my rival to the army;
Already has the rumor reached the camp.

   *Agrippina.* I make him emperor? Can you believe it?
What motive could I have? What could I want?
What honor could I look for in his court?
If under your reign malice spares me not,
If my accusers dog my steps and dare
Attack the mother of their emperor,
How should I fare within a stranger's court?
They would reproach me, not with futile words,
With trumped-up charges, doomed at birth to fail,
But with my crimes committed for your sake,
And I could all too easily be convicted.
You do not trick me with your smooth evasions.
You are ungrateful, and you always were.
My love and care, even from your tenderest years,
But drew from you a feigned affection. Nothing
Could touch your heart; your hardness should have stopped
The springs of kindness. Ah, how miserable
Am I! By what misfortune is it fated
That all my love should serve to make me hateful!
I have an only son. Ye gods who hear me,
Have I made any vows except for him?
Remorse, fear, danger, nothing held me back.
I conquered scorn; I turned away my eyes
From evils which were prophesied for me.
I did my best. You reign. I am content.
Now with the freedom you have taken from me,
If you desire it, take my life as well,
Provided that the people in their anger
Deprive you not of that which cost me dear.

*Nero.* Speak then. What is it you would have me do?

*Agrippina.* Punish the insolence of my accusers;
Calm the resentment of Britannicus;
Let Junia have the husband of her choice;
Let both be free; let Pallas stay in Rome;
And suffer me to see you when I will.
       *(Perceiving Burrus at the back of the stage)*
Lastly, let Burrus, who has come to hear us,
No longer dare to stop me at your door.

*Nero.* Madam, I hope my gratitude may stamp
Henceforth, your power upon all the court.
And I already bless this happy coldness,
Which makes the fire of our love burn brighter.
Whatever Pallas did, it is forgotten;
My quarrel with Britannicus is over.
As for this passion which has come between us,
I make you arbiter, and you shall judge us.
Go then, and bear good tidings to my brother.
Guards, let my mother's orders be obeyed.

### Scene III. *Nero and Burrus*

*Burrus.* How charming, Sire, the spectacle, which these
Embraces offer to my eyes! You know
If ever my voice has been raised against her,
If ever I sought to cleave you from her love,
Or merited this unjust wrath of hers.

*Nero.* To tell you plainly, I mistrusted you.
Burrus, I thought you two in league together.
Her enmity restores my trust in you.
She is too eager after triumph, Burrus.
If I embrace my rival, 'tis to crush him.

*Burrus.* What, Sire?

*Nero.*                Enough of this. I need his ruin

To set me free from Agrippina's fury.
For while he breathes I am but half alive.
She makes me weary with his hateful name,
And I shall not permit her insolence
To promise him my throne a second time.
   *Burrus.* And must she soon weep for Britannicus?
   *Nero.* By evening I shall never fear him more.
   *Burrus.* What motive has inspired you with this plan?
   *Nero.* My love, my honor, my safety, and my life.
   *Burrus.* No, tell me what you will, this foul design
Was never, Sire, conceived in your own breast.
   *Nero.* Burrus!
   *Burrus.* Great Heaven! must I learn it from your lips?
Do you not quake yourself at hearing it?
Have you considered whose blood it is you spill?
Is Nero weary of ruling in all hearts?
What do you think that men will say of you?
   *Nero.* What, bound forever to a blameless past,
Shall I consider such a fickle love
As chance may give, and in a day remove?
Shall I submit my wishes to their will?
Is it to please them I am emperor?
   *Burrus.* Sire, is it no source of satisfaction
That all the public good is owed to you?
It is for you to choose; you still are master.
Blameless thus far, you could be always so;
The way is plain, and nothing holds you back;
Yours but to march from virtue on to virtue.
But if you follow where your flatterers lead,
Then, Sire, your way leads on from crime to crime.
Successive cruelties must back your harshness,
And you must bathe your reeking arms in blood.
Britannicus dying will excite the zeal

Of all his friends, too ready now to quarrel,
And his avengers will find new defenders,
Who after they have died will have successors.
You will touch off a fire you cannot quench.
Feared of all men, you will have all to fear,
To tremble always even while you punish,
And count your subjects all for enemies.

Ah, does the happy life of your first years
Cause you to hate your youthful innocence?
Do you recall the joy that marked their course?
How tranquilly they passed! How sweet it is
To think on them, and whisper to yourself:
"Now everywhere my people love and bless me;
No subject trembles at my name, and Heaven
Has never heard it mingled with their tears.
No sullen glances follow my appearance,
But everywhere hearts flutter when I pass."

Such were your pleasures once. What change, O gods!
The meanest blood was precious to you then.
And I recall a day once, when the senate,
Sitting in judgment, pressed you to subscribe
Your name upon a criminal's death warrant;
But you berated them for too much harshness,
And, saddened by the burden of a crown,
You said: "I would I knew not how to write."

No, take my counsel, or my death shall spare me
The sight and sorrow of this sad decay.
I shall not stay, Sire, to outlive your glory,
If you are bent upon so black a deed.
                    (*Casts himself at Nero's feet*)
Lo, I am ready! Strike before you go.

Pierce through this heart which never can consent.
Summon the cruel men who have misled you
To come and try their faltering hand on me—
I see my tears have touched my emperor;
His native goodness shudders at this crime.
Oh, lose no time. Tell Burrus who they are,
These traitors who dare give you such advice:
Summon your brother; in his arms forget—
 *Nero.* What are you asking?
 *Burrus.*      No! He does not hate you.
He is deceived. I know his innocence,
And I shall pledge his loyalty for him.
I'll run to him to press this happy meeting.
 *Nero.* Let him attend me in my rooms with you.

### Scene IV. *Nero and Narcissus*

 *Narcissus.* Sire, I have arranged this righteous murder.
The poison is prepared. Renowned Locusta
Took special pains in brewing it for me.
She killed a slave before my very eyes—
A sword is slower to cut off a life
Than this new poison she has given me.
 *Nero.* Enough, Narcissus. I commend your pains,
But have no wish that you should press them further.
 *Narcissus.* What, has your hatred for Britannicus
So weakened?
 *Nero.*    Yes, Narcissus, we are friends.
 *Narcissus.* Sire, I would not turn you from your course.
But he has been so late a prisoner,
This wrong will long be green within his heart.
There are no secrets time does not reveal.
He will discover that he should have had
Poison from me, prepared at your command.

I pray the gods may turn him from such purpose,
But he, perhaps, will dare what you dare not.

    *Nero.* His heart is pledged, and I shall conquer mine.

    *Narcissus.* And Junia's marriage? Does that seal the bond?
Will you, Sire, make this sacrifice for him?

    *Nero.* You show too much concern. Let be what will,
I reckon him no longer with my foes.

    *Narcissus.* Sire, Agrippina counted upon this,
She has restored her empire over you.

    *Nero.* What has she said? What would you say to me?

    *Narcissus.* She has boasted of it publicly.

    *Nero.*                                        Of what?

    *Narcissus.* That she need only see you for a moment,
And all this fury, all this deadly wrath,
Would yield to temperate silence; you yourself
Would first consent to peace, happy that she
Should deign in kindness to forget the past.

    *Nero.* Tell me, Narcissus, what am I to do?
Right gladly would I punish her presumption,
And if I had my will, this rash success
Would soon be followed by regret unending.
But what would be the verdict of the world?
Would you have me follow in the steps of tyrants,
And Rome, forgetting all the noble names
It knows me by, remember me at last
Only by that of poisoner? This vengeance
Would stamp me in their eyes a fratricide.

    *Narcissus.* Would you be guided, Sire, by Rome's caprice?
Think you that men will always hold their tongues?
Is it your proper province to lend ear
To what they say, and let your own desires,
Because of it, fade from your memory?
Dare you oppose no wishes but your own?

But, Sire, you do not understand these Romans—
No, not at all—their talk is more restrained.
You weaken your control with so much caution;
They soon will think that you have cause to fear them.
They have been long accustomed to the yoke,
And kiss the hand that rivets on their chains.
You will discover they are always willing
To do your pleasure. This servility
Wearied Tiberius. I, myself, invested
With borrowed power, which with my liberty,
I had from Claudius, tried a hundred times,
During my hey-day, to exhaust their patience,
But never found it lacking. Why should you
Fear the black odium of a poisoning?
Destroy your brother, and desert your sister:
Rome, prodigal of victims for its altars,
Would find them crimes if they were innocent,
And you shall see men rank as luckless days
The birthdays of your brother and your sister.

   *Nero.* Once more, Narcissus, it must not be done.
I promised Burrus, I was forced to yield.
And I would not break faith with him and give
His virtue arms that he may use against me.
My courage fails before his arguments,
And yet I did not listen tranquilly.

   *Narcissus.* Burrus, sire, speaks not his simple mind.
He works his virtue shrewdly to his interest—
Or rather all of them have but one thought:
They see their powers shattered by this stroke;
You would be free, and at your feet these masters
Would bow their proud heads like the rest of us.
Do you not know what things they dare to say?
"Nero, in truth, was never born to rule.

He speaks, he does, what we prescribe for him.
Burrus directs his heart, and Seneca
Controls his spirit. He has no ambition,
No special gift or talent, but to drive
A chariot in the circus, to compete
For prizes which he should disdain to take,
To make himself a spectacle in Rome,
Performing in the theater and singing
Songs he hopes the rabble will admire.
Meanwhile his soldiers, ever and anon,
Force the applause that so delights his ear."
Will you not silence such remarks as these?

    *Nero.* Come, let us go and plan what we shall do.

## ACT V

### Scene I. *Britannicus and Junia*

    *Britannicus.* Yes, madam, Nero—strange as it may seem—
Is waiting in my room to welcome me.
He has invited all the youth of court
That in a festal spirit we may seal
Our oaths before their eyes, and so revive
Our love amid a general rejoicing.
He sets aside his passion, from which springs
Our enmity, and makes of you sole judge
And master of his fate. As for myself,
Though banished from the glory of my fathers,
Though he usurps their rank before my eyes,
In ceasing to oppose my love, he yields
To me the dear delight of pleasing you;
And in my heart I secretly forgive him,
And grant him all the rest without regret.

No more shall I be exiled from your beauty.
I look without alarm upon those eyes
Which neither grief nor terror could persuade,
Which sacrificed for me the imperial throne.
Ah, Junia—but what new fear is this?
Why are you silent in this hour of joy?
Why do your eyes, your lovely, sad eyes, look
So longingly towards heaven while I speak?
What do you fear?

 *Junia.*     I do not know myself—
And yet I fear—

 *Britannicus.*  You love me?

 *Junia.*       Yes, I love you.

 *Britannicus.* Nero no longer bars our happiness.

 *Junia.* But can you answer to me for his faith?

 *Britannicus.* Do you suspect him of some secret hate?

 *Junia.* But lately Nero loved me, swore your death;
He shuns me now and calls you to his side.
Can such a change be but a moment's work?

 *Britannicus.* This change is Agrippina's work. She thought
My death would bear her ruin in its wake.
Thanks to the foresight of her jealous heart,
Our bitterest enemies have fought for us.
I trust the passion which I saw in her;
I trust in Burrus; I believe his master.
I think that he, like me, cannot play false,
Hates openly or does not hate at all.

 *Junia.* Judge not his heart by yours, for you and he
Pursue two different courses. I have known
Nero and his court but one short day,
Yet I have learned, if I dare speak of it,
How different are their words from what they think;
How little mouth and heart agree in them;

How lightly they betray their promises!
How strange a dwelling, this, for me and you.

   *Britannicus.* But if his love be feigned or true, if you
Fear Nero, is he not himself afraid?
No, no, he will not by so base a crime,
Dare to arouse the people and the senate
Against himself. He owns his latest wrong.
Even Narcissus knows of his remorse.
Ah, my dear princess, had he told you how—

   *Junia.* May not Narcissus be a traitor too?

   *Britannicus.* Why would you have my heart hold out
   against him?

   *Junia.* How can I tell? But when your life is touched,
Suspicion falls on all, in everyone
I fear to find a traitor. I fear Nero;
I fear the evil fate that follows me.
I feel a dark presentiment of danger,
That makes me tremble when you leave my sight.
Suppose this peace which so rejoices you
Concealed a secret snare against your life;
If Nero, angered by our mutual love,
Had chosen night to cover up his vengeance,
And while I see you here prepares to strike—
If I should never see you more—my prince—

   *Britannicus.* You weep, dear princess, can it be your heart
Is so concerned for me that on a day
So glorious for you, when Nero thought
To dazzle you with his imperial splendor,
Here where I am shunned and he is courted,
You still prefer my misery to his pomp?
That on this very day, here in his palace,
You can refuse an empire for yourself,
And weep, my love, for me? Oh, dry your tears,

Your precious tears. I will come quickly back,
And all our fears will vanish. If I stay
Too long my going, I will rouse suspicion.
Adieu! I go. My heart so filled with love,
Amid the joy of these unseeing youths,
Will have not eyes nor ears but for my princess.
   *Junia.* Prince—
   *Britannicus.*      They wait for me, and I must go.
   *Junia.* Oh, stay at least until they send for you.

#### Scene II. *Agrippina, Britannicus, Junia*

   *Agrippina.* Why do you tarry, prince? Go quickly. Nero
Complains impatiently at your delay.
His festive company waits anxiously
To show its joy when you embrace each other.
Let not his ardor cool. Go now! You, Junia,
And I will go to find Octavia.
   *Britannicus.* Go, my fair Junia, and with mind at ease
Embrace my sister, who is waiting for you.
As soon as possible I shall return,
And thank you, madam, for your kindnesses.

#### Scene III. *Agrippina and Junia*

   *Agrippina.* Unless I am mistaken, Junia,
Some farewell tears have dimmed your shining eyes.
Tell me what trouble clouds your happiness.
Do you distrust the peace I brought about?
   *Junia.* After the sorrows which this day has cost me,
Can I so quickly reassure my heart?
I scarcely can believe this miracle;
And if I fear that even your good works
Will meet some obstacle, 'tis but because
I know how quickly things can change at court,
And fear is the companion of love.

*Agrippina.* Enough. I spoke, and the whole face of things
Was altered. You have now no cause to fear.
I'll answer for this peace pledged in my presence.
Nero has given me his certain word.
Ah, could you but have seen with what affection
He sealed again the promise of his faith;
How longingly he held me in his arms
At our farewell. He scarce could let me go.
His easy goodness, written on his face,
First spoke of trivial matters, then forgetting
His royal pride, he was a boy again,
Telling his troubles on his mother's breast.
But soon, returning to his graver manner,
He was the emperor speaking with his mother;
And in my hands he placed his confidence,
The secrets which control the fates of men.
No, I must here confess it to his honor,
He hides no black resentment in his heart.
Our enemies alone warped his good-nature,
And through his kindness turned his mind against us.
But in its turn their influence now declines:
Once more shall Rome see Agrippina rule,
It hails already my return to favor.
But meanwhile let us find Octavia,
And share with her the remnants of a day,
So fearful once, so happily concluded.
But what is that I hear? What means this tumult?
What are they doing?

    *Junia.*              Now Heaven save Britannicus!

SCENE IV. *Agrippina, Junia, Burrus*

*Agrippina.* Where are you going, Burrus? Stop! What
  means—

*Burrus.* Madam, 'tis done. Britannicus is dying.
*Junia.* My prince!
*Agrippina.* Dying?
*Burrus.*                    Say rather he is dead!
*Junia.* Forgive me, madam, this outburst of grief.
I go to help him or to follow him.

SCENE V. *Agrippina and Burrus*

*Agrippina.* Ah, Burrus, what a crime!
*Burrus.*                    It is the end.
I must desert the emperor and the court.
   *Agrippina.* Felt he no horror at his brother's blood?
   *Burrus.* His plan was subtler. When the emperor
First saw his brother coming, he arose
And threw his arms around him. All were silent.
Then suddenly Cæsar lifted up the cup,
And spoke for all to hear: "To crown this day
With happy auguries, my hand pours out
The first drops from this cup, and on the gods
I call with this libation to descend
And look with favor on our pledge of love."
Britannicus accepts the pledge. Narcissus
Refills the cup he holds, but as his lips
No more than touch the rim—madam, a sword
Could not have been more swift and powerful—
The light dims from his eyes, and on his couch,
Lifeless and cold, he falls. Imagine then
What consternation struck the company;
Half of the guests rushed out with shrieks of fear,
But those with more experience in the court
Adapted their expressions to the look
They saw in Cæsar's eyes. Meanwhile he lay
Unmoved upon his couch, and utterly

Without astonishment he said: "This illness,
Which terrifies you with its violence,
Has often and with no especial peril
Attacked him since his infancy." Narcissus
Tried vainly to appear concerned. His joy,
In spite of him, was all too evident.
For my part, let the emperor, if he will,
Punish my boldness. Through the press I strode,
And left his hateful court. My heart o'erwhelmed
By treachery so base, I went to mourn
Britannicus, the emperor, and Rome.

    *Agrippina.* He comes. Now you shall see if I inspired him.

## Scene VI. *Agrippina, Nero, Burrus, Narcissus*

    *Nero.* You!

    *Agrippina.*     Stop, Nero, I must speak with you.
Britannicus is dead. I heard the cries.
I know his murderer.

    *Nero.*             Who, madam?

    *Agrippina.*                    You!

    *Nero.* I? I? See how suspicion stirs within you!
There is no crime that I cannot commit!
If one believes you, madam, Claudius
Himself was done to death by me. His son
Was dear to you; his death may well distress you.
I cannot answer for the strokes of fate.

    *Agrippina.* No! No! Britannicus is dead by poison!
Narcissus gave it; you commanded it!

    *Nero.* Madam!—But who has dared to tell you this?

    *Narcissus.* Why, Sire, should this suspicion so affront you?
Britannicus had secret projects, madam,
Which would have given you better cause for grief.
His aim was higher far than Junia's hand.

He would have made you suffer for your kindness.
You were deceived in him, and soon or late,
He meant to be revenged for all his wrongs.
If fate has helped you in your own despite,
Or Cæsar, knowing the conspiracies
Against your life, trusted my loyalty,
Leave weeping, madam, to your enemies;
Let them deplore however much they please
This villain's death, but you—

   *Agrippina.*           Go on, Nero.
With ministers like these you should win glory.
Go on! You have already gone too far
To turn back now. Your hand, as a beginning,
Is reddened with your brother's blood, and I
Foresee that next your blow will strike your mother.
Deep in your secret heart I know you hate me.
You would be free from gratitude's hard yoke.
But I shall make my death of little use
To your designs. Think not that, dying, I
Shall leave you peaceful. Rome, the sky above,
The very light of day you have from me,
Will keep me everywhere before your eyes.
Regrets will follow you like vengeful furies,
And you will try with fresh atrocities
To set your heart at rest; so fury, feeding
Upon itself, will mark your every day
With some new bloodshed. But I hope at last
That Heaven, weary of your cruelties,
Will add your life to all your other victims;
That after wallowing in their blood and mine,
You'll find yourself compelled to shed your own;
And that your name descend to future times
An insult to the cruelest of tyrants.

That is the fate my heart predicts for you.
Farewell, you may go now.
    *Nero.*                  Narcissus, come.

### Scene VII. *Agrippina and Burrus*

  *Agrippina.* Ah, god, how false have my suspicions been!
Condemning Burrus to believe Narcissus!
Did you remark the furious looks which Nero
Left with me for farewell? The die is cast.
No cruelty is great enough to stop him.
The stroke foretold me is about to fall,
And it will overwhelm you in your turn.
  *Burrus.* Ah, madam, I have lived a day too long.
Would Heaven his hand had been so kindly cruel
As to expend on me this new-born fury!
Would that he had not showed me by this crime
The certain sign of Rome's impending ruin!
Not that this deed alone makes me despair,—
He might through jealousy have killed his brother—
But if I must explain my sadness, madam,
It is that Nero saw him die unmoved.
In his indifferent eyes there was already
The look of one inured to crime from birth.
Let him complete his work and put to death
A rash adviser who cannot endure him.
So far from wishing to avoid his wrath,
The swiftest doom is now the most desired.

### Scene VIII. *Agrippina, Burrus, Albina*

  *Albina.* Ah, madam—sir—go save the emperor,
Save Cæsar from the strength of his own madness.
He sees himself forever robbed of Junia.
  *Agrippina.* What! Has Junia taken her own life?

*Albina.* To heap eternal sorrow upon Cæsar,
She made herself, still living, dead for him.
You know how hurriedly she left this spot.
She feigned that she was going to sad Octavia;
But soon she took a different way, where I
Could watch her as she sped. Distractedly,
She passed the palace gates. Then first she saw
Augustus' statue, and she clasped its knees,
The while her tears bedewed its marble feet.
"O prince," she prayed, "by these knees which I clasp,
Protect this hour the last one of your line:
Rome, in your very palace, has seen destroyed
The only one of all your family
Who might have been like you. Now he is dead,
They would compel me to be false to him.
But that my faith with him may live unstained,
I give myself to the immortal gods,
With whom your goodness lets you share their altars."
Meanwhile the people, wondering at the sight,
Rush in from every side and throng around her,
And in their pity at her grief and tears,
With one voice promise to defend her vow.
They lead her to the temple where so long
Our virgins, sworn to serve at Vesta's altar,
Guard faithfully the precious flame which burns
Forever for our gods. Cæsar looks on
And sees them leave, nor dares to interfere.
More rash, Narcissus, who would please his master,
Rushes to Junia's side and fearlessly
Would stop her with his sacrilegious hand.
A thousand mortal blows avenge his insult.
And Junia is spattered with his blood.
Cæsar in dumb surprise at such an outburst,

Leaves him to those who have surrounded him,
And so returns. All flee his sullen silence.
The name of Junia alone escapes
His lips. He paces vaguely up and down;
He dares not lift his downcast eyes to heaven;
And there is fear if night and solitude
Are left to work on his distracted spirit,
If you delay too long to go and help him,
His grief may hurry him to suicide.
Time presses! Run! or in a fit of passion,
He will destroy himself.

   *Agrippina.*             That would be just.
But, Burrus, let us go and see how far
His grief is like to drive him, let us see
What change remorse will work in him, if he
Henceforth will listen to a wiser counsel.

   *Burrus.* I would to heaven this crime might be his last.

**FINIS**

PHÆDRA

by

JEAN RACINE

# CHARACTERS

Theseus . . . . . *Son of Ægeus and King of Athens.*

Phædra . . . . . *Wife of Theseus and Daughter of Minos and Pasiphaë*

Hippolytus .*Son of Theseus and Antiope, Queen of the Amazons*

Aricia . . . . . .*Princess of the blood royal of Athens*

Œnone . . . . .*Nurse of Phædra*

Theramenes .*Tutor of Hippolytus*

Ismene . . . . . .*Friend of Aricia*

Panope . . . . .*Waiting-woman of Phædra*

Guards

The scene is laid in Trœzen, a town of the Peloponnesus.

# ACT I

*(Enter Hippolytus and Theramenes)*

*Hippolytus.* My mind is settled, dear Theramenes,
And I must stay no more in lovely Trœzen,
Racking my soul in doubt and mortal anguish.
I am ashamed of my long idleness.
Look you, my father gone six months and more—
One so dear gone,—and to what fate befallen
I do not know, nor do I know what corner
Of all the wide earth hides him!

*Theramenes.*                    Ah, my prince,—
And where, then, would you seek him? I have sailed
Over the seas on either side of Corinth.
Where Acheron is lost among the Shades
I asked, indeed, if aught were known of Theseus!
And to content you, I have gone to Elis,
Rounded Tœnarus, sailed to the far waters
Where Icarus once fell. What newer hope . . . ?
Under what favored sky would you think now
To trace his footsteps? Who knows if your father
Wishes the secret of his absence known?
Perhaps while we are trembling for his life
The hero calmly plots a fresh intrigue,
And only waits till the deluded lady—

*Hippolytus.* Peace, good Theramenes! Respect his name.
The waywardness of youth is his no longer,
And nothing so unworthy should detain him.
Now for a long time, Phædra has held that heart

Inconstant once, and she need fear no rival.

And if I seek him, it is but my duty.

I leave a place I dare no longer see!

   *Theramenes.* Indeed! When, prince, did you begin to
    dread

These peaceful haunts, so dear to happy childhood,

Where I have often known you rather stay

Than face the tumult and the pomp of Athens?

What danger do you shun? Or is it grief?

   *Hippolytus.* All things are changed. That happy past is
    gone.

Since then, the gods sent Phædra!

   *Theramenes.*                           Now I see!

It is the queen whose sight offends you. Yes,—

For with a step-dame's spite she schemed your exile

At her first sight of you. But then, her hatred

Is somewhat milder, if not wholly vanished.

A dying woman—one who longs for death!

What danger can she bring upon your head?

Weary of life, and weary of herself,—

Sick with some ill she will not ever speak of,—

Can Phædra then lay plots?—

   *Hippolytus.*                           I do not fear

The hatred of the queen. There is another

From whom I fly, and that is young Aricia,

The sole survivor of an impious race.

   *Theramenes.* What! You become her persecutor, too?

The gentle sister of the cruel sons

Of Pallas, did not share their perfidy.

Why should you hate such charming innocence?

   *Hippolytus.* If it were hate, I should not need to fly.

   *Theramenes.* Then will you tell me what your flying
    means?

ᴈ this the proud Hippolytus I see?
Love's fiercest foe alive?—the fiercest hater
Of Theseus' well-worn yoke?—Now can it be
That Venus, scorned, will justify your father?
And is Hippolytus, like other mortals,
To bow, perforce, and offer incense to her?—
And can he love? ...

   *Hippolytus.*       My friend, you must not ask me.
You who have known my heart through all my life,
And known it to be proud and most disdainful,—
You will not ask that I should shame myself
By now disowning all that I professed.
My mother was an Amazon,—my wildness,
Which you think strange, I suckled at her breast,
And as I grew, why, Reason did approve
What Nature planted in me. Then you told me
The story of my father, and you know
How, often, when I listened to your voice
I kindled, hearing of his noble acts,—
And you would tell how he brought consolation
To mortals for the absence of Alcides,
And how he cleared the roads of monsters,—robbers,—
Procrustes, Cercyron, Sciro, Sinnis slain,
Scattered the Epidaurian giant's bones,
And how Crete ran with blood of the Minotaur!
But when you told me of less glorious deeds,—
Troth plighted here and there and everywhere,
Young Helen stolen from her home at Sparta,
And Peribœa's tears in Salamis,
And many other trusting ones deceived,
Whose very names he cannot now remember,—
Lone Ariadne, crying to the rocks,—
And last of all this Phædra, bound to him

By better ties,—You know that with regret
I heard, and urged that you cut short the tale.
I had been happier, could I erase
This one unworthy part of his bright story
Out of my memory. Must I in turn
Be made love's slave, and brought to bend so low?
It is the more contemptible in me,
For no such brilliance clings about my name
As to the name of Theseus,—no monsters quelled
Have given me the right to share his weakness.
And if I must be humbled for my pride,
Aricia should have been the last to tame me!
Was I not mad that I should have forgotten
Those barriers which must keep us far apart
Eternally? For by my father's order
Her brothers' blood must never flow again
In a child of hers. He dreads a single shoot
From any stock so guilty, and would bury
Their name with her; so even to the tomb
No torch of Hymen may be lit for her.
Shall I espouse her rights against my father,
Provoke his wrath, launch on a mad career?—

　　*Theramenes.* But if your time has come, dear prince, the
　　　　gods
Will care but little for your guiding reason.
Theseus would shut your eyes;—he but unseals them.
His hatred kindles you to burn, rebellious,
And only lends his enemy new charms.
Then, too, why should you fear a guiltless passion?
Do you not dare this once to try its sweetness,
Rather than follow such a hair-drawn scruple?—
Afraid to stray where Hercules has wandered?—
What heart so stout that Venus has not won it?

And you, so long her foe, where would you be
Had your own mother, always scorning love,
Never been moved with tenderness for Theseus?
What good to act a pride you do not feel?
If you are changed, confess it! For some time
You have been seldom seen urging the car
With wild delight, rapid, along the shore,
Or, skillful in the art that Neptune taught,
Making th' unbroken steed obey the bit.
The forest has flung back our shouts less often.
A secret burden, cast upon your spirits,
Has dimmed your eye.—Can I then doubt your love?
It is in vain that you conceal your hurt.
Tell me, has not Aricia touched your heart?
   *Hippolytus.* Theramenes, I go to find my father.
   *Theramenes.* Will you not see the queen before you leave?
   *Hippolytus.* So I intend. And you may tell her so.
Yes, I will see her, since it is my duty.
But what new ill vexes her dear Œnone?
(Enter Œnone)

   *Œnone.* Alas, my lord, what grief was e'er like mine?
The queen has almost touched the gates of death.
It is in vain I watch her night and day,
In my very arms this secret malady
Is killing her—her mind is all disordered.
She rises from her bed, weary yet restless,
Pants for the outer air, yet she commands me
That none should see her in her misery.
She comes!
   *Hippolytus.* That is enough. I shall not vex her
Nor make her see the face of one she hates.
   (*Exeunt Hippolytus and Theramenes. Enter Phædra*)
   *Phædra.* Yes, this is far enough. Stay here, Œnone.

My strength is failing. I must rest a little.
I am dazzled with the light; it has been long
Since I have seen it. Ah, and my trembling knees
Are failing me—

    *Œnone.* Dear Heaven, I would our tears
Might bring relief.

    *Phædra.* And how these clumsy trinkets,
These veils oppress me! Whose officious hand
Tied up these knots, and gathered all these coils
Over my brow? All things conspire against me
And would distress me more!

    *Œnone.* That which you wish
This moment, frets you next! Did you not ask
A minute past, that we should deck you out,
Saying you felt your energy return,
Saying you sickened of your idleness,
And wished to go and see the light of day?
You sought the sun, and now you see it here,—
And now you would be hidden from its shining!

    *Phædra.* O splendid author of a hapless race,—
You whom my mother boasted as her father,—
Well may you blush to see me in such plight.
For the last time I look on thee, O Sun!

    *Œnone.* So! And are you still in love with death?
Will you not ever make your peace with life,
And leave these cruel accents of despair?

    *Phædra.* I wish that I were seated in the forest.
When may I follow with delighted eye,
Through glorious dust, flying in full career,—
A chariot?—

    *Œnone.* Madam?

    *Phædra.* Have I lost my wits?
What did I say? Where am I? Ah, and where

Do my vain wishes wander? For the gods
Have made me mad! And now I blush, Œnone,—
I hide my face, for you have seen too clearly
The grief and shame, that, quite in spite of me,
Will overflow my eyes.

 *Œnone.* If you must blush,
Blush at the silence that inflames your grief.
Deaf to my voice, you will not have my care.
Then will you have no pity on yourself,
But let your life be ended in mid-course?
What evil spell has drained its fountains dry?
Night-shadows thrice have darkened all the heavens
Since sleep came to your eyes, and now three times
The dawn has chased the darkness back again
Since your pale lips knew food. You faint, are languid,—
What awful purpose have you in your heart?
How do you dare attempt to lose your life
And so offend the gods who gave it you,—
And so prove false to Theseus and your marriage?—
Yes, and betray your most unhappy children,
Bending their necks yourself, beneath the yoke?
That day, be sure, which robs them of their mother
Will give his high hopes back to the stranger's son,—
To that proud enemy of you and yours,
Born of an Amazon,—Hippolytus!—

 *Phædra.* You gods!

 *Œnone.* Ah, this is a reproach to move you!

 *Phædra.* Unhappy one, what name have your lips spoken?

 *Œnone.* Your anger is most just, and it is well
That hated name can rouse such rage! Then live,
And hear again the claims of love and duty!
Live, then,—and stop this son of Scythia
From crushing down your children by his sway,

Ruling the noblest offspring of the gods,—
The purest blood of Greece! Never delay!
Death threatens every moment! Now restore
Your shattered strength, while the dim torch of life
Burns, and can yet be fanned into a flame.

    *Phædra.* I have endured its guilt and shame too long.

    *Œnone.* Why? What remorse is gnawing at your heart?
What crime can have disturbed you so? Your hands
Have not been stained with the blood of innocence.

    *Phædra.* No, I thank Heaven my hands are free from
        stain,—
I would my soul were innocent as they!

    *Œnone.* Why then, what awful plan have you been
        scheming,
At which your conscience still should be afraid?

    *Phædra.* Have I not said enough? Spare me the rest!
I die to save myself a full confession.

    *Œnone.* Die, then,—and keep a silence more than
        human!—
But seek some other hand to close your eyes,
For I will go before you to the Shades.
There are a thousand highways always open,
And since you have so little faith in me,
I'll go the shortest! When has my love failed you?
Remember, in my arms you lay, new-born.
For you I left my country and my children,—
And is this payment for my service to you?

    *Phædra.* What will you gain from words that are so bitter?
Were I to speak, horror would freeze your blood.

    *Œnone.* What can you say more terrible to me
Than to behold you die before my eyes?

    *Phædra.* If you should know my sin, I still should die,
But with guilt added—

*Œnone.* Oh, my dearest lady,
By all the tears that I have wept for you,
By these poor knees I clasp, now ease my mind
From doubt and torture!

*Phædra.* As you wish. Then rise.

*Œnone.* I hear you. Speak.

*Phædra.* Ah, how shall I begin?

*Œnone.* Leave off your fears,—you hurt me with distrust.

*Phædra.* O malice of great Venus! Into what madness,
What wild distractions, did she cast my mother!

*Œnone.* Let them be blotted from all memory,
Buried in silence, for all times to come.

*Phædra.* My sister, Ariadne, what was the love
Which brought you death, forsaken on lone shores?

*Œnone.* Madam, what deep pain is it prompts reproaches
Thus against all your kin—?

*Phædra.* It is her will—
It is the will of Venus, and I perish,
Last and least happy of a family
Where all were wretched!

*Œnone.* Do you love?

*Phædra.* I feel
All of its fever—

*Œnone.* Ah! For whom?

*Phædra.* Now hear
The final horror. Yes, I love. My lips
Tremble to name him.

*Œnone.* Whom?

*Phædra.* And do you know him?—
He whom I tortured long,—the Amazon's son!

*Œnone.* Hippolytus! Great gods!

*Phædra.* Yes, you have named him.

*Œnone.* Blood freezes in my veins! O cursed race!

Ill-omened journey! Land of misery,
Why did we ever reach these dangerous shores?
   *Phædra*. My wound is not a new one. Scarcely had I .
Been bound to Theseus by our marriage tie,
With peace and happiness seeming so well secured,
Until at Athens I saw my enemy.
I looked, I first turned pale, then blushed to see him,
And all my soul was in the greatest turmoil;
A mist made dim my sight, and my voice faltered,
And now my blood ran cold, then burned like fire.
In all my fevered body I could feel
Venus, whose fury had pursued so many
Of my sad race. I sought to shun her torments
With fervent vows. I built a shrine for her,
And there, 'mid many victims did I seek
The reason I had lost; but all for nothing.
I found no remedy for pain of love!
I offered incense vainly on her altars,
I called upon her name, and while I called her,
I loved Hippolytus, always before me!
And when I made her altars smoke with victims,
'Twas for a god whose name I dared not utter,—
And still I fled his presence, only to find him—
(The worst of horrors)—in his father's features!
At last I raised revolt against myself,
And stirred my courage up to persecute
The enemy I loved. To banish him
I wore a harsh and jealous step-dame's manner,
And ceaselessly I clamored for his exile,
Till I had torn him from his father's arms!
I breathed once more, Œnone. In his absence
The days passed by less troubled than before—
Innocent days! I hid my bitter grief,

Submitted to my husband, cherished the fruits
Of our most fatal marriage,—and in vain!
Again I saw the one whom I had banished,
Brought here by my own husband, and again
The old wound bled. And now it is not love
Hid in my heart, but Venus in her might
Seizing her prey. Justly I fear my sin!
I hate my life, and hold my love in horror.
I die:—I would have kept my name unsullied,
Burying guilty passion in the grave;
But I have not been able to refuse you;
You weep and pray, and so I tell you all,
And I shall be content, if as I perish,
You do not vex me with unjust reproaches,
Nor vainly try to snatch away from death
The last faint sparks of life, yet lingering!

(*Enter Panope*)

*Panope.* I wish that I might hide sad tidings from **you**,
But 'tis my duty, madam, to reveal them.
The hand of death has seized your peerless husband.
You are the last to hear it.

*Œnone.* What is this?

*Panope.* The queen begs Heaven for the safe **return**
Of Theseus, but she trusts, indeed, in vain—
She is deceived. Hippolytus, his son,
Has learned from vessels newly come to port
That Theseus is dead.

*Phædra.* Oh gods!

*Panope.* At Athens
Opinions are divided; some would have it
Your child should rule, and some, despite the law,
Are bold, and dare support the stranger's son,
While one presuming faction, it is said,

Would crown Aricia, and the house of Pallas.
I thought it well to warn you of this danger.
Hippolytus is ready, now, to start,
And if he chance to show himself in Athens,
The crowd, I fear, will follow in his lead.

 *Œnone.* It is enough. The queen has heard your message,
And she will not neglect your timely warning.

(Exit Panope)

Dear lady, I had almost ceased from urging
That you should wish to live. I thought to follow
My mistress to that tomb from which my pleading
Had failed to turn her,—but this new misfortune
Changes the aspect of affairs, and prompts us
To take fresh measures. Madam, Theseus is gone,
And you must fill his place. He leaves a son,—
Slave if you die, but if you live, a king!
Upon whom can he lean, but you, his mother?
There is no hand but yours to dry his tears.
Live then, for him, or else his guiltless weeping
Will move the gods to wrath against his mother.
Live, for no blame is in your passion now.
The king is dead, you bear the bonds no longer
Which made your love a thing of crime and horror.
You need no longer dread Hippolytus,
For you may see him, now, without reproach.
Perhaps, if he is certain of your hatred,
He means to lead the rebels. Undeceive him!
Soften his callous heart, and bend his pride!
King of this fertile land, his portion lies
Here in his Trœzen, yet he knows the laws,—
They give your son these walls Minerva built,
Aye, and protects,—but if a common foe
Threatens you both, you had best be united.

For you must thwart Aricia!
  *Phædra.* I consent.
Yes, I will live, if life can yet be mine,—
If my affection for a son has power
To rouse my sinking heart, at such a dangerous hour !
                 (*Exeunt*)


## ACT II

### (*Enter Aricia and Ismene*)

  *Aricia.* Hippolytus has asked to see me here?
Hippolytus has asked to bid farewell?
'Tis true, Ismene? You are not deceived?
  *Ismene.* This is the first result of Theseus' death,
And you may look to see from every side
Hearts that he kept away, now turning to you.
Aricia soon shall find all Greece low-bending
To do her homage.
  *Aricia.* Then it is not only
An idle tale? Am I a slave no longer?
Have I no enemies?
  *Ismene.* The gods, Aricia,
Trouble your peace no more, for Theseus' soul
Is with your brothers, now.
  *Aricia.* Does rumor tell
How Theseus died?
  *Ismene.* Tales most incredible
Are spread. Some say, that, seizing a new bride,
The faithless man was swallowed by the waves.
Others have said, and this report prevails,
That he, together with Pirithous,
Went to the world below, seeking the shores

Of Cocytus, showing his living self
To the pale ghosts, but could not leave the gloom,
For they who enter there abide forever.

   *Aricia.* Can I believe a mortal may descend
Into that gulf before his destined hour?
What lure could ever overcome its terrors?

   *Ismene.* Nay, he is dead; 'tis only you who doubt it
The men of Athens all bewail his loss.
Trœzen already hails Hippolytus,
And Phædra, fearing for her children's rights,
Asks counsel of such friends as share her troubles,
Here in this palace!

   *Aricia.* Will Hippolytus
Prove kinder than his father, make my chains light,
And pity my misfortunes?

   *Ismene.* Yes, I think so.

   *Aricia.* Indeed, I think you do not know him well,
Or you would not believe a heart so hard
Could ever pity, or could look on me
As one not sharing in the scorn he feels
For all our sex. Does he not still avoid
Whatever place we go?

   *Ismene.* I know the stories
Of proud Hippolytus, but I have seen him
When he was near to you, and watched to see
How one supposed so cold would bear himself.
I found his manners not at all like those
Which I had looked to see, for in his face
Was great confusion, at your slightest glance.
He could not turn his languid eyes away,
But still looked back again to gaze at you.
Love is a word that may offend his pride,
But though the tongue deny it, looks betray!

*Aricia.* How eagerly my heart hears what you say,
Though it may be delusion, dear Ismene!
Did it seem possible to you, who know me,
That I, poor toy of unrelenting fate,
Fed upon bitter tears by night and day,
Could ever taste the maddening draught of love?
I am the last frail offspring of my race—
My royal race, the Children of the Earth,
And of them, I alone survive war's fury.
Yes, I have lost six brothers, in their youth,—
Mown by the sword, cut off in their first flower!
They were the hope of an illustrious house.
Earth drank their blood with sorrow; it was kin
To his whom she brought forth. And well you know,
Since then, no heart in Greece could sigh for me,
Lest, by a sister's flame, her brothers' ashes
Might chance to blaze again. And, too, you know
How I disdained the cautions of my captor,
His care, and his suspicion, and you know
How often I have thanked the king's injustice,
Since I had never loved the thought of love.
He happily confirmed my inclinations,—
But then, I never yet had seen his son!
It is not merely that my eye is caught,
And that I love him for his grace and beauty,—
Charms which he does not know, or seems to scorn,—
I love him for a kind of wealth that's rarer.
He has his father's virtues, not his faults.
I love, and I must grant it, that high pride
Which never stooped beneath the yoke of love.
Phædra gains little glory from a lover
Free of his sighs; I am too proud, I think,
To share devotion with a thousand others,

Or enter in a door that's never shut.
But to make one who never stooped before
Bend his proud neck,—to pierce a heart of stone,
And bind one captive, whom his chains astonish,
Who struggles vainly in his pleasant bonds,—
That takes my fancy, and I long for it.
The god of strength was easier disarmed
Than this Hippolytus, for Hercules
Yielded so often to the eyes of beauty
That he made triumph cheap. But, dear Ismene,
I take too little heed of a resistance
Which I may never quell. If I am humbled,
And if I find defeat, then you will hear me
Speak ill of that same pride I so admire!
What! can he love? And have I been so happy
That I have bent—?

    *Ismene.* He comes,—and you shall hear him.
            *(Enter Hippolytus)*

    *Hippolytus.* Lady, before you go, it is my duty
To tell you of the changes of your fortune.
What I have feared is true; my sire is dead.
Yes, his long stay was what I had supposed it.
For only death, which came to end his labors,
Could keep him hidden from the world so long.
The gods at last have doomed Alcides' friend—
His friend, and his successor. Since your hatred
I think will grant his virtues, it can hear
Some praise for him, without resenting it,
Knowing that it is due. I have one hope
To soothe me in my sorrow. I can free you.
Now I revoke the laws, whose strictness moved me
To pity for you; you are your own mistress
Of heart and hand. Here in my heritage,

In Trœzen, here where Pittheus once reigned,
'And where I now am king, by my own right,
I leave you free, free as myself,—and more.

   *Aricia.* Your kindness is too great; it overcomes me.
A goodness which will pay disgrace with honor
Can give a greater force than you would think
To the harsh laws from which you would release me.

   *Hippolytus.* Athens, not knowing how to fill the throne
Left empty, speaks of you, and then of me,
And then of Phædra's son.

   *Aricia.*            Of me, my lord?

   *Hippolytus.* I know that by the law it is not mine,
For Greece reproaches me my foreign mother.
But if my brother were my only rival,
My rights are clearly truer ones than his,
So that I should not care for twists of the law.
There is a juster claim to check my boldness.
I yield my place to you, or rather, grant
That you should have it,—you should hold the sceptre,
Bequeathed to you from Earth's great son, Erectheus.
It came, then, to Ægeus, and the city
Which was protected and increased by him
Was glad to welcome such a king as Theseus,
Leaving your luckless brothers out of mind.
Now Athens calls you back within her walls.
Long strife has cost her groans enough already,
Her fields are glutted with your kinsmen's blood,
Fattening those same furrows whence it sprang.
I will rule here in Trœzen; Phædra's son
Has his rich kingdom waiting him in Crete.
Athens is yours, and I will do my best
To bring to you the votes which are divided
Between us two.

*Aricia.*    I fear a dream deceives me.
For I am stunned, my lord, at what I hear.
Am I, indeed, awake? Can I believe
Such generosity as this? What god
Has put it in your heart? Well you deserve
That fame you have, yet it falls short of you.
For me, you will be traitor to yourself!
Was it not grace enough never to hate me,
To have been free so long from enmity,
Which some have harbored—
    *Hippolytus.*        Hate you? I to hate **you**?
However darkly you have seen my pride,
Did you suppose a monster gave me birth?
What savagery, what hatred, full of venom
Would not become less evil, seeing you?
Could I resist this charm which caught my soul—
    *Aricia.* Why, what is this, sir?
    *Hippolytus.* I have said too much
Not to say more. No prudence can resist
The violence of passion. Now, at last,
Silence is broken. I must tell you now
The secret that my heart can hold no longer.
You see before you an unhappy victim
Of hasty pride,—a prince who begs compassion.
For I was long the enemy of love.
I mocked his fetters, I despised his captives,
And while I pitied these poor, shipwrecked mortals,
I watched the storms, and seemed quite safe on land.
And now I find that I have such a fate,
And must be tossed upon a sea of troubles!
My boldness is defeated in a moment,
And all my boasted pride is humbleness.
For nearly six months past, ashamed, despairing,

Carrying with me always that sharp arrow
Which tears my heart, I struggle quite in vain
To free me, both from you and from myself.
I leave your presence;—leaving, I find you near,
And in the forest's darkness see your form.
Black night, no less than daylight brings the vision
Of charms that I avoid. All things conspire
To make Hippolytus your slave. The fruit
Of all my sighs is only that I cannot
Find my own self again. My bow, my spear,
Please me no longer. I have quite forgotten
My chariot, and the teaching of the Sea God.
The woods can only echo back my groans,
Instead of flinging back those joyous shouts
With which I urged my horses. Hearing this,
A tale of passion so uncouth, you blush
At your own handiwork. These are wild words
With which I offer you my heart, a captive
Held, strangely, by a silken jess. And yet
The off'ring should be dearer to your eyes,
Since such words come as strangers to my lips.
Nor do not scorn my vows, so poorly spoken
Since, but for you, they never had been formed.

(*Enter Theramenes*)

*Theramenes.* My lord, I came to tell you of the queen.
She comes to seek you.

*Hippolytus.* Me?

*Theramenes.* And what she wishes
I do not know. I speak at her request,
For she would talk with you before you go.

*Hippolytus.* What shall I say to her? Can she expect—?

*Aricia.* You cannot, noble prince, refuse to hear her,
Though you are sure she is your enemy.

There is a shade of pity due her tears.

   *Hippolytus.* Shall we part so? And will you let me leave
     you
Not knowing if I have offended you,—
The goddess I adore,—with all this boldness?
Or if this heart, which I now leave with you—

   *Aricia.* Go now, my prince, and do whatever deeds
Your generosity would have you do.
Make Athens own my sceptre. All these gifts
I will accept. But the high throne of Empire
Is not the thing most precious to my eyes!

        (*Exeunt Aricia and Ismene*)

   *Hippolytus.* Friend, are we ready?—But the queen is
    coming.
See that the ship is trimmed and fit to sail.
Hurry, gather the crew, and hoist the signal,
And then return, the sooner to release me
From a most irksome meeting.

       (*Exit Theramenes. Enter Phædra and Œnone*)

   *Phædra* (*to Œnone*). Look, I see him!
My blood forgets to flow,—tongue will not speak
What I have come to say!

   *Œnone.* Think of your son.
And think that all his hopes depend on you.

   *Phædra.* They tell me that you leave us, hastily.
I come to add my own tears to your sorrow,
And I would plead my fears for my young son.
He has no father, now; 'twill not be long
Until the day that he will see my death,
And even now, his youth is much imperiled
By a thousand foes. You only can defend him.
And in my inmost heart, remorse is stirring,—
Yes, and fear, too, lest I have shut your ears

Against his cries; I fear that your just anger
May, before long, visit on him that hatred
His mother earned.

    *Hippolytus.* Madam, you need not fear.
Such malice is not mine.

    *Phædra.* I should not blame you
If you should hate me; I have injured you.
So much you know;—you could not read my heart.
Yes, I have tried to be your enemy,
For the same land could never hold us both.
In private and abroad I have declared it;—
I was your enemy! I found no peace
Till seas had parted us; and I forbade
Even your name to be pronounced to me.
And yet, if punishment be meted out
Justly, by the offense;—if only hatred
Deserves a hate, then never was there woman
Deserved more pity, and less enmity.

    *Hippolytus.* A mother who is jealous for her children
Will seldom love the children of a mother
Who came before her. Torments of suspicion
Will often follow on a second marriage.
Another would have felt that jealousy
No less than you; perhaps more violently.

    *Phædra.* Ah, prince, but Heaven made me quite exempt
From what is usual, and I can call
That Heaven as my witness! 'Tis not this—
No, quite another ill devours my heart!

    *Hippolytus.* This is no time for self-reproaching, madam.
Perhaps your husband still beholds the light,
Perhaps he may be granted safe return
In answer to our prayers; his guarding god
Is Neptune, whom he never called in vain.

*Phædra.* He who has seen the mansions of the dead
Returns not thence. Since Theseus has gone
Once to those gloomy shores, we need not hope,
For Heaven will not send him back again.
Prince, there is no release from Acheron;—
It is a greedy maw,—and yet I think
He lives and breathes in you,—and still I see him
Before me here; I seem to speak to him—
My heart—! Oh, I am mad! Do what I will,
I cannot hide my passion.

    *Hippolytus.* Yes, I see
What strange things love will do, for Theseus, dead,
Seems present to your eyes, and in your soul
A constant flame is burning.

    *Phædra.* Ah, for Theseus
I languish and I long, but not, indeed,
As the Shades have seen him, as the fickle lover
Of a thousand forms, the one who fain would ravish
The bride of Pluto;—but one faithful, proud,
Even to slight disdain,—the charm of youth
That draws all hearts, even as the gods are painted,—
Or as yourself. He had your eyes, your manner,—
He spoke like you, and he could blush like you,
And when he came across the waves to Crete,
My childhood home, worthy to win the love
Of Minos' daughters,—what were you doing then?
Why did my father gather all these men,
The flower of Greece, and leave Hippolytus?
Oh, why were you too young to have embarked
On board the ship that brought your father there?
The monster would have perished at your hands,
Despite the windings of his vast retreat.
My sister would have armed you with the clue

To guide your steps, doubtful within the maze.—
But no—for Phædra would have come before her,
And love would first have given me the thought,
And I it would have been, whose timely aid
Had taught you all the labyrinthine ways!
The care that such a dear life would have cost me!
No thread could satisfy my lover's fears.
I would have wished to lead the way myself,
And share the peril you were sure to face.
Yes, Phædra would have walked the maze with you,—
With you come out in safety, or have perished!

   *Hippolytus.* Gods! What is this I hear? Have you forgotten
That Theseus is my father and your husband?

   *Phædra.* Why should you fancy I have lost remembrance
And that I am regardless of my honor?

   *Hippolytus.* Forgive me, madam! With a blush I own
That I mistook your words, quite innocent.
For very shame I cannot see you longer—
Now I will go—

   *Phædra.* Ah, prince, you understood me,—
Too well, indeed! For I had said enough.
You could not well mistake. But do not think
That in those moments when I love you most
I do not feel my guilt. No easy yielding
Has helped the poison that infects my mind.
The sorry object of divine revenge,
I am not half so hateful to your sight
As to myself. The gods will bear me witness,—
They who have lit this fire within my veins,—
The gods who take their barbarous delight
In leading some poor mortal heart astray!
Nay, do you not remember, in the past,
How I was not content to fly?—I drove you

Out of the land, so that I might appear
Most odious—and to resist you better
I tried to make you hate me—and in vain!
You hated more, and I loved not the less,
While your misfortunes lent you newer charms.
I have been drowned in tears and scorched by fire!
Your own eyes might convince you of the truth
If you could look at me, but for a moment!
What do I say? You think this vile confession
That I have made, is what I meant to say?
I did not dare betray my son. For him
I feared,—and came to beg you not to hate him.
This was the purpose of a heart too full
Of love for you to speak of aught besides.
Take your revenge, and punish me my passion!
Prove yourself worthy of your valiant father,
And rid the world of an offensive monster!
Does Theseus' widow dare to love his son?
Monster indeed! Nay, let her not escape you!
Here is my heart! Here is the place to strike!
It is most eager to absolve itself!
It leaps impatiently to meet your blow!—
Strike deep! Or if, indeed, you find it shameful
To drench your hand in such polluted blood,—
If that be punishment too mild for you,—
Too easy for your hate,—if not your arm,
Then lend your sword to me.—Come! Give it now!—

  *Œnone.* What would you do, my lady? Oh, just gods?
But someone comes;—go quickly. Run from shame.
You cannot fly, if they should find you thus.

     (*Exeunt Phædra and Œnone. Enter Theramenes*)
  *Theramenes.* Is that the form of Phædra that I see
Go hurrying? What are these signs of sorrow?

Where is your sword? Why are you pale and shaken?
　*Hippolytus.* Friend, let us fly. Indeed, I am confused
With greatest horror and astonishment.
Phædra—but no; gods, let this dreadful secret
Remain forever buried and unknown.
　*Theramenes.* The ship is ready if you wish to sail,
But Athens has already cast her vote.
Their leaders have consulted all the tribes.
Your brother is elected;—Phædra wins!
　*Hippolytus.* Phædra?
　*Theramenes.* A herald bringing a commission
Has come from Athens, placing the reins of power
In Phædra's hands. Her son is king.—
　*Hippolytus.* O gods,—
O ye who know her, is it thus, indeed,
That ye reward her virtue?
　*Theramenes.* Meanwhile rumor
Is whispering that Theseus is not dead,—
That there are those who saw him in Epirus,—
But I have searched, and I know all too well—
　*Hippolytus.* No matter. Let no chances be neglected.
This rumor must be hunted to its source,
And if it be not worthy of belief
Let us then sail, and at whatever cost,
We'll trust the sceptre to deserving hands.
　　　　　　*(Exeunt)*


## ACT III

### *(Enter Phædra and Œnone)*

　*Phædra.* Ah, let them take away the worthless honors
They bring to me;—why urge that I should see them?

What flattery can soothe my wounded heart?
Far rather hide me. I have said too much.
My madness bursting like a stream in flood,
I spoke what never should have reached his ears.
Oh gods! The way he heard me! How reluctant
To take my meaning,—dull and cold as marble,
And only eager for a quick retreat!
And how his blushes made my shame the deeper!
Why did you turn me from the death I sought?
Ah, when his sword was pointed at my breast,
Did he grow pale?—or try to snatch it from me?
That I had touched it was enough for him
To make it seem forever horrible,
And to defile whatever hand should hold it.

 *Œnone.* When you will brood upon your bitter grief,
You only fan a fire that must be quenched.
Would it not more become the blood of Minos
To find you peace in cares that are more noble?—
And in defiance of this wretch, who flies
From what he hates, reign on the throne you're offered?

 *Phædra.* I reign?—And shall I hold the rod of empire,
When reason can no longer reign in me?
When I have lost control of mine own senses?
When I do gasp beneath a shameful yoke?
When I am dying?—

  *Œnone.* Fly!

  *Phædra.* I cannot leave him.

  *Œnone.* You dare not fly from one you dared to banish?

  *Phædra.* That time is past. He knows how I am frenzied,
For I have overstepped my modesty,..
And blazoned out my shame before his eyes.
Against my will, hope crept into my heart.
Did you not call my failing powers to me?

Was it not you, yourself, called back my soul
Which fluttered on my lips, and with your counsel
Lent me new life? Who told me I might love him?

   *Œnone.* Blame me or blame me not for your misfortunes,—
What could I not have done if it would save you?
But if your anger ever was aroused
By insult, can you pardon him his scorn?
How cruel were his eyes, severe and fixed,
Surveying you, half prostrate at his feet!
How hateful, then, his savage pride appeared!
Why did not Phædra see as I saw then?

   *Phædra.* This pride that you detest may yield to time.
The rudeness of the forest clings about him,
For he was bred there by the strictest laws.
Love is a word he never knew before.
Perhaps it was surprise that stunned him so;—
There was much vehemence in all I said.

   *Œnone.* Remember that his mother was barbaric—
   *Phædra.* She was a Scythian, but she learned to love
   *Œnone.* He has a bitter hate for all our sex.
   *Phædra.* Well, then no rival ever rules his heart.
Your counsel comes a little late, Œnone.
Now you must serve my madness, not my reason.
Love cannot find a way into his heart,
So let us take him where he has more feeling.
The lure of power seemed somewhat to touch him.
He could not hide that he was drawn to Athens,—
His vessels' prows were pointed there already,
With sails all set to run before the breeze.
Go, and on my behalf, touch his ambition,—
Dazzle his eyes with prospects of the crown.
The sacred diadem shall grace his brow,—
My highest honor is to set it there.

And he shall have the power I cannot keep.
He'll teach my son how men are ruled.—It may be
That he will deign to be a father to him.
He shall control both son and mother;—try him,—
Try every means to move him, for your words
Should meet more favor than my own could find.
Urge him with groans and tears,—say Phædra's dying,
Nor blush to speak in pleading terms with him.
My last hope is in you,—do what you will,
I'll sanction it,—the issue is my fate!

*(Exit Œnone)*

*Phædra (alone).* Venus implacable, thou seest me shamed,
And I am sore confounded. Have I not
Been humbled yet enough? Can cruelty
Stretch farther still? Thine arrows have struck home!
It is thy victory! Wouldst gain new triumphs?—
Then seek an enemy more obdurate,—
Hippolytus neglects thee, braves thine anger.
He never bows his knee before thine altars.
Thy name offends his proud, disdainful hearing.
Our interests are alike,—avenge thyself,
Force him to love—But what is this, Œnone?
Already back? Then it must be he hates me,
And will not hear you speak—

*(Enter Œnone)*

*Œnone.* Yes, you must stifle
A love that's vain, and best call back your virtue.
The king we thought was dead will soon appear
Here to your eyes. Yes, Theseus will be here,
For he has come again. The eager people
Are hastening to see him. I had gone
As you commanded, seeking for the prince,
When all the air was torn,—a thousand shouts—

*Phædra.* My husband living! 'Tis enough, Œnone.
I owned a passion that dishonors him.
He is alive. I wish to know no more.
   *Œnone.* What is it?
   *Phædra.* What I prophesied to you,—
What you refused to hear, while with your weeping
You overcame repentance. Had I died
I had deserved some pity, earlier.
I took your counsel, and I die dishonored.
   *Œnone.* You die?
   *Phædra.* Just Heavens! What I have done today!
My husband comes, and with him comes his son,
And I shall see the witness of my passion,
The object of my most adulterous flame
Watch with what face I make his father welcome,
Knowing my heart is big with sighs he scorned,
And my eyes wet with tears that could not move him.
Will his respect for Theseus make him hide it?—
Conceal my madness?—not disgrace his father?
And do you think he can repress the horror
Which he must have for me? A fruitless silence!
I know my treason, and I lack the boldness
Of those abandoned women, who can feel
Tranquillity in crime,—can show a forehead
All unashamed. I know my madness well,
Recall it all. I think that these high roofs
And all these walls can speak. They will accuse me.
They only wait until my husband comes,
And then they will reveal my perfidy.
'Tis death alone can take away this horror.
Is it so great an ill to cease to live?
Death holds no fear for those in misery.
I tremble only for the name I leave,—

My son's sad heritage. The blood of Jove
Might justly swell the pride of those who boast it,
But what a heavy weight a mother's guilt
Leaves for her children! Yes, I dread that scorn
For my disgrace, which will be cast on them
With too much truth. I tremble when I think
How they will never dare to raise their heads,
Crushed with that curse.—
   *Œnone.* Nay, do not doubt my pity.
There never was a juster fear than yours.
Then why do you expose them to this shame?
And why must you accuse yourself, destroying
The one hope left. It will be said of Phædra
That she well knows of her own perfidy,
That she has fled from out her husband's sight,—
And proud Hippolytus may well rejoice
That, dying, you should lend his tale belief.
What answer can I make him? It will be
For him, a story easy to deny,
And I shall hear him, while triumphantly
He tells your shame to every open ear.
Why, I had sooner Heaven's fire consumed me!
Deceive me not! And do you love him still?
What think you now of this contemptuous prince?
   *Phædra.* As of a monster fearful to mine eyes!
   *Œnone.* Why do you give him easy victory?
You are afraid! Dare to accuse him first!
Say he is guilty of the charge he brings
This day against you. Who shall say it's false?
All things conspire against him. In your hands
His sword, which he most happily forgot,—
Your present trouble, and your past distress,—
Your warnings to his father,—and his exile

Which you accomplished with your earnest prayers—
   *Phædra.* So! You would have me slander innocence!
   *Œnone.* My zeal asks nothing from you but your silence.
I also tremble. I am loath to do it.
I'd face a thousand deaths more willingly.
But since, without this bitter deed, I lose you,
And since, for me, your life outweighs all else,
Why, I will speak. Theseus, however angry,
Will do no worse than banish him again.
A father, punishing, remains a father.
His anger will be soothed with easy penance.
But even if some guiltless blood be spilt,
Is not your honor of a greater worth,—
A treasure far too precious to be risked?
You must submit, no matter what is needful,
For when your reputation is at stake,
Then you must sacrifice your very conscience.
But someone comes. 'Tis Theseus—
   *Phædra.* Look, I see
Hippolytus most stern, and in his eyes
There is my ruin written. I am helpless.
My fate is yours. Do with it as you will.
     *(Enter Theseus, Hippolytus and Theramenes)*
   *Theseus.* Fortune will fight no longer with my wishes,
But to your arms it brings me back—
   *Phædra.* Wait, Theseus.
Nay, do not hurry to profane caresses
One time so sweet, which I am now not worthy
Even to taste of, for you have been wronged.
Fortune has proved most spiteful. In your absence
It has not spared your wife. I am not fit
To meet you tenderly, and from this time

I only care how I shall bear my shame.

(Exeunt Phædra and Œnone)

*Theseus.* Strange welcome for your father, is it not?
What does it mean, my son?

    *Hippolytus.* Why, only Phædra
Can solve that mystery. If I can move you
By any wish, then let me never see her.
Hippolytus begs leave to disappear,—
To leave the home that holds your wife, forever.

   *Theseus.* You, my son! Leave me?

   *Hippolytus.* 'Twas not I who sought her.
You were the one to lead her to these shores!
My lord, at your departure you thought fit
To leave Aricia and the queen in Trœzen,
And I, myself, was charged with their protection.
But now, what cares will need to keep me here?
My idle youth has shown what skill it has
Over such petty foes as roam the woods.
May I not leave this life of little glory,—
Of ease—and dip my spear in nobler blood?
Before you reached my age, more than one tyrant,
More than one monster had already felt
The force of your good arm. You had succeeded
In whipping insolence; you had removed
All of the dangers lurking on our coasts.
The traveler no longer feared for outrage,
And Hercules, himself, who knew your deeds,
Relied on you, and rested from his labors.
But I—the son of such a noble father,—
I am unknown, and I am far behind
Even my mother's footsteps. Let my courage
Have scope to act. If there is yet some monster
Escaped from you, then let me seek for glory,

Bringing the spoils to you; or let it be
That memory of death well met with courage
Shall keep my name a living one,—shall prove
To all the world I am my father's son.

   *Theseus.* Why, what is this? What terror can have seized
    you?
What makes my kindred fly before my face?
If I return to find myself so feared,
To find so little welcome in my home,
Then why did Heaven free me from my prison?
My only friend, misled by his own passion
Set out to rob the tyrant of Epirus,—
To rob him of his wife! Regretfully
I gave the lover aid. Fate blinded us,—
Myself as well as him. The tyrant seized me,
Defenseless and unarmed. With tears I saw
Pirithous cast forth to be devoured
By savage beasts, that lapped the blood of men.
He shut me in a gloomy cave, far down,
Deep in the earth, near to the realm of Pluto.
I lay six months, before the gods had pity,
Then I escaped the eyes that guarded me.
I purged the world of this, its enemy,
And he, himself has fed his monsters' hunger.
But when I come, with an expectant joy,
When I draw close to all that is most precious
Of what the gods have left me,—when my soul
Looks for its happiness in these dear places,
Then I am welcomed only with a shudder,
With turning from me, and with hasty flight.
And since it seems that I inspire such terror,
Would I were still imprisoned in Epirus!
Phædra complains that I have suffered outrage.

Who has betrayed me? Speak! Was I avenged?
Why was I not? Has Greece, to whom mine arm
Has often brought good help, sheltered my foe?
You do not answer. Is it that my son,—
My own son—has he joined mine enemies?
I'll enter, for I cannot bear to wonder.
I'll learn at once the culprit and the crime,
And Phædra must explain her trouble to me.

(Exit)

*Hippolytus.* What mean these words? They freeze my
  very blood!
Will Phædra, in her frenzy, blame herself,—
Make sure of her destruction? And the king,—
What will he say? O gods! The fatal poison
That love has spread through all my father's house!
I burn with fires his hatred disapproves.
How changed he finds me from the son he knew!
My mind is much alarmed with dark forebodings,
But surely innocence need never fear.
Come, let us go, and in some other place
Consider how I best may move my father
To make him tender, and to tell a love
Troubled, but never vanquished, by his frown.

(Exeunt)

## ACT IV

(Enter Theseus and Œnone)

*Theseus.* Ah, what is this I hear? Presumptuous traitor!
And would he have disgraced his father's honor?
With what relentless footsteps Fate pursues me!
I know not where I go, nor where I am!

My kindest love, how very ill repaid!
Bold scheme! Oh most abominable thought!
A wretch who did not shrink from violence
To reach the object of his evil passion!
I know this sword,—it served to arm his fury,—
The sword I gave him for a nobler use!
And could the sacred ties of blood not stop him?
And Phædra,—was she loath to have him punished?
She held her silence. Was it to spare his guilt?

*Œnone.* Only to spare a most unhappy father.
She knew it shameful that her eyes had kindled
So infamous a love,—had prompted him
To such a crime,—and Phædra would have died.
I saw her raise her arm, and ran to save her.
To me alone you owe it that she lives.
And since I pity her, and pity you
I came, unwilling, to explain her tears.

*Theseus.* The traitor! Well indeed might he turn pale!
It was for fear he trembled when he saw me!
I was amazed that he should show no gladness.
The coldness of his greeting chilled my love.
But was this guilty passion that consumes him
Declared before I banished him from Athens?

*Œnone.* Remember, sire, how Phædra urged it on you.
It was illicit love that caused her hatred.

*Theseus.* And then this flame burst out again at Trœzen?

*Œnone.* Sire, I have told you all there is. The queen
Is left to bear her grief alone too long.
Let me now leave you. I will wait on her.

(*Exit. Enter Hippolytus*)

*Theseus.* Ah, there he is! Great gods! That noble manner
Might well deceive an eye less fond than mine!
Why should the sacred mark of virtue shine

Bright on the forehead of an evil wretch?
Why should the blackness of a traitor's heart
Not show itself by sure and certain signs?

   *Hippolytus.* My father, may I ask what fatal cloud
Has troubled so the face of majesty?
Dare you not trust this secret to your son?

   *Theseus.* Traitor, how dare you show yourself before me?
Monster, whom Heaven's bolts have spared too long!
A last survivor of that robber band
Whereof I cleansed the earth, your brutal lust
Scorned to respect even my marriage bed!
And now you dare,—my hated foe,—to come
Here to my presence, here where all things are filled
And foul with infamy, instead of seeking
Some unknown land, that never heard my name.
Fly, traitor, fly! Stay not to tempt my wrath!
I scarce restrain it. Do not brave my hatred.
I have been shamed forever; 'tis enough
To be the father of so vile a son,
Without your death, to stain indelibly
The splendid record of my noble deeds.
Fly! And unless you yearn for punishment
To make you yet another villain slain,
Take heed that this sun, shining on us now
Shall see your foot no more upon this soil.
I say it once again,—fly!—and in haste!
Rid all my realms of your detested person.
On thee,—on thee, great Neptune, do I call!
If once I cleared thy shores of murderers,
Remember, then, thy promise to reward me
For these good deeds, by granting my first prayer.
I was held long in close captivity.
I did not then demand thy mighty aid,

For I have saved so great a privilege
To use in greatest need. That time is come.
And now I ask,—avenge a wretched father!
I leave this traitor subject to thy wrath.
I ask that thou shouldst quench his fires in blood,
And by thy fury, I will judge thy favor!

   *Hippolytus.* Phædra accuses me of wanton passion!
A final horror to confuse my soul!
Such blows, unlooked for, falling all at once,
Have crushed me, choked me, struck me into silence!

   *Theseus.* Traitor, you thought that in a timid silence
Phædra would cover your brutality.
But, though you fled, you still should not have left her
Holding the sword that seals your condemnation.
Or rather, to complete your perfidy,
You should have robbed her both of speech and life!

   *Hippolytus.* Most justly angered at so black a lie,
I might be pardoned, should I speak the truth.
But it concerns your honor to conceal it.
Welcome that reverence which stops my tongue,
And, without seeking to increase your troubles,
Look closely at my life, as it has been.
Great crimes come never singly; they are linked
To sins that went before. Who once has sinned
May, at the last, do greater violence
To all that men hold sacred. Vice, like virtue,
Grows in small steps, and no true innocence
Can ever fall at once to deepest guilt.
No man of virtue, in a single day,
Can turn himself to treason, murder, incest!
I am the son of one both chaste and brave.
I have not proved unworthy of my birth.
Pittheus, one by all men reckoned wise,

Deigned to instruct me, when I left her keeping.
I do not wish to boast upon my merits,
But if I may lay claim to any virtue,
I think I have displayed, beyond all else,
That I abhor those sins with which you charge me.
Look you, Hippolytus is known in Greece
As one so continent he's thought austere,
And all men know how I abstain, unbending.
The daylight is not purer than my heart.
Then how could I, if burning so profanely,—

　　*Theseus.* Villain, it is that very pride condemns you!
I see the hateful reason for your coldness,
For only Phædra charmed your shameless eyes.
Your heart, quite cold to other witcheries,
Refused the pure flame of a lawful love.

　　*Hippolytus.* No, father, I have hidden it too long.
This heart has not disdained its sacred flame.
Here, at your feet, I'll tell my real offense.
I love, and love, indeed, where you forbid it.
My heart's devotion binds me to Aricia,—
The child of Pallas has subdued your son!
Her I adore, rebellious to your laws.
For her alone I breathe my ardent sighs.

　　*Theseus.* You love her? Gods! But no,—I see the truth.
You play this crime to justify yourself.

　　*Hippolytus.* Sir, for six months I kept me from her
　　　presence,
And still I love her. I have come to tell it,—
Trembling I come—! Can nothing free your mind
Of such an error? Can my oaths not soothe you?
By Heaven—Earth,—by all the powers of Nature—

　　*Theseus.* The wicked will not ever shrink from lying.
Be still, and spare me tiresome vows and pleadings,

Since your false virtue knows no other way.

*Hippolytus.* Although you think it false and insincere,
Phædra has cause enough to know it true.

*Theseus.* Ah, how your boldness rouses all my anger!

*Hippolytus.* What is my term and place of banishment?

*Theseus.* Were you beyond the Pillars of Alcides,
Your perjured presence still were far too near me!

*Hippolytus.* What friends will pity me, if you forsake me
And think me guilty of so vile a crime?

*Theseus.* Go seek for friends who praise adultery,
And look for those who clap their hands at incest!—
Low traitors, lawless,—steeped in infamy,—
Fit comforters for such an one as you!

*Hippolytus.* Are incest and adultery the words
Which you will cast at me? I hold my peace.
Yet think what mother Phædra had—remember
Her blood, not mine, is tainted with these horrors!

*Theseus.* So then! Before my eyes your rage bursts out,
And loses all restraint. Go from my sight!—
This last time I will say it,—traitor, go!
And do not wait until a father's anger
Drives you away in public execration!

(*Exit Hippolytus*)

*Theseus (alone).* Wretch! Thou must meet inevitable
ruin!
Neptune has sworn by Styx,—an oath most dreadful
Even to gods,—and he will keep his promise.
Thou canst not ever flee from his revenge.
I loved thee, and in spite of this offense
My heart is moved by what I see for thee.
Nay, but thy doom is but too fully earned.
Had father ever better cause for rage?
O you just gods, who see my crushing grief,

Why was I cursed with such an evil son?

(*Enter Phædra*)

   *Phædra.* I come to you, my lord, in proper dread,
For I have heard your voice raised high in anger,
And much I fear that deeds have followed threats.
Oh, spare your child, if there is still some time!
Respect your race, your blood, I do beseech you.
I would not hear that blood cry from the earth!
Save me the horror and the lasting shame
Of having caused his father's hand to shed it!

   *Theseus.* No, madam, I am free from such a stain.
But still the wretch has not escaped my vengeance.
The hand of an Immortal holds his doom,
And pledges his destruction. 'Tis a debt
That Neptune owes me. You shall be avenged.

   *Phædra.* A debt to you? Prayers made in anger—

   *Theseus.* Fear not.

They will not fail. But join your prayers to mine,
And paint his crimes for me in all their blackness,
To fan my sluggish wrath to whitest heat.
You do not know of all his villainy.
His rage against you feeds itself on slanders.
Your words, he says, are full of all deceit.
He says Aricia has his heart and soul,
That he loves only her—

   *Phædra.* Aricia?—

   *Theseus.* Yes.

He said it to my face:—an idle pretext!
A trick I am not caught by. Let us hope
That Neptune does swift justice. I am going
Now to his altars, urging he keep his oath.

(*Exit Theseus*)

*Phædra* (*alone*). So he is gone! What words have struck
  mine ears?
What smothered fires are burning in my heart?
What fatal stroke falls like a thunder-bolt?
Stung with remorse that would not give me peace,
I tore myself from out Œnone's arms
And hurried here to help Hippolytus,
With all my soul and strength. Who knows, indeed,
But that new-found repentance might have moved me
To speak in accusation of myself?—
And if my voice had not been choked with shame,
Perhaps I might have told the frightful truth.
Hippolytus can feel—but not for me!
Aricia has his heart, his plighted word!
You gods! I thought his heart could not be touched
By any love, when, deaf to all my tears,
He armed his eye with scorn, his brow with threats.
I thought him strong against all other women,
And yet another has prevailed upon him!
She tamed his pride, and she has gained his favor!
Perhaps he has a heart that's quick to melt,
And I alone am she he cannot bear!
Then shall I charge myself with his protection?

(*Enter Œnone*)

*Phædra.* Dear nurse, and do you know what I have
  learned?
*Œnone.* No, but in truth I come with trembling limbs.
I dreaded what you planned when you went out,
And fear of fatal madness turned me pale.
*Phædra.* Who would have thought it, nurse? I had a rival.
*Œnone.* A rival?
*Phædra.* Yes, he loves. I cannot doubt it.
This wild Hippolytus I could not tame,—

Who scorned to be admired, and who was wearied
With lovers' sighs,—this tiger whom I dreaded
Fawns on the hand of one who broke his pride.
Aricia found the entrance to his heart!

    *Œnone.* Aricia?

    *Phædra.* 'Tis a torture yet untried!
Now for what other pains am I reserved?
All I have suffered,—ecstasies of passion,
Longings and fears, the horrors of remorse,
The shame of being spurned with contumely,
Were feeble tastes of what is now my torment.
They love each other! By what secret charm
Have they deceived me? When and where and **how**
Did they contrive to meet? You knew it all,—
And why, then, was I kept from knowing of it?
You never told me of their stolen hours
Of love and of delight. Have they been seen
Talking together often?—did they seek
The forest shadows? Ah, they had full freedom
To be together. Heaven watched their sighs.
They loved,—and never felt that they were guilty.
The morning sun shone always clear for them,
While I,—an outcast from the face of Nature,
Shunned the bright day, and would have hid **myself,**—
Death the one god whom I dared ask for aid!
I waited for the freedom of the grave.
My woe was fed with bitterness, and watered
With many tears. It was too closely watched.
I did not dare to weep without restraint,
And knowing it a solace perilous,
I feared it, and I hid my mortal terror
Beneath a face most tranquil. Oftentimes
I stopped my tears, and made myself to smile—

*Œnone.* What fruit can they desire from fruitless love?
For they can meet no more.
    *Phædra.* That love will stay,
And it will stay forever. While I speak—
O dreadful thought—they laugh and scorn my madness
And my distracted heart. In spite of exile,
In spite of that which soon must come to part them,
They make a thousand oaths to bind their union.
Œnone, can I bear this happiness
Which so insults me? I would have your pity.
Yes, she must be destroyed. My husband's fury
Against her hated race shall be renewed.
The punishment must be a heavy one.
Her guilt outruns the guilt of all her brothers,
I'll plead with Theseus, in my jealousy,—
What do I say? Oh, have I lost my senses?
Is Phædra jealous? will she, then, go begging
For Theseus' help? He lives,—and yet I burn.
For whom? Whose heart is this I claim as mine?
My hair stands up with horror at my words,
And from this time, my guilt has passed all bounds!
Hypocrisy and incest breathe at once
Through all I do. My hands are ripe for murder,
To spill the guiltless blood of innocence.
Do I still live, a wretch, and dare to face
The holy Sun, from whom I have my being?
My father's father was the king of gods;
My race is spread through all the universe.—
Where can I hide? In the dark realms of Pluto?
But there my father holds the fatal urn.
His hands award the doom irrevocable.—
Minos is judge of all the ghosts in hell.
And how his awful shade will start and shudder

When he shall see his daughter brought before him,
And made confess such many-colored sins,
Such crimes, perhaps, as hell itself knows not!
O father, what will be thy words at seeing
So dire a sight? I see thee drop the urn,
Turning to seek some punishment unheard of,—
To be, thyself, mine executioner!
O spare me! For a cruel deity
Destroys thy race. O look upon my madness,
And in it see her wrath. This aching heart
Gathers no fruit of pleasure from its crime.
It is a shame which hounds me to the grave,
And ends a life of misery in torment.

    *Œnone.* Ah, madam, drive away this groundless fear.
Look not so hard upon a little sin.
You love. We cannot conquer destiny.
Why, you were drawn as by a fatal charm;—
Is that a marvel we have never seen?
Has love, then, come to triumph over you,
And no one else? By nature man is weak.
You are a mortal,—bow to mortal fortune.
You chafe against a yoke that many others
Have borne before you. They upon Olympus,—
The very gods themselves, who make us tremble
For our poor sins, have burned with lawless passions.

    *Phædra.* What words are these? What counsels do you
      give me?
Why will you still pour poison in mine ears?
You have destroyed me. You have brought me back
When I should else have left the light of day.
You made me to forget my solemn duty,
And see Hippolytus, whom I had shunned.
What have you done? Why did those wicked lips

Slander his faultless life with blackest lies?
It may be you have murdered him. By now
The prayer unholy of a heartless father
May have been granted. I will have no words!
Go, monster! Leave me to my sorry fate.
May the just gods repay you properly,
And may your punishment remain forever
To strike with fear, all such as you, who strive
To feed the frailty of the great with cunning,
To push them to the very brink of ruin
To which their feet incline,—to smooth the path
Of guilt. Such flatterers the gods, in anger,
Bestow on kings as their most fatal gift!

(Exit Phædra)

  *Œnone* (*alone*). O gods! What is there I've not done to
   serve her?
And this is the reward that I have won!

(Exit)

## ACT V

(Enter Hippolytus and Aricia)

  *Aricia.* Can you keep silent in this mortal danger?
Your father loves you. Will you leave him so—
When he is thus deceived? If you are cruel,—
If, in your heart, you will not see my tears,
Why then, content,—and do not ever see me.
Abandon poor Aricia,—but at least
If you must go, make sure your life is safe.
Defend your honor from a shameful stain,
And force your father to recall his prayers.
There still is time. Why, for a mere caprice,

Should you leave open way for Phædra's slanders?
Let Theseus know the truth.

   *Hippolytus.* Could I say more
And not expose him to a great disgrace?
How should I dare, by speaking what I know,
To make my father's brow blush red with shame?
You only know the hateful mystery.
I have not showed my heart to any other
But you and Heaven. Judge, then, if I love you,
Since you have seen I could not hide from you
All I would fain have hidden from myself!
Remember under what a seal I spoke.
Forget what I have said, if that may be,
And never let so pure a mouth give voice
To such a secret. Let us trust to Heaven
To give me justice, for the gods are just.
For their own honor they will clear the guiltless.
The time will come for Phædra to be punished.
She cannot always flee the shame she merits.
I ask no other favor than your silence.
In all besides, I give my wrath free scope.
Make your escape from this captivity,
Be bold, and come with me upon my flight.
Oh, do not stay on this accursèd soil
Where virtue breathes the air of pestilence.
To hide your leaving, take the good advantage
Of all this turmoil, roused by my disgrace.
I promise you the means of flight are ready.
You have, as yet, no other guards than mine.
Defenders of great strength will fight our quarrel.
Argos has open arms, and Sparta calls us.
Let us appeal for justice to our friends,
And let us not stand by while Phædra joins us

Together in one ruin, driving us
Down from the throne,—and swells her son's possessions
By robbing us. Come, take this happy chance.
What fear can hold you back? You seem to pause.
Only your better fortune makes me urge
That we be bold. When I am all a-fire,
Why are you ice? Are you afraid to follow
One who is banished?
    *Aricia.* Ah, but such an exile
Would be most dear to me. For with what joy
I'd live, if I could link my fate to yours,
And be forgot by all the world. But still
We are not bound by that sweet tie together.
Then how am I to steal away with you?
I know the strictest honor need not stop me
From seeking freedom from your father's hands,
For this, indeed, is not my parents' home,
And flight is lawful, when one flies from tyrants.
But you, sir, love me, and my virtue shrinks—
    *Hippolytus.* No, no! To me your honor is as dear
As it is to yourself. A nobler purpose
Brings me to you. I ask you leave your foes
And follow with your husband. That same Heaven
Which sends these woes, sets free the pledge between us
From human hands. There are not always torches
To light the face of Hymen. Come with me—
Beside the gates of Trœzen is a temple,
Amid the ancient tombs of princes, buried.
They who are false can never enter there,
And there no mortal dares make perjured oaths,
For instant punishment will come on guilt.
There is not any stronger check to falsehood
Than what is present there,—fear of a death

That cannot be escaped. There we shall go,
If you consent, and swear eternal love,
And call the god who watches there to witness
Our solemn vows, and ask his guarding care.
ĭ will invoke the holiest of powers—
The chaste Diana and the Queen of Heaven,—
Yes, all the gods, who know my inmost heart,
Will answer for my sacred promises.

    *Aricia.* Here is the king. Away—make no delay.
I linger yet a while to hide my flight.
Go you, and leave me with some trusted one
To lead my timid footsteps to your side.

        (*Exit Hippolytus. Enter Theseus and Ismene*)

    *Theseus.* O gods, throw light upon my troubled mind!
Show me the truth which I am seeking here.

    *Aricia* (*to Ismene*). Be ready, dear Ismene, for our flight.

        (*Exit Ismene*)

    *Theseus.* Your color changes, and you seem confused.
Madam,—what dealing had my son with you?

    *Aricia.* Sire, he was bidding me his last farewell.

    *Theseus.* It seems your eyes can tame that stubborn pride,
And the first sighs he breathes are paid to you.

    *Aricia.* I cannot well deny the truth; he has not
Inherited your hatred and injustice,—
He does not treat me as a criminal.

    *Theseus.* That is to say,—he swore eternal love.
Do not depend on such a fickle heart.
He swore as much to others, long before.

    *Aricia.* He, Sire?

    *Theseus.* You stop the roving of his taste.
How should you bear so vile a partnership?

    *Aricia.* And how can you endure that wicked slanders
Should make so pure a life seem black as pitch?

How do you know so little of his heart?
Do you so ill distinguish innocence
From the worst guilt? What mist before your eyes
Can make them blind to such an open virtue?
Ah! 'Tis too much to let false tongues defame him!
Repent! Call back again your fatal prayers.
Oh, be afraid, lest Heaven in its justice
Hate you enough to hear your wish and grant it!
The gods, in anger, often take our victims,—
And oftentimes they punish us with gifts!
   *Theseus.* No, it is vain to seek to hide his guilt.
Your love is blind to his depravity.
But I have witnesses beyond reproach,—
Tears I have seen,—true tears, that may be trusted.
   *Aricia.* Take heed, my lord. Although your mighty hand
Has rid the world of many beasts and monsters,
You have not slain them all,—there's one alive!—
Your son, himself, forbids that I say more,
And since I know how much he still reveres you,
I know that I should cause him much distress
If I should dare to finish. I shall act
Like reverence,—and to be silent,—leave you.
              *(Exit Aricia)*
   *Theseus (alone).* What is there in her mind? What
     hidden meaning
Lurks in a speech begun, then broken short?
Would both deceive me with a vain pretense?
Have they conspired to put me to this torture?
And yet, for all that I am most severe,
What plaintive voice is crying in my heart?
I have a secret pity that disturbs me.
Œnone must be questioned, once again,
For I must see this crime in clearer light.

Guards, bid Œnone come to me,--alone.

*(Enter Panope)*

*Panope.* I do not know the purpose of the queen,
Yet, seeing her distress, I fear the worst;—
Despair most fatal, painted on her features,—
Death's pallor is already in her face.
Œnone, shamed and driven from her sight,
Has thrown herself into the ocean's depths.
What moved her to so rash a deed, none knows,
And now the waves forever hide her from us.

*Theseus.* What is it that you say?

*Panope.* Her sad fate adds
New trouble to the queen's tempestuous soul.
Sometimes, to soothe her secret pain, she clasps
Her children to her, bathes them with her tears,—
Then suddenly forgets her mother's love,
And thrusts them from her with a look of horror.
She wanders back and forth with doubtful steps,
Her eye looks vacantly, and will not know us.
She wrote three times, and thrice she changed her mind,
And tore the letter when it scarce was started.
Be willing then to see her, Sire,—to help her.

*(Exit Panope)*

*Theseus.* Œnone dead, and Phædra bent on dying?
Oh, call my son to me again, great Heaven!
Let him defend himself, for I am ready
To hear him, now. Oh, haste not to bestow
Thy fatal bounty, Neptune. Rather my prayers
Should stay unheard forever. Far too soon
I raised too cruel hands, and I believed
Lips that may well have lied! Ah, what may follow?

*(Enter Theramenes)*

*Theseus.* 'Tis you, Theramenes? Where is my son?

I gave him to your keeping in his childhood,—
But why should tears be flowing from thine eyes?
How is it with my son—?
  *Theramenes.* You worry late.
It is a vain affection. He is dead.
  *Theseus.* O gods!
  *Theramenes.* Yes, I have seen the very flower
Of all mankind cut down; and I am bold
To say that never man deserved it less.
  *Theseus.* My son! My son is dead! When I was reaching
My arms to him again, then why should Heaven
Hasten his doom? What sudden blow was this?
  *Theramenes.* When we had scarcely passed the gates of
    Trœzen,—
He, silent in his chariot, his guards
Downcast and silent, too, all ranged around him,—
He turned his steeds to the Mycenian road,
And, lost in thought, allowed the reins to lie
Loose on their backs, and his high-mettled chargers,
One time so eager to obey his voice,
Now seemed to know his sadness and to share it.
Then, coming from the sea, a frightful cry
Shatters the troubled air with sudden discord;
And groaning from the bosom of the earth
Answers the crying of that fearful voice.
It froze the blood within our very hearts!
Our horses hear, and stand with bristling manes.
Meanwhile there rises on the watery plain
A mountain wave, mighty, with foaming crest.
It rolls upon the shore, and as it breaks
It throws before our eyes a raging monster.
Its brow is armed with terrifying horns
And all its body clothed with yellow scales.

In front it is a bull, behind, a dragon,
Turning and twisting in impatient fury.
It bellows till the very shores do tremble.
The sky is struck with horror at the sight.
The earth in terror quakes; breath of the beast
Poisons the air. The very wave that brought it
Runs back in fear. All fly, forgetting courage
Which cannot help,—and in a nearby temple
Take refuge,—all but brave Hippolytus.
A hero's worthy son, he stays his horses,
Seizes his darts, and rushing forward, hurls
A missile with sure aim, and wounds the beast
Deep in the flank. It springs, raging with pain,
Right to the horses' feet, and roaring, falls,
Writhes in the dust, shows them his fiery throat,
And covers them with flame and smoke and blood.
Fear lends them wings; deaf to his voice for once,
Heeding no curb, the horses race away.
Their master tires himself in futile efforts.
Each courser's bit is red with blood and foam.
Some say a god, in all this wild disorder,
Is seen, pricking their dusty flanks with goads.
They rush to jagged rocks, urged by this terror.
The axle crashes, and the hardy youth
Sees his car broken, shattered into bits.
He himself falls, entangled in the reins.—
Forgive my grief. That cruel sight will be
For me, the source of never-ending tears.
I saw thy luckless son,—I saw him, Sire,
Dragged by those horses that his hands had fed.
He could not stop their fierce career,—his cries
But added to their terror. All his body
Was soon a mass of wounds. Our anguished cries

Filled the whole plain. At length the horses slackened.
They stopped close by the ancient tombs which mark
The place where lie the ashes of his fathers.
I ran there panting, and behind me came
His guard, along a track fresh-stained with blood,
Reddening all the rocks; locks of his hair
Hung dripping in the briers,—gory triumphs!
I came and called him. Stretching out his hand,
He opened dying eyes, soon to be closed.
"The gods have robbed me of a guiltless life."
I heard him say, "Take care of sad Aricia,
When I am dead. Friend, if my father mourn
When he shall know his son's unhappy fate,—
One accused falsely,—then, to give me peace,
Tell him to treat his captive tenderly,
And to restore—" The hero's breath had failed,
And in my arms there lay a mangled body,—
A thing most piteous, the bleeding spoil
Of Heaven's wrath,—his father could not know him.
    *Theseus.* Alas, my son:—my hope, now lost forever!
The gods are ruthless. They have served me well,
And I am left to live a life of anguish
And of a great remorse.
    *Theramenes.* And then Aricia,
Flying from you, came timidly to take him
To be her husband, there, before the gods.
And coming close, she saw the grass, all reeking,
All bloody red, and (sad for a lover's eyes!)
She saw him, lying there, disfigured, pale,—
And for a time she knew not her misfortune.
She did not know the hero she adores.
She looked and asked, "Where is Hippolytus?"
Only too sure. at last, that he was lying

Before her there, with sad eyes, silently
Reproaching Heaven, she groaned, and shuddering
Fell fainting, all but lifeless, at his feet.
Ismene, all in tears, knelt down beside her,
And called her back to life, a life of nothing
But sense of pain. And I to whom the light
Is only darkness, now, come to discharge
The duty he imposed on me: to tell you
His last desire,—a melancholy task.—
But here his mortal enemy is coming.

(*Enter Phædra and Guards*)

*Theseus.* Madam, you've triumphed, and my son is killed!
Ah, but what room have I for fear! How justly
Suspicion racks me that in blaming him
I erred! But he is dead; accept your victim,
Rightly or wrongly slain. Your heart may leap.
For me, my eyes shall be forever blind.
Since you have said it, I'll believe him guilty.
His death is cause enough for me to weep.
It would be folly, should I seek a light
Which could not bring him back to soothe my grief,
And which might only make me more unhappy.
I will go far from you and from this shore,
For here the vision of my mangled son
Would haunt my memory, and drive me mad.
I wish I might be banished from the world,
For all the world must rise in judgment on me.
Even my glory weights my punishment,
For if I bore a name less known to men,
'Twere easier to hide me. Ah, I mourn
And hate all prayers the gods have granted me.
Nor will I ever go to them again
With useless pleadings. All that they can give

Is far outweighed by what they took from me.

   *Phædra.* My lord, I cannot hear you and be silent.
I must undo the wrong that he has suffered,—
Your son was innocent.

   *Theseus.* Unhappy father!
And I condemned him for a word of yours!
You think I can forgive such cruelty—?

   *Phædra.* Moments are precious to me; let me speak.
'Twas I who cast an eye of lawless passion
On chaste and dutiful Hippolytus.
The gods had lit a baleful fire in me,
And vile Œnone's cunning did the rest.
She feared Hippolytus,—who knew my madness,—
Would tell you of that passion which he hated.
And so she took advantage of my weakness
And hastened, that she might accuse him first.
She has been punished now, but all too lightly.
She sought to flee my anger,—cast herself
Into the waves. The sword had long since cut
My thread of life, but still I heard the cry
Of slandered innocence, and I determined
To die a slower way, and first confess
My penitence to you. There is a poison
Medea brought to Athens, in my veins.
The venom works already in my heart.
A strange and fatal chill is spreading there.
I see already, through a gathering mist,
The husband whom I outrage with my presence.
Death veils the light of Heaven from mine eyes,
And gives it back its purity, defiled.

   *Panope.* She dies, my lord.

   *Theseus.* I would the memory
Of her disgraceful deed might perish with her!

Ah! I have learned too late! Come, let us go,
And with the blood of mine unhappy son
Mingle our tears,—embrace his dear remains,
Repenting deeply for a hated prayer.
Let him have honor such as he deserves,
And, to appease his sore-offended spirit,
No matter what her brothers' guilt has been,
From this day forth, Aricia is my daughter.

(Exeunt)

FINIS

ATHALIAH

A Tragedy Founded Upon Holy Scripture

by

JEAN RACINE

## CHARACTERS

JOASH ...............*King of Judah and Son of Ahaziah*

ATHALIAH ............*Widow of Joram, and Grandmother of Joash*

JEHOIADA .............*The High Priest*

JEHOSHEBA ..........*Aunt of Joash, and Wife of the High Priest*

ZACHARIAH ..........*Son of Jehoiada and Jehosheba*

SALOME ..............*Sister of Zachariah*

ABNER ...............*One of the Chief Officers of the Kings of Judah*

AZARIAH, ISHMAEL ....*and the three other Chiefs of the Priests and Levites*

MATTAN .............*An Apostate priest; Chief Priest of Baal*

NABAL ...............*Confidential friend of Mattan*

HAGAR ...............*An attendant of Athaliah*

*Band of Priests and Levites*

*Attendants of Athaliah*

*Nurse of Joash*

*Chorus of young Maidens of the Tribe of Levi*

The scene is laid in the Temple at Jerusalem, in an antechamber of the High Priest's dwelling

# ACT I

## Scene I. *Jehoiada and Abner*

*Abner.* Yea, to the Temple of the Lord I come,
To worship with the solemn rites of old,
To celebrate with thee the famous day
When from the holy mount our Law was giv'n.
How times are changed! Soon as the sacred trump
With joyous blast announced this day's return,
The Temple porticoes, with garlands gay,
Could not contain the crowds of the devout;
Before the altar they in order due,
Bringing the earliest harvest of their fields,
Offered those firstfruits to the Lord of all;
Nor were there priests enough for sacrifice.
A woman's will has dared to check these throngs,
And turn'd the day's bright glory into gloom.
Scarce dare a few most zealous worshippers
Recall for us some shadow of the past;
The rest are all forgetful of their God,
Or, e'en to Baal's altars flocking now,
In shameful orgies learn to bear their part,
And curse the Name on which their fathers call'd.
My soul is troubled,—naught will I conceal—
Lest Athaliah visit upon thee
Her vengeance, spurn all remnant of respect,
And tear thee from the altar of the Lord.
   *Jehoi.* Whence comes to thee this presage dark today?

*Abner.* Holy and righteous, how canst thou escape?
Long has she hated that rare constancy
Which adds new brilliance to thy mitred brow;
Long has she treated thy religious zeal
As obstinate sedition and revolt.
The shining virtues of thy faithful spouse
Have earned the special hatred of the Queen.
If Aaron's priesthood has devolved on thee,
Thy wife is sister to our latest king.
Mattan moreover, that apostate priest,
His foul desertion from our altars crowns
With eager persecution of all good,
And, worse than Athaliah, spurs her on.
'Tis not enough that in a foreign garb
The Levite serves at Baal's altar now,
This Temple is to him a sore offence,
And he would fain destroy the God he left.
No means he leaves untried to ruin thee,
And undermines with praise no less than blame.
He feigns for thee a treacherous kindliness,
Masking the blackness of his venom thus.
Sometimes he prompts the Queen to dread thy power,
And sometimes, looking to her lust for gold,
Pretends that somewhere known to thee alone,
Thou hidest treasures David has amass'd.
For two days past the proud imperious Queen
Has seem'd as though consumed by baffled spite.
I saw her yesterday with furious eyes
Glare at this sacred place, and mark'd her well,
As if within the Temple's deep recess
Lurk'd God's avenger arm'd to punish her.
The more I think thereon, the less I doubt
On thee her wrath is ready now to burst,

And that, with all her mother's thirst for blood,
E'en in His shrine she will defy our God.

*Jehoi.* He who enchains the fury of the waves
Knows how to curb the plots of wicked men.
Submitting humbly to His holy will,
I fear my God, and know no other fear.
And yet, I thank thee, Abner, for thy zeal
That o'er my peril keeps a watchful eye.
I see injustice chafes thine inmost heart,
Thou art a faithful son of Israel still.
For that may Heaven be bless'd! But secret wrath
And passive worth, thou art content with these?
Is faith sincere, if it declines to act?
An impious foreigner for eight long years
Has David's throne usurp'd, with all its rights,
Unpunished waded in our princes' blood,
Foul murderess of the children of her son,
And e'en against our God has raised her arm.
And thou, a pillar of this trembling state,
Bred in the camp of good Jehoshaphat,
Under his son Hehoram in command,
On whom alone our towns in terror lean'd
When Ahaziah's unexpected death
Scatter'd his armies before Jehu's face,
Say'st thou—"I fear the Lord and own His truth!"
Lo, by my mouth to thee the Lord replies,—
"What boots it that thou boast zeal for My Law?
Thinkest to honour Me by barren vows?
What fruit have I of all thy sacrifice?
Need I the blood of heifers and of goats?
Thy princes' blood cries out, and is not heard.
Break, break, all compact with impiety,
Root up the crimes amidst My people rife,

And come and sacrifice thy victims then."

*Abner.* What can I do? The people have lost heart,
Judah is cow'd, and Benjamin is weak;
The day that saw their royal line extinct
Extinguish'd all their ancient valour too.
The Lord Himself, they say, withdraws from us,
Tho' once so jealous of His People's praise;
He sees unmoved their majesty abased,
And His compassion is at last worn out.
No more for us His mighty arm outstretch'd
With countless marvels terrifies our foes;
His Ark is dumb,—utters no oracle.

*Jehoi.* Yet when did miracles abound as now?
When by more signs has God display'd His power?
Will ye have always eyes that cannot see,
Ungrateful people? Shall His mightiest deeds
Strike on your ears, nor ever move your hearts?
Say, my dear Abner, must I needs repeat
The wonders brought to pass in these our days;
The signal fall of Israel's tyrant kings,
And God found faithful to perform His threats;
Ahab destroy'd, and with his blood defiled
The plot of land which murder had usurp'd;
Hard by that fatal field Jezebel slain,
A Queen down trampled under horse's hoofs,
The dogs that lick'd up her inhuman blood,
The mangled limbs of her dishonour'd corpse;
The troop of lying prophets brought to shame,
The fire from heav'n that on the altar fell;
Elijah's voice ruling the elements,
The skies thereby shut up, the earth like brass,
For three whole years left without rain or dew;
The dead arising at Elisha's word?

Recall, O Abner, these portentous signs,
God is today as He has always been.
He can unfold His glory when He will,
And ever in His mind His people dwell.

*Abner.* But where the promises so often made
To David and to Solomon his son?
Alas! We hoped that from their fruitful stock
Kings were to issue in a numerous train;
That over every nation, tribe, and tongue
One of their lineage should extend his sway,
Should everywhere make war and strife to cease,
And at his footstool see earth's proudest kings.

*Jehoi.* And why distrust the promises of Heaven?

*Abner.* That son of David, where shall he be found?
Can Heav'n itself restore the living sap
Of that dry tree, now wither'd at the root?
E'en in his cradle Athaliah slew
The babe, and eight years after can he live?
Ah! might it be her fury miss'd its aim,
That of our royal blood some drop escaped—

*Jehoi.* What would'st thou do?

*Abner.*                                O happy day for me!
How gladly would I go to meet my king!
Doubt not that to his feet our eager tribes,—
But wherefore mock me with these idle dreams?
Ill-fated heir of our victorious kings,
We had but Ahaziah, with his sons;
By Jehu's darts I saw the father slain,
And thou his sons by his own mother murder'd.

*Jehoi.* I cannot now explain; but when the sun
Shall the third portion of his course complete,
Bringing the morning hour that bids to prayer,
Hither return and with the self-same zeal.

Then God may prove to thee by gracious deeds
His word is faithful still, and never fails.
So, for this solemn day I must prepare
And dawn already gilds the temple roof.

*Abner.* What gracious deed is this, to me unknown?
Tow'rd thee Jehosheba directs her steps;
I leave thee, and will join the faithful band
Brought hither by this solemn festival

### SCENE II. *Jehoiada and Jehosheba*

*Jehoi.* Princess, the time is come for us to speak.
Thy happy theft can be no longer hid.
The insults of the enemies of God,
Abusing this our silence, have too long
Charged with unfaithfulness His promises.
Nay more; success has animated rage,
And Athaliah would to Baal burn,
E'en in God's courts, incense idolatrous.
Rear'd in His Temple 'neath th' Almighty's wing,
'Tis ours to show the King thine hands have saved.
He'll prove himself courageous as his sires,
Already in his wit beyond his age.
Ere I unfold his wondrous destiny,
I offer him to God by Whom kings reign;
Then, gathering straight our Levites and our priests,
I will proclaim their masters' long lost heir.

*Jehosh.* Knows he his name and noble fortune yet?

*Jehoi.* He owns no other than Eliakim,
And thinks himself some foundling left to die,
Whom I in pity treated as my son.

*Jehosh.* Ah! from what perils I deliver'd him!
What danger is he now to meet once more!

*Jehoi.* What! Fails thy faith already in alarm?

*Jehosh.* My lord, I yield me to thy counsels wise.
Since first I snatch'd this precious babe from death,
I placed his welfare in thy careful hands;
Yea, dreading e'en the fervour of my love,
I shun his presence where and when I can,
For fear lest my unguarded heart betray
My secret with the tears I cannot check.
Three days and nights I thought that duty bade
Devote to weeping and impassion'd prayer.
Yet may it be allowed me now to ask,
What friends thou hast ready to take thy side?
Abner, brave Abner, will he lend his aid?
Say, has he sworn to stand beside his King?
 *Jehoi.* Abner, though on his faith we may rely,
Knows not as yet that any King is ours.
 *Jehosh.* Who is to guard young Joash? Wilt thou trust
Obed or Amnon with so high a charge?
My father's kindness they have often proved,—
 *Jehoi.* And sold themselves to Athaliah's will.
 *Jehosh.* Whom to her hirelings wilt thou then oppose?
 *Jehoi.* Have I not said? Our Levites and our priests.
 *Jehosh.* I know that, secretly assembled near,
Their numbers have been doubled by thy care;
That full of love for thee, horror for her,
A great oath binds them, ere the trial come,
To David's heir when he shall be reveal'd.
But though with loyal ardour they may burn,
Can they unaided vindicate their king?
Is zeal enough to cope with such a task?
Doubt not the Queen, when the first rumour spreads
Of Ahaziah's son in hiding here,
Will gather all her savage troops around,
Besiege the Temple, and break down its gates.

Against such foes will sanctity avail,
And holy hands raised to the Lord in prayer?
Their province is to intercede for guilt,
No blood but that of victims have they shed;
Joash, perchance, sore wounded in their arms,—

  *Jehoi.* Contest as naught the God who fights for us?
God, who protects the orphan's innocence,
And e'en in weakness manifests His might;
God, who hates tyrants, and in Jezreel swore
He would root out Ahab and Jezebel;
Who, striking Joram, husband of their child,
And Joram's son, their family pursued;
Whose threatening arm, though for a time withheld,
Over that impious race is ever stretch'd?

  *Jehosh.* Yea, 'tis His righteous sentence on them all
That makes me tremble for my brother's son.
Who knows if he, inheriting their guilt,
Was not at birth condemn'd to share their fate?
Or whether God exempts him from the curse,
And will for David's sake his pardon seal?
Ah! his sad state when Heaven gave him me
Returns each moment to alarm my soul.
With slaughter'd princes was the chamber full;
Dagger in hand, th' inexorable Queen
To bloodshed urged her barbarous soldiery,
And eagerly her murderous course pursued!
Young Joash, left for dead, there met my eyes;
I seem to see his terror-stricken nurse
Still vainly crouching at the assassin's feet,
His drooping form clasp'd to her feeble breast.
I took him stain'd with blood. Bathing his face
My copious tears restored his vanish'd sense;
And, whether yet with fear or fond caress,

I felt the pressure of his tender arms.
Great God, forbid my love should be his bane,
Last relic of the faithful David now.
Bred in Thine House, and taught to love Thy Law.
He knows no other Father than Thyself.
If, ready to attack a murderous Queen,
Faith falters trembling at the danger nigh;
If flesh and blood, disquieted this day,
Have shed too many tears, alarm'd for him;
Heir of Thy holy promise, guard him well,
And for such weakness punish only me!

*Jehoi.* Thy tears, Jehosheba, no blame deserve,
But God would have us trust Him as a Father.
He visits not with blind resentment sins
Of impious ancestors on pious sons.
All that remains of faithful Israel still
Will come today here to renew their vows;
Deep as their reverence for David's race,
They hold abhorr'd the child of Jezebel;
Joash will move them with his modest grace,
Seeming to light anew the glorious past;
And the Lord's Voice, making our cause His own,
Will in His Temple to their hearts appeal.
Two faithless kings in turn have Him defied,
Now must a monarch to the throne be raised
Whose grateful memory shall bless the day
When God by His own priests his rights restored.
Who pluck'd him from th' oblivion of the tomb,
And David's lamp rekindled when put out.
Great God, if Thy foreknowledge sees him base,
Bent to forsake the paths that David trod,
Then let him be like fruit ere ripeness pluck'd
Or flower wither'd by a noisome blast!

But if this child, obedient to Thy will,
Is destined to advance Thy wise designs,
Now let the rightful heir the sceptre sway,
Give to my feeble hands his pow'rful foes,
And baffle in her plots a cruel Queen.
Vouchsafe, my God, on Nathan and on her
That spirit of blind foolishness to pour
Which leads deluded monarchs to their fall!
No more; fare well. Our children with them bring
Maidens, of holiest stock the hallow'd seed.

SCENE III. *Jehosheba, Zachariah, Salome, Chorus*

*Jehosh.* Dear Zachariah, go, nor stay thy steps,
Accompany thy venerable sire.
    Daughters of Levi, young and faithful band,
Whom with His zeal the Lord already fires,
Who come so often here to share my sighs,
Children, my only joy in griefs profound;
These gay festoons and coronets of flow'rs
Once well accorded with our stately feasts,
But now, alas, when shame and sorrow reign,
What offering is more fit than one of tears!
Already do I hear the solemn trump,
Soon will the Temple doors be opened wide,
While thither I myself prepare to go,
Sing, praise the God whose presence here ye seek.

SCENE IV. *The Chorus*

*All the Chorus* [*sings*].

His glory fills the universe sublime,
Lift to this God for aye the voice of prayer!
He reign'd supreme before the birth of Time;
    Sing of His loving care.

### One Voice [alone].

Vainly unrighteous force
Would still His people's praise that must have course;
  His Name shall perish ne'er.
Day tells to day His pow'r, from time to time;
His glory fills the universe sublime;
  Sing of His loving care.

### All the Chorus [repeats].

His glory fills the universe sublime;
  Sing of His loving care.

### One Voice [alone].

He paints the flow'rs with all their lovely hues;
  The fruit to ripeness grows,
  For daily He bestows
The day's warm sunshine, and the night's cool dews,
Nor does the grateful earth t' o'erpay the debt refuse.

### Another Voice.

The sun at His command spreads joy around,
  'Tis from His bounteous nand its light proceeds;
But in His Law, so pure, so holy found,
  We hail His richest gift to meet our needs.

### Another.

Oh! mount of Sinai, let the memory stay
Of that for ever great and famous day,
  When on thy flaming head,
In clouds conceal'd, the Lord reveal'd
To mortal eyes a ray from His own glory shed.
Tell us, why glow'd those lightning fires up there,

Why roll'd the smoke, why peal'd in troubled air
  Thunder and trumpet's blare?
Came He that, back to primal Chaos hurl'd,
On its foundations of past ages whirl'd,
  Came He to shake the world?

### *Another.*

He came that He to Israel might reveal
Th' immortal lustre of His holy Law;
He came that to their hearts He might appeal,
To claim their lasting love, based upon reverent awe.

### *All the Chorus.*

O Law divine and full of grace!
  Justice and goodness all supreme!
  What reason and what joy extreme,
Our love and trust in such a God to place!

### *One Voice* [*alone*].

From slavery's yoke He did our fathers save,
And for their desert-food sweet manna gave;
To us He gives His Laws, all gifts above
Save of Himself; for all He only claims our love.

### *The Chorus.*

Justice and goodness all supreme!

### *The Same Voice.*

For them divided He the waters of the sea,
From the dry dock He made the torrent stream;
To us He gives His Laws, all gifts above
Save of Himself, for all He only claims our love.

### The Chorus.

O Law divine and full of grace!
  What reason, and what joy extreme,
Our love and trust in such a God to place!

### Another Voice [alone].

You who can only know a servile fear,
Whose thankless souls God's goodness fails to move;
Does it to you so hard a task appear,
  So difficult to love?
Slaves dread the tyrant's lash that makes them smart,
But children feel a love that binds the heart;
To share God's lavish bounty you are fain,
  But not to love again!

### All the Chorus.

O Law divine and full of grace!
  Justice and goodness all supreme!
  What reason and what joy extreme,
Our love and trust in such a God to place!


## ACT II

### Scene I. *Jehosheba, Salome, Chorus*

*Jehosh.* Maidens, it is enough; your songs must cease;
'Tis time for us to join the public prayers.
The hour is come to celebrate the feast,
And in our turn before the Lord appear.

Scene II. *Jehosheba, Zachariah, Salome, and Chorus*

*Jehosh.* What do I see? My son, what brings thee back?
So pale and breathless, whither dost thou run?
  *Zach.* Mother!
  *Jehosh.*        Speak, then!
  *Zach.*                The Temple is profaned!
  *Jehosh.* What?
  *Zach.* And the altar of the Lord forsaken!
  *Jehosh.* I tremble. Quickly tell thy mother all.
  *Zach.* My father, the High Priest, with all due rites
Presented to the Lord, Who feeds mankind,
The first loaves of the harvest we have reap'd,
And then, while offering with blood-stain'd hands
The smoking inwards of the victims slain;
And, standing by his side, Eliakim
Help'd me to serve him, clad in linen stole;
While with the blood of sacrifice the priests
Sprinkled the altar and the worshippers;
There rose a tumult, and the people turn'd,
Sudden astonishment in every eye.
A woman—is to name her blasphemy?—
A woman—it was Athaliah's self.
  *Jehosh.*                  Great Heav'n!
  *Zach.* Within the court reserved for men
This woman enters with uplifted brow,
Yea, and attempts to pass the limit set,
Where none but Levites have a right to come.
The people fly, all scatter'd in dismay;
My father—ah, what wrath blazed from his eyes!
Moses to Pharaoh seem'd less terrible,—
"Go, Queen," my father said, "and leave this place,
Bann'd to thy sex and thine impiety!

Comest to brave the majesty of God?"
And then the Queen fiercely confronting him,
Seem'd as in act to utter blasphemies;
I know not if the Angel of the Lord
Appear'd before her with a glittering sword,
But straight her tongue seem'd frozen in her mouth,
And all her boldness utterly abash'd;
She could not move her eyes, in terror fix'd
And strange surprise on young Eliakim.

 *Jehosh.* What! Did he stand there in her very sight?
 *Zach.* We both stood gazing on that cruel Queen,
Stricken with equal horror at our hearts;
But soon the priests encompass'd us around,
And forced us to withdraw. I came to thee,
To tell the outrage done; I know no more.

 *Jehosh.* Ah! she would doubtless tear him from our arms
E'en at God's altar hunting for her prey.
Perchance, ere now, this child of many tears—
Oh God, remember David, see and save!

 *Sal.* Who is he, thus to cause your tears to flow?
 *Zach.* Why should his life be threaten'd? Can it be?
 *Sal.* What can the boy have done to enrage the Queen?
 *Zach.* What fear they from a helpless orphan child?
 *Jehosh.* She comes! She must not see us, let us go.

SCENE III. *Athaliah, Abner, Hagar, Attendants of Athaliah*

 *Hag.* Madam, why stay in such a place as this,
Where every sight offends and wounds thine eye?
Leave to the priests this temple where they dwell;
Fly from this scene of tumult; and within
Thy palace, lull each troubled sense to rest.

 *Ath.* I cannot. Thou dost see me vex'd and weak.
Go thou, send word to Mattan that he come

With haste: oh! happy still, if by his aid
I find that peace I seek, and seek in vain!
[*She seats herself.*]

SCENE IV. *Athaliah, Abner, Attendants of Athaliah*

*Abner.* Madam, forgive me if I dare defend him,
His zeal should not surprise you. For the God,
Whom we adore, Himself ordain'd it so,
And gave us charge to guard His altar well;
The work of sacrifice to Aaron's sons,
And to the Levites place and task assign'd;
To their descendants strictly He forbade
All fellowship with other deities.
Art thou the wife and mother of our kings,
A stranger to our customs on this point?
Dost thou not know our laws? And must today—
But Mattan comes: with him I leave thee now.

*Ath.* We need thy presence, Abner. Let it pass,
Jehoiada's presumptuous insolence,
With all that heap of superstitions vain
Which bid you keep your Temple to yourselves:
A subject far more urgent wakes alarm.
I know that from a child, rear'd in the camp,
Abner is generous, knowing how to pay
Alike to God and King the debt he owes.
Remain.

SCENE V. *Athaliah, Abner, Mattan, Attendants of Athaliah*

*Mat.* Great Queen, is this a place for thee?
What trouble stirs, what terror chills thine heart?
What dost thou in the midst of enemies?
Darest thou this unhallowed fane approach?
Hast thou that bitter hatred cast away—

*Ath.* Both of you lend me an attentive ear.
I do not wish now to recall the past,
Nor give account to you for blood I shed.
A sense of duty prompted all my acts.
Nor will I take for judge a hasty crowd;
Whate'er they may presume to spread abroad,
My vindication Heav'n has made its care.
My pow'r, establish'd on renown'd success,
Has magnified my name from sea to sea;
Jerusalem enjoys profoundest peace;
The wandering Arab Jordan sees no more
Ravage his borders with continual raids;
Nor boasts Philistia over Judah now,
And Syria owns me for a sister Queen.

Lastly the traitor, who destroy'd my House,
And e'en to me thought to extend his rage,
Jehu, fierce Jehu, in Samaria quails
Before a mighty rival's rapid strokes,
Whom I incited to attack my foe;
And thus th' assassin leaves me mistress here,
To reap the fruits of policy in peace.

But for some days a gnawing care has come,
To check the flood of my prosperity.
A dream (why should a dream disquiet me?)
Preys on my heart, and keeps it ill at ease;
I try to banish it; it haunts me still.

'Twas deepest night, when horror falls on man,
My mother Jezebel before me stood,
Richly attired as on the day she died,
Her pride undaunted by misfortune's touch.
That borrow'd brightness still her features wore,
Which she would paint upon her wither'd face,

To hide the ravages of ruthless age:
  "Tremble," she said, "child worthy of myself;
O'er thee too triumphs Judah's cruel god,
And thou must fall into his dreadful hands,
Whereat I grieve." With these alarming words,
Her spectre o'er my bed appear'd to bend;
I stretch'd my hands to clasp her; but I found
Only a hideous mass of flesh and bones,
Horribly bruised and mangled, dragg'd thro' mire,
Bleeding and torn, whose limbs the dogs of prey
Were growling over with devouring greed.
  *Abner.* Great God!
  *Ath.* While thus disturb'd, before me rose
The vision of a boy in shining robe,
Such as the Hebrew priests are wont to wear.
My drooping spirits at his sight revived:
But while my troubled eyes, to peace restored,
Admired his noble air and modest grace,
I felt the sudden stroke of murderous steel
Plunged deeply by the traitor in my breast.
Perhaps to you this dream, so strangely mix'd,
May seem a work of chance, and I myself,
For long ashamed to let my fears prevail,
Referr'd it to a melancholy mood;
But while its memory linger'd in my soul,
Twice in my sleep I saw that form again,
Twice the same child before my eyes appear'd
Always about to stab me to the heart.
  Worn out at last by horror's close pursuit,
I went to claim Baal's protecting care,
And, kneeling at his altars, find repose.
How strangely fear may sway our mortal minds!

And instinct seem'd to drive me to these courts,
To pacify the god whom Jews adore;
I thought that offerings might appease his wrath,
That this their god might grow more merciful.
Baal's High Priest, my feebleness forgive!
I enter'd; and the sacrifice was stay'd,
The people fled, Jehoiada in wrath
Advanced to meet me. As he spake, I saw
With terror and surprise that self-same boy
Who haunts me in my dreams. I saw him there;
His mien the same, the same his linen stole,
His gait, his eyes, each feature of his race;
It was himself; beside th' High Priest he walk'd,
Till quickly they removed him from my sight.

That is the trouble which detains me here,
And thereon would I fain consult you both.
Mattan, what means this omen marvellous?

*Mat.* Coincidence so strange fills me with dread.

*Ath.* But, Abner, hast thou seen this fatal child?
Who is he? What his family, his tribe?

*Abner.* Two children at the altar lend their aid,
One is the High Priest's son, the other is
To me unknown.

               *Mat.* Why hesitate to act?
Your Majesty must needs secure them both.
'Tis known how I regard Jehoiada,
Seeking no vengeance for my private wrongs,
In all my warnings studying to be fair;
But, after all, were this indeed his son,
Would he one moment let the guilty live?

*Abner.* Of what crime can a child be capable?

*Mat.* Heav'n show'd him with a dagger in his hand;

And Heav'n is just and wise, nor works in vain.
What more dost want?

*Abner.*                    But, trusting to a dream
Say, would'st thou have us bathe in infant blood?
Ye know not yet his father nor his name.

*Mat.* Enough for fear! I have considered all.
If from illustrious parentage he springs,
His ruin should be hasten'd by his rank;
If fate has placed him in a lot obscure,
What matters it if worthless blood be spilt?
Must kings keep pace when justice lags behind?
On promptitude their safety oft depends;
No irksome scruples need their freedom check;
To be suspected is all one with guilt.

*Abner.* Mattan! Is this the language of a priest?
Nursed in the lap of war, in carnage reared,
Stern agent of the vengeful wrath of Kings,
'Tis I who now must urge misfortune's plea!
And thou, who owest him a father's love,
A minister of peace in times of wrath,
Cloaking resentment with pretended zeal
Dost chafe that blood should flow so tardily!
Thou badest me, Madam, speak my honest thought:
What, then, is this that moves thy fear so much?
A dream, a feeble child, whom, it may be
Too readily thy fancy recognised.

*Ath.* Abner, I will admit I may be wrong,
Heeding too much, perchance, an idle dream.
More closely then must I behold that child,
And at my leisure scan his features well.
Let both the boys be brought before me now.

*Abner.* I fear—

*Ath.* What! Can they fail to grant me this?
What reason could they have to say me no?
'Twould rouse suspicion. Bid Jehosheba,
Or else her husband bring the children here;
I can at pleasure use a monarch's tone.
Abner, I tell thee candidly, your priests
Have cause to bless my kindness hitherto;
I know how far they freely have discuss'd
My conduct, and abused my sovereign power;
And yet they live, and yet their temple stands.
But soon, I feel, the limit may be pass'd;
Jehoiada must curb his savage zeal,
And not provoke my wrath a second time.
Go.

SCENE VI. *Athaliah, Mattan, Attendants of Athaliah*

*Mat.* I may now at last in freedom speak,
And clearly set the truth before thine eyes.
A growing monster in this temple lurks;
A tempest threatens, wait not till it breaks.
Ere daylight Abner with th' High Priest conferr'd;
Thou knowest well his love for David's line.
What if Jehoiada should in their ranks
Foist this young child with whom Heav'n threatens thee,
His son or not—

*Ath.* Thou hast unseal'd eyes,
And Heaven's warning vision grows distinct.
But I would fain be free from every doubt:
Children will readily betray their thoughts,
One word will oft disclose some deep design.
Let me, dear Mattan, see him, question him,
Go thou, meanwhile, and secret orders give
That all my Tyrians quickly arm themselves.

Scene VII. *Joash, Athaliah, Jehosheba, Zachariah, Abner,*
*Salome, two Levites, Chorus, Attendants of Athaliah*

*Jehosh.* [*to the two Levites*]. Keep constant watch, ye
  servants of the Lord,
Over these children, precious and beloved.
  *Abner* [*to* Jehosheba]. Take courage,
    Princess; they shall be my charge.
  *Ath.* Heav'ns! the more closely I examine him,—
'Tis he! And horror seizes me again.
                    [*Pointing to Joash.*]
Wife of Jehoiada, is this thy son?
  *Jehosh.* He, Madam?
  *Ath.*                    He.
  *Jehosh.*                    His mother? No, not I.
                [*Pointing to Zachariah.*]
There is my son.
  *Ath.* [*to* Joash]. Who is thy father, child?
Answer, thyself.
  *Jehosh.*        Heav'n till this very day—
  *Ath.* Why in such haste to answer for the boy?
It is for him to speak.
  *Jehosh.*            From one so young
What revelation canst thou hope to gain?
  *Ath.* The young are innocent; and simple truth
Their honest frankness knows not to disguise:
Let him explain all that concerns himself.
  *Jehosh.* [*aside*]. Great God, put now Thy wisdom in his
    mouth!
  *Ath.* What is thy name?
  *Joash.*                    My name's Eliakim.
  *Ath.* Thy father?

*Joash.*                    Fatherless, they say, I am,
Cast since my birth upon the arms of God;
I never knew my parents, who they were.

*Ath*. Hast thou no parents?

*Joash.*                          They abandon'd me.

*Ath*. How? and how long ago?

*Joash.*                          When I was born.

*Ath*. Where is thy home? This can at least be told.

*Joash*. This Temple is my home; none else I know.

*Ath*. Where wast thou found? Hast thou been told of
   that?

*Joash*. 'Midst cruel wolves, ready to eat me up.

*Ath*. Who placed thee in this temple?

*Joash.*                            One unknown,
She gave no name, nor was she seen again.

*Ath*. Whose guardian hands preserved thine infant years?

*Joash*. When did God e'er neglect His children's needs?
The feather'd nestlings He provides with food,
And o'er all nature spreads His bounty wide.
Daily I pray; and with a Father's care
He feeds me from the sacred offerings.

*Ath*. New wonder comes to trouble and perplex!
The sweetness of his voice, his infant grace
Unconsciously make enmity give way
To—can it be compassion that I feel!

*Abner*. Madam, is this thy dreaded enemy?
'Tis evident thy dreams have played thee false;
Unless thy pity, which now seems to vex,
Should be the fatal blow that terrified.

*Ath*. [*to Joash and Jehosheba*]. Why are ye leaving?

*Jehosh.*                          Thou hast heard his tale:
His presence longer might be troublesome.

*Ath*. [*to Joash*]. Nay, child, come back.
   What dost thou all the day?

*Joash.*          I worship God, and hear His Law explain'd;
His holy volume I am taught to read,
And now to write it has my hand begun.

   *Ath.* What says that Law?

   *Joash.*                              That God requires our love
Avenges, soon or late, His Name blasphemed,
Is the protector of the fatherless,
Resists the proud, the murderer punishes.

   *Ath.* I understand. But all within these walls,
How are they occupied?

   *Joash.*                    In praising God.

   *Ath.* Does God claim constant service here and prayer?

   *Joash.* All else is banish'd from His hoiy courts.

   *Ath.* What pleasures hast thou?

   *Joash.*                              Where God's altar stands,
I sometimes help th' High Priest to offer salt
Or incense, hear His lofty praises sung,
And see His stately ritual perform'd.

   *Ath.* What! Hast thou pastime none more sweet than that?
Sad lot for one so young; but come with me,
And see my palace and my splendour there.

   *Joash.* God's goodness then would from my memory fade.

   *Ath.* I would not force thee to forget Him, child.

   *Joash.* Thou dost not pray to Him.

   *Ath.*                              But thou shalt pray.

   *Joash.* There I should hear another's name invoked.

   *Ath.* I serve my god: and thou shalt worship thine.
There are two powerful gods.

   *Joash.*                    Thou must fear mine;
He only is the Lord, and thine is naught.

   *Ath.* Pleasures untold will I provide for thee.

   *Joash.* The happiness of sinners melts away.

   *Ath.* Of sinners, who are they?

*Jehosh.*                    Madam, excuse
A child—

    *Ath.* I like to see how ye have taught him;
And thou hast pleased me well, Eliakim,
Being, and that past doubt, no common child.
See thou, I am a queen, and have no heir;
Forsake this humble service, doff this garb,
And I will let thee share in all my wealth;
Make trial of my promise from this day;
Beside me at my table, everywhere,
Thou shalt receive the treatment of a son.

    *Joash.* A son!
    *Ath.*                    Yes, speak.
    *Joash.*                    And such a Father leave
For—

    *Ath.* Well, what?
    *Joash.*                    Such a mother as thyself!
    *Ath.* [*to Jehosheba*]. His memory is good; in all he says
I recognise the lessons ye have given.
Yea, this is how, corrupting guileless youth,
Ye both improve the freedom ye enjoy,
Inciting them to hatred and wild rage,
Until they shudder but to hear my name.

    *Jehosh.* Can our misfortunes be conceal'd from them?
All the world knows them; are they not thy boast?

    *Ath.* Yea; with just wrath, that I am proud to own,
My parents on my offspring I avenged.
Could I see sire and brother massacred,
My mother from the palace roof cast down,
And the same day beheaded all at once
(Oh, horror!) fourscore princes of the blood;
And all to avenge a pack of prophets slain,
Whose dangerous frenzies Jezebel had curb'd?

Have Queens no heart, daughters no filial love,
That I should act the coward and the slave,
Too pitiful to cope with savages,
By rendering death for death, and blow for blow?
David's posterity from me received
Treatment no worse than had my father's sons!
Where should I be today, had I not quell'd
All weakness and a mother's tenderness,
Had not this hand of mine like water shed
My own heart's blood, and boldly check'd your plots?
Your god has vow'd implacable revenge;
Snapt is the link between thine house and mine,
David and all his offspring I abhor,
Tho' born of mine own blood I own them not.

    *Jehosh.* Thy plans have prospered. Let God see, and judge!

    *Ath.* Your god, forsooth, your only refuge left,
What will become of his predictions now?
Let him present you with that promised King,
That Son of David, waited for so long,—
We meet again. Farewell. I go content:
I wished to see, and I have seen.

    *Abner* [*to Jehosheba*]. The trust I undertook to keep, I
    thus resign.

SCENE VIII. *Joash, Jehosheba, Zachariah, Salome, Jehoiada*
*Abner, Levites, the Chorus*

    *Jehosh.* [*to Jehoiada*]. My lord, did'st hear the Queen's
    presumptuous words?

    *Jehoi.* I heard them all, and felt for thee the while.
These Levites were with me ready to aid
Or perish with you, such was our resolve.

           [*To Joash, embracing him.*]
May God watch o'er thee, child, whose courage bore,

Just now, such noble witness to His Name.
Thy service, Abner, has been well discharged:
I shall expect thee at th' appointed hour.
I must return, this impious murderess
Has stain'd my vision, and disturb'd my prayers;
The very pavement that her feet have trod
My hands shall sprinkle o'er with cleansing blood.

## Scene IX. *Chorus*

### *One of the Maidens Forming the Chorus.*

What star has burst upon our eyes?
What shall this wondrous child become one day?
  Vain pomp and show he dares despise,
  Nor lets those charms, where danger lies,
Lead his young feet from God astray.

### *Another Voice.*

While all to Baal's altar flock,
And for the Queen their faith disown,
A child proclaims that Israel's Rock
Is the eternal God alone,
And though this Jezebel may mock,
Elijah's spirit he has shown.

### *Another Voice.*

Who will the secret of thy birth explain?
Dear child, some holy prophet lives in thee again!

### *Another Voice.*

Thus grew the gentle Samuel of yore,
  Beneath the shadow of God's dwelling-place;
  And he became the hope of Israel's race,
To guide and comfort; this be thou and more!

### *Another Voice.*

Oh! blest beyond compare,
The child who knows His love,
Who early hears His voice, and keeps with care
The teaching he receives from God above!
Far severed trom the world, from birth endued
With all the gifts of Heaven,
No evil influence has imbued
His innocence with sin's infectious leaven.

### *All the Chorus.*

A happy youth he spends,
Whom the Lord teaches, whom the Lord defends?

### *The Same Voice* [*alone*].

As in sequester'd vale,
Where a clear streamlet flows,
Shelter'd from every stormy gale
Darling ot Nature, some young lily grows.
Far severed from the world, from birth endued
With all the gifts of Heaven,
No evil influence has imbued
His innocence with sin's infectious leaven.

### *All the Chorus.*

Blest more than tongue can tell,
'The child whom God inclines to keep His statutes well!

### *One Voice* [*alone*].

With faltering steps doth dawning Virtue tread
'Mid countless perils that beset the way;
What hindrances and snares for him are spread

Who seeks Thee, Lord, and fears from innocence to stray!
   Where can Thy saints a shelter find,
   With foes in front and foes behind?
Sinners fill all the earth, my God, look where we may.

### Another Voice.

Palace and City, David loved so well,
O Mount, where God Himself long deigned to dwell,
What has thy crime that draws down vengeance been?
What sayest thou, dear Zion, to behold,
Seated where sat thy kings from days of old,
   An impious foreign Queen?

### All the Chorus.

What sayest thou, dear Zion, to behold
   An impious foreign Queen,
Seated where sat thy kings from days of old?

### The Same Voice.

   Where once the Lord was bless'd,
     Father and God confess'd,
   Where David's holy strains so sweet had been,
   What sayest thou, dear Zion, to behold
   Cursing the Name thy kings adored of old,
Praising her own false gods, an impious foreign Queen?

### One Voice [alone].

How often, Lord, how often yet shall we
Against Thee rising up the wicked see?
They with unhallow'd feet Thy courts defile,
And all who worship Thee as fools revile.
How often, Lord, how often yet shall we
Against Thee rising up the wicked see?

### Another Voice.

Ah, what avails, say they, this virtue stern,
   That from sweet Pleasure's voice
   Morosely bids you turn?
Your God does naught for you to justify your choice.

### Another Voice.

Where Pleasure leads, laughter and song be ours,
   Thus speak those impious throngs:
Care for the future to dull fools belongs,
To passion give the reins, cull the sweet flow'rs;
Too quickly at the best years take their flight,
Who knows if he shall see tomorrow's light?
Let us today enjoy life's fragrant bowers!

### All the Chorus.

Let tears and terrors, Lord, their portion be,
These outcast wretches, who shall never see
Thy holy city with eternal glory crown'd;
   Be ours, on whom Thy beams immortal shine,
     To hymn Thy gifts divine,
Be ours with voice of praise Thy majesty to sound!

### One Voice [alone].

Of all their false delights what will remain
To souls absorb'd therein? As visions vain,
   That vanish with the dawning day,
   When they awaken with dismay!
While for the poor Thy table shall be spread,
Deep shall they drain the cup of judgment dread
That Thou shalt offer to all such as they,
   When Mercy's hour has fled.

### *All the Chorus.*

Oh, wakening of dismay
From dream too quickly sped,
From error's dangerous sway!

## ACT III

#### Scene I. *Mattan, Nabal, the Chorus*

*Mat.* Go, damsels: let Jehosheba be told
That Mattan would in private speak with her.

#### *One of the Maidens of the Chorus.*

Mattan! May God in Heav'n confound his plots!
  *Nab.* They all disperse in flight without reply!
  *Mat.* Let us draw near.

#### Scene II. *Zachariah, Mattan, Nabal*

  *Zach.*     Rash man, where would'st thou go?
Beware thou do not step beyond this spot;
This is a dwelling sacred to the priests;
Our laws forbid all common entrance here.
Who seekest thou? This solemn day, my sire
Shuns contact with impure idolatry,
And prostrate now before Jehovah's shrine,
My mother will not have her pray'r disturb'd.
  *Mat.* My son, be not distress'd, we will wait here.
To your illustrious mother I would speak;
I come charged with a message from the Queen.

### Scene III. *Mattan, Nabal*

*Nab.* Their very children ape their insolence!
But what means Athaliah now to do?
Whence springs this indecision in her plans?
This morn, rebuff'd by that presumptuous priest,
When dreams had warn'd of danger from a child,
Her mind was to destroy Jehoiada,
And in this temple Baal's altar place,
With thee to serve him; in thy joy I shared,
Hoping to gain my part in the rich spoil.
What made her change her fickle purpose thus?

*Mat.* She has not been herself these two days past.
No more is she the bold, clear sighted Queen,
With spirit raised above her timid sex,
Whose rapid action overwhelm'd her foes,
Who knew the value of an instant lost:
Fear and remorse disturb that lofty soul;
She wavers, falters, all the woman now.
Not long ago I fill'd with bitter wrath
Her heart already moved by threats from Heav'n,
And she, intrusting vengeance to my care,
Bade me assemble all her guard in haste;
But whether that young child, before her brought,
(A poor, unhappy foundling, as they say,)
Assuaged the terror that her dream had caused,
Or seeing in the boy some secret charm,
I find her shaken in her dire resolve,
Postponing vengeance to some future day;
And fatal strife in all her counsels reigns.
"I have inquired," said I, "about that child,
And hear strange boasts of royal ancestry,
How to the malcontents, from time to time,

The High Priest shows him, bids the Jews expect
In him a second Moses, and supports
His speech with lying oracles." These words
Made her brow flush. Swiftly the falsehood work'd.
"Is it for me," she said, "to pine in doubt?
Let us be rid of this perplexity.
Convey my sentence to Jehosheba:
Soon shall the fire be kindled, and the sword
Deal slaughter, soon their Temple shall be razed,
Unless, as hostage for their loyalty,
They yield this child to me."

   *Nab.*               For one unknown,
Whom chance, may be, has thrown into their arms,
Will they behold their Temple buried low—

   *Mat.* Ah! but no mortals have such pride as they.
Rather than to my hands resign a child,
Whom to his God Jehoiada has vow'd,
He will endure to die the worst of deaths,
Besides, they manifestly love this child,
And, if I construe right the Queen's account,
Jehoiada knows more than he will say
Touching his birth. Refusal I foresee,
In any case, with fatal consequence,
The rest be my concern; with fire and sword
To wipe this odious Temple from my eyes
Is my last hope.

   *Nab.* What prompts so fierce a hate?
Is it consuming zeal for Baal's cause?
Myself a child of Ishmael, as thou knowest,
I worship neither thine, nor Israel's god.

   *Mat.* Dost think, my friend, that any senseless zeal
For a dumb idol could my judgment blind,—
A perishable log, that worms destroy

In spite of all my efforts, day by day?
From birth devoted to the God, who here
Is worshipp'd, Mattan still might be his priest,
If but the love of grandeur, thirst for pow'r,
Could be consistent with his stringent yoke.
Nabal, I hardly need to thee recall
The quarrel 'tween Jehoiada and me,
When against him I dared the censer claim;
They made some stir, my struggle, tears, despair.
Vanquish'd, I enter'd on a new career,
And bound me, soul and body, to the Court,
By slow degrees I gain'd the ear of kings,
And soon my voice was deem'd oracular.
Their hearts I studied, flatter'd each caprice,
And sprinkled flow'rs for them on danger's brink.
Nothing to me was sacred that they craved,
Measure and weight I alter'd as they will'd.
As often as Jehoiada's blunt speech
Boldly offended their fastidious ears,
So often I had pow'r and skill to charm;
Concealing from their eyes unpleasant truths,
Gilding their savage passion with fair tints.
And lavish more than all of human blood.

At length was raised by Athaliah's hands
A temple to the god she introduced.
Jerusalem with tears the outrage saw;
The sons of Levi, stricken with alarm,
Appeal'd to Heaven with indignant cries.
I only, leading cowards in my train,
Deserter from their Law, that act approved,
And Baal's priesthood thereby merited.
Thus made my rival's formidable foe,
I donn'd the mitre; march'd along, his peer.

Still, I confess, e'en at my glory's height,
Harass'd by memories of the God I left,
Some fear remain'd to discompose my soul,
And this it is that fans and feeds my rage:
Happy if, wreaking vengeance on His shrine,
I may reduce His wrath to impotence,
And amidst ruin, desolation, death,
Lose my remorse in plenitude of crime!
Here comes Jehosheba.

SCENE IV. *Jehosheba, Mattan, Nabal*

*Mat.* Sent by the Queen
To bring back peace, and hatred drive away,
Be not surprised that I should thee accost,
Princess, whose gentle spirit comes from Heav'n,
A rumour, which of falsehood I suspect,
Supports the warning that a dream had giv'n,
Accusing the High Priest of dangerous plots,
And raising in the Queen a storm of ire.
I wish not here to vaunt my services,
Knowing Jehoiada to me unjust;
But good for evil is a due return.
In short, I come commission'd to speak peace.
Live, keep your feasts without a shade of fear.
For your obedience she but asks a pledge,—
(My efforts to dissuade her have been vain),
This orphan, whom she says that she has seen.

*Jehosh.* Eliakim?

*Mat.* Whereat I feel some shame
On her account, making an idle dream
Of too much moment. But unless ye give
This child to me forthwith, her mortal foes
Ye prove yourselves. Your answer she awaits,

Impatient.

*Jehosh.* These, then, are her words of peace!

*Mat.* And can ye for one moment hesitate
By slight concession such a boon to gain?

*Jehosh.* Strange would it be, if Mattan, free of guile,
Could trample down th' injustice of his heart,
And, after being of all ill contriver,
Could be the author of some shade of good!

*Mat.* What is your grievance? Has the Queen, in rage,
Sent to tear Zachariah from your arms?
He is your son; the other why so dear?
This fondness, in my turn, surprises me.
What treasure find ye there of priceless worth?
Has Heav'n in him sent a deliverer?
Bethink you, your refusal may confirm
A secret rumour that begins to grow.

*Jehosh.* What rumour?

*Mat.*                           That illustrious is his birth,
And that thy husband hatches some grand part
For him to play.

*Jehosh.*              And Mattan, by this tale
That soothes his rage—

*Mat.* Princess, it is for thee
To disabuse my mind. I know thou would'st,
As falsehood's ruthless foe, resign thy life
Sooner than sully thy sincerity
By the least word that is opposed to truth.
Hast thou no clue then to this mystery?
Is his birth buried in the deepest night?
Knowest thou not thyself from whom he sprang?
Whose hands they were that gave him to thy spouse?
I pause for answer; ready to believe thee.
Give glory, Princess, to the God thou servest.

*Jehosh.* Base man, it suits thee well to dare to name
A God whom thou hast taught men to blaspheme!
Can such a wretch as thou invoke His truth,
Thou on the seat of foul corruption throned,
Where falsehood reigns and spreads its poison round,
Whose lip with treachery and imposture teems!

SCENE V. *Jehoiada, Jehosheba, Mattan, Nabal*

*Jehoi.* Where am I? Is this Baal's priest I see?
Does David's daughter with a traitor talk,
And turn a listening ear? Dost thou not fear
That 'neath his feet should gape a gulf profound,
And flames forth issuing straight scorch and consume thee,
Or these walls crush thee falling upon him?
What would he? Why this bold effrontery?
Why comes God's foe to taint this holy air?

*Mat.* To rail is but to be Jehoiada!
Yet might he well, in reverence for the Queen,
Show greater prudence, and forbear to insult
The chosen envoy of her high command.

*Jehoi.* With what ill-omened tidings art thou charged?
What dreadful mission brings such messenger?

*Mat.* Jehosheba has heard the royal will.

*Jehoi.* Then get thee from my presence, impious wretch;
Go, and fill up the measure of thy crimes,
Soon will God make thee join the perjured crew
Of Dathan, Doeg, and Ahithophel;
The dogs He fed with fallen Jezebel,
Waiting to glut their fury upon thee,
Besiege thy door, all howling for their prey.

*Mat.* [*in confusion*]. Ere the day close—which of us is
    to be—
'Twill soon be seen—but, Nabal, let us go.

*Nab.* Where dost thou stray? Is then thy sense distraught?
There lies thy way.

Scene VI. *Jehoiada, Jehosheba*

*Jehosh.* The storm's about to burst:
The angry Queen demands Eliakim.
Already they begin to penetrate
The mystery of his birth and thy designs,
Mattan could all but tell his father's name.

*Jehoi.* Who to the traitor can have giv'n a clue?
Thine agitation may have told too much.

*Jehosh.* I have done all I could to master it:
And yet, believe me, danger presses close.
Let us reserve this child for happier times.
While still our wicked foes deliberate,
Ere they come round to tear him from our arms,
Let me, my lord, hide him a second time:
The gates stand open, and the way is free.
To wildest deserts must I carry him?
Ready am I. I know a secret path,
By which, without a chance of being seen,
Crossing the Kedron's torrent with the lad,
The wilderness I'll gain, where wept of old
David, in flight from his rebellious son,
And seeking safety from pursuit like us.
I shall fear less for him lions and bears—
But why reject Jehu's good offices?
Is not the counsel sound that I unfold?
Let us in Jehu's charge this treasure place,
And one may reach his realm this very day;
The way that leads to him is short. Nor starts
The heart of Jehu from compassion's touch;

The name of David he in honour holds.
Ah! lives there king so cruel and so hard,
Unless his mother were a Jezebel,
Who would not pity such a suppliant's cry?
Must not all monarchs make his cause their own?

*Jehoi.* What timid counsels, and how boldly urged!
Canst thou then place thy hopes in Jehu's aid?

*Jehosh.* Does God forbid all forethought and all care?
Condemns He not too blind a confidence?
Making mankind fulfill His holy ends,
Is it not God Himself arms Jehu's hands?

*Jehoi.* Jehu, whom God in His deep wisdom chose,
Jehu, on whom I see thy hopes are based,
Ungratefully forgets His benefits;
Ahab's fierce daughter he has left in peace,
And follows the vile steps of Israel's kings,
Keeps up the shrines of Egypt's bestial god,
And on high places rashly dares to burn
An incense that the Lord our God abhors.
Jehu too surely lacks the upright heart,
And clean hands, needed to promote His cause.
No, we must cling to God, and Him alone.
We must not hide but plainly show the boy,
With royal diadem around his brow;
I e'en intend to advance the appointed hour.
Ere Mattan can mature his counterplot.

SCENE VII. *Jehoiada, Jehosheba, Azariah, followed by
the Chorus, and a number of Levites*

*Jehoi.* Well, Azariah, is the Temple closed?

*Aza.* I have seen all the gates securely barr'd.

*Jehoi.* Remain there none but thou and thine allies?

*Aza.* Twice have I gone all round the sacred courts,

All have fled hence, nor think they of return,
Scatter'd by panic like a flock of sheep;
The holy tribe are left sole worshippers.
Never, since they escaped from Pharaoh's pow'r,
Has such dismay as this the people seized.

   *Jehoi.* Faint-hearted people, born for slavery,
Bold only against God! Let us pursue
The work we have in hand. But who still keeps
These children in our midst?

   *One of the Maidens Forming the Chorus.* Could we, my
      lord.
Sever ourselves from you? No strangers we
Here, in God's House, where ranged beside thee stand
Our fathers and our brothers.

   *Another Maiden.*                If to avenge
The shame of Israel we lack Jael's pow'r,
Who pierced the temples of God's impious foe,
We may at least for Him our lives lay down;
When for His threaten'd shrine your arms shall fight,
At least our tears may to His throne appeal.

   *Jehoi.* Lo, what avengers of Thy holy cause,
O Wisdom infinite,—these priests and babes!
But, Thou supporting, who can make them fall?
Thou canst, at will, recall us from our graves,
Canst wound and heal, canst kill and make alive.
They put no trust in merits of their own,
But in Thy Name, for them so oft invoked,
Thy promise to the holiest of their kings,
This Temple where Thou dost vouchsafe to dwell,
Destined to last long as the sun in heaven.

   Why throbs my heart with holy ecstasy?
Is it God's Spirit thus takes hold of me,
Glows in my breast, speaks, and unseals mine eyes?

Before me spread dim distant ages rise.
Ye Levites, let your melodies conspire
To fan the fiame of inspiration's fire.

    *The Chorus* [*singing to the accompaniment of musical in-
       struments*]. Lord, be Thy voice to our dull ears con-
       veyed,
    Thy holy message to our hearts be borne,
      As to the tender blade
    Comes, in the spring, the freshness of the morn!

*Jehoi.* Ye heavens hear my voice; thou earth give ear:
That the Lord sleeps, no more let Israel fear:
The Lord awakes! Ye sinners, disappear!

    [*The music begins again, and Jehoiada immediately
           resumes.*]

How has pure gold changed into worthless lead?
What Pontiff's blood is at the altar shed?
Weep, Salem; faithless city, weep in vain!
Thy murderous hands have God's own prophets slain:
Therefore His love for thee hath banish'd been,
Thine incense is to Him a smoke unclean.
Oh, whither are these tender captives led?
    The Lord the queen of cities hath discrown'd,
    Cast off her kings, her priests in fetters bound;
    Within her streets no festal throngs are found:
The Temple falls! high leap the flames with cedar fed!
Jerusalem, sad spectacle of woe,
    How in one day thy beauty disappears!
    Would that mine eyes might be a fount of tears,
      To weep thine overthrow!

*Aza.* Oh, holy shrine!
*Jehosh.* Oh, David!
*The Chorus.*           Lord, restore
Favour to Thine own Zion, as of yore!

*The music begins again, and Jehoiada, a moment after-*
*wards, breaks in upon it.*

*Jehoi.* What new Jerusalem is this draws nigh,
With beams of light that from the desert shine?
She bears upon her brow a mark divine:
Ye peoples, raise your joyous song on high!
Zion is born anew, far fairer to the eye,
From every side a gathering crowd I view,
Children that thine own bosom never knew;
    Jerusalem arise, lift up thine head!
Thy glory fills with wonder all these kings,
Each monarch of the earth his homage brings,
    Her mightiest kiss the dust where thou dost tread;
    All press to hail the light around thee shed.
Blessèd be he whose soul with ardour glows
        To see fair Zion rise!
        Drop down your dews, ye skies,
And let the earth her Saviour now disclose!
    *Jehosh.* Ah, whence may we expect a gift so rare,
If those, from whom that Saviour is to spring,—
    *Jehoi.* Prepare, Jehosheba, the royal crown,
Which David wore upon his sacred brow:
                    [*To the Levites.*]
And ye, to arm yourselves, come, follow me
Where are kept hidden, far from eyes profane,
That dread array of lances, and of swords,
Which once were drench'd with proud Philistia's blood,
And conquering David, full of years and fame,
Devoted to the Lord Who shelter'd him.
Can we employ them for a nobler use?
Come; and I will myself distribute them.

### Scene VIII. *Salome, the Chorus*

*Sal.* What fearful scenes, my sisters, must we see!
These arms, great God, strange sacrifice portend:
What incense, what firstfruits do they intend
To offer on Thine altar unto Thee?

*One of the Maidens of the Chorus.* What sight is this to
meet our timid eyes!
Who would have thought that we should e'er behold
Forests of spears arise.
And swords flash forth, where Peace has dwelt from days of
old?

*Another.* How comes it that, when danger is at hand,
Our city shows such dull indifference?
How comes it, sisters, that for our defence
E'en valiant Abner leads no succouring band?

*Sal.* Ah! In a Court that owns no other laws
Than force and violence,
Who would embrace the inauspicious cause
Of youthful innocence?
Baseness and blind submission there provide
High honours that to virtue are denied.

*Another Maiden.* When danger and disorder grimly
frown,
For whom thus bring they forth the consecrated crown?

*Sal.* The Lord hath deign'd to speak
But vainly do we seek
His prophet's utterance to comprehend.
Arms He destructions upon us to wreak?
Or arms He to defend?

*All the Chorus* [*sings*]. Promise and threat! What may
this mystery be?
What evil and what good in turn foretold!

How with such anger can such love agree?

 Who shall the clue unfold?

*One Voice* [*alone*]. Zion shall perish in devouring flame
And all her beauty shall be overthrown.

*Another Voice.* Zion's defence is in Jehovah's Name,
His deathless word her sure foundation stone.

*The First Voice.* I see her glory sink before mine eyes!

*The Second Voice.* The spreading radiance of her light I
 see!

*The First Voice.* Plunged in the deepest gulf of misery!

*The Second Voice.* Zion uplifts her forehead to the skies!

*The First Voice.* What ruin!

*The Second Voice.* Endless life to her belongs!

*The First Voice.* What cries of pain!

*The Second Voice.* Hark to victorious song!

*A Third Voice.* Cease these perplexing thoughts to trace,
God will the mystery solve, we know not how.

 *All Three Voices.* Before His wrath in reverence let us
 bow,

 And let our hopes His love embrace.

*Another Voice.* The heart whose love is thine,

 My God, who can disturb its peace?

Thy will supreme its guiding star doth shine,

 With beams that never cease:

What happiness in earth or heav'n can be

Like peace that keeps in sweet tranquillity,

 The heart that loveth Thee?

## ACT IV

SCENE I. *Joash, Jehosheba, Zachariah, Salome, a Levite,*
*the Chorus*

*Sal.* With step majestic, by my mother's side,
Comes with my brother young Eliakim.
Sisters, what bear they wrapp'd within those veils?
What means that sword carried in front of them?

*Jehosh.* [to *Zachariah*]. My son, with reverence on this
table place
The awful volume of our holy Law.
And thou, my sweet Eliakim, lay here,
Close to the book of God, this diadem.
Levite, it is Jehoiada's command,
Let David's sword be placed beside his crown.

*Joash.* Dear Princess, tell me, what new sight is this?
The sacred scroll, the sword, the diadem?
Since God within His Temple shelter'd me,
No preparation have I seen like this.

*Jehosh.* Soon will thy wondering doubts be clear'd, my son.

*Joash.* Try not that diadem upon my brow!
'Tis profanation of the glorious dead!
The King who wore it claims more reverence.
A poor unhappy child, left for the bears—

*Jehosh.* [*trying the crown upon him*]. Let be, my son;
thus has it been enjoin'd.

*Joash.* But do I hear thee sob? Princess, thy cheeks
Are wet with tears! What pity touches thee?
Am I, as Jephthah's daughter was of old,
To be presented for a sacrifice,
And, by my death, appease the wrath of God?

A son has naught his Father may not claim.
Ah me!

*Jehosh.* Lo, here is one who will declare God's will
To Thee, alone: fear not.

Come, let us go.

### Scene II. *Joash, Jehoiada*

*Joash.* [*running into the High Priest's arms*]. Father!
*Jehoi.* My son!

*Joash.* What preparation's here?

*Jehoi.* 'Tis right, my son, that thou should'st know the
truth,
And, sooner than all others, learn God's will,
His purpose for His people and for thee.
Arm thee with courage, and renew thy faith.
The time is come to prove that fervent zeal
Which I have cherish'd in thy heart with care,
And to discharge the debt due to thy God.
Art thou resolv'd to show a generous mind?

*Joash.* Yea, ready if He will to give my life.

*Jehoi.* Oft hast thou heard the story of our kings;
Dost bear in mind, my son, how strict the laws
A king must follow, worthy of the crown?

*Joash.* Wise kings, for thus hath God Himself declared,
Will not rely on riches and on gold,
But fear the Lord their God, regarding still
His precepts, and His judgments, and His laws,
Nor yoke oppressive on their brethren lay.

*Jehoi.* But wert thou bound to copy one such king,
Which would'st thou choose to imitate, my son?

*Joash.* There seems to me none worthy to compare
With faithful David, full of love divine.

*Jehoi.* Thou would'st not follow then the erring steps

Of faithless Joram and his impious son?

*Joash.* Father!

*Jehoi.* Proceed, and tell me all thy mind.

*Joash.* Whoso resembles them perish as they!

[*Jehoiada prostrates himself at his feet.*]

Father, why dost thou kneel before my face?

*Jehoi.* I pay thee the respect I owe my King.

Joash, prove worthy of thine ancestor,

Of David.

*Joash.* Am I Joash?

*Jehoi.* Thou shalt know

How graciously God foil'd the savage plot

Of Athaliah, saving thee from death,

Already with the dagger in thy breast.

Nor from her fury art thou yet escaped:

With the same eagerness that would erewhile

Have slain in thee her son's posterity,

Her cruelty is bent on thy destruction,

Nor does a change of name elude pursuit.

But 'neath thy standard I have gather'd here,

Prompt to avenge thee, an obedient band.

Enter, brave captains of the holy seed,

Honour'd by sacred service in your turns.

SCENE III. *Jehoiada, Joash, Azariah, Ishmael, and the three other chiefs of the Levites*

*Jehoi.* [*continues*]. Lo there, the king's avengers 'gainst his foes!

And there, ye priests, behold your promised King!

*Aza.* Why, 'tis Eliakim!

*Ish.* Is that sweet child—

*Jehoi.* The rightful heir of Judah's kings, the last
Of hapless Ahaziah's lineage,
Call'd by the name of Joash, as ye know.
All Judah, like yourselves, bewail'd the fate
Of that fair tender flow'r, so soon cut down,
Believing him with all his brethren slain.
With them he met the traitor's cruel knife:
But Heaven turn'd aside the mortal stroke,
Kept in his heart the smouldering spark of life.
And let my wife, eluding watchful eyes,
Convey him in her bosom, bathed in blood,
And hide him in the Temple with his nurse,
I being sole accomplice of her theft.

*Joash.* Ah, how, my father, can I e'er repay
The kindness and the love so freely giv'n?

*Jehoi.* The time will come to prove that gratitude.
Look then upon your King, your only hope!
My care has been to keep him for this hour;
Servants of God, 'tis yours that care to crown.
The child of Jezebel, the murderess queen,
Inform'd that Joash lives, will soon be here,
Opening for him the tomb a second time,
His death determined, though himself unknown.
Priests, 'tis for you her fury to forestall,
And Judah's shameful slavery to end,
Avenge your princess slain, your Law restore,
Make Benjamin and Judah own their King.
The enterprise, no doubt, is dangerous,
Attacking a proud queen upon her throne,
Who rallies to her standard a vast host
Of hardy strangers and of faithless Jews:
But He who guides and strengthens me is God.
Think, on this child all Israel's hope depends.

The wrath of God already marks the Queen;
Here have I muster'd you, in her despite,
Nor lack ye warlike arms as she believes.
Haste, crown we Joash, and proclaim him King,
Then, our new Prince's valiant soldiers, march,
Calling on Him with Whom all victory lies,
And, waking loyalty in slumbering hearts,
E'en to her palace track our enemy.
What hearts, so sunk in sloth's inglorious sleep,
Will not be roused to follow in our steps,
When in our sacred ranks they see advance
A King whom God has at His altar fed,
Aaron's successor, and a train of priests
Leading to battle Levi's progeny.
And in those self-same hands, by all revered,
The arms that David hallow'd to the Lord?
Our God shall spread His terror o'er His foes.
Shrink not from bathing you in heathen blood;
Hew down the Tyrians, yea, and Jacob's seed.
Are ye not from those famous Levites sprung
Who, when inconstant Israel wickedly
At Sinai worshipp'd the Egyptian god,
Their dearest kinsmen slew with righteous zeal,
And sanctified their hands in traitors' blood,
Gaining the honour, by this noble deed,
Of serving at the altars of the Lord?
    But I perceive your zeal already fired;
Swear then upon this holy volume, first,
Before this King whom Heav'n restores today,
To live, to fight, yea, or to die for him!
    *Aza.* Here swear we, for ourselves and brethren all,
To establish Joash on his father's throne,
Nor, having taken in our hands the sword,

To lay it down till we have slain his foes.
If anyone of us should break this vow,
Let him, great God, and let his children feel
Thy vengeance, from Thine heritage shut out,
And number'd with the dead disown'd by Thee!

   *Jehoi.* And thou, my King, wilt thou not swear to be
Faithful to this eternal Law of God?

   *Joash.* How could I ever wish to disobey?

   *Jehoi.* My son,—once more to call thee by that name,—
Suffer this fondness, and forgive the tears
Prompted by too well founded fears for thee.
Far from the throne, in ignorance brought up
Of all the poisonous charms of royalty,
Thou knowest not th' intoxicating fumes
Of pow'r uncurb'd, and flattery's magic spells;
Soon will she whisper that the holiest laws,
Tho' governing the herd, must kings obey;
A monarch owns no bridle but his will;
All else must bow before his majesty;
Subjects are rightly doom'd to toil and tears,
And with a rod of iron should be ruled,
For they will crush him if they be not crush'd.
Thus will fresh pitfalls for your feet be dug,
New snares be spread to spoil your innocence,
Till they have made you hate the truth at last,
By painting virtue in repulsive guise.
Alas! our wisest king was led astray.
Swear on this book, before these witnesses,
That God shall be thy first and constant care;
Scourge of the evil, refuge of the good,
That you will judge the poor as God directs;
Rememb'ring how, in simple linen clad,
Thou wast thyself a helpless orphan child.

*Joash.* I promise to observe the Law's commands,
If I forsake Thee, punish me, my God.
  *Jehoi.* I must anoint thee with the holy oil.
Jehosheba, thou mayest show thyself.

SCENE IV. *Joash, Jehoiada, Jehosheba, Zachariah Salome,*
*Azariah, Ishmael, the three other chiefs of the Levites,*
*the Chorus*

  *Jehosh.* [*embracing Joash*]. My King, and son of David!
  *Joash.* Mother, dear,
My only mother! Zachariah, come,
Embrace thy brother.
  *Jehosh.* [*to Zachariah*]. Kneel before thy King.
    [*Zachariah casts himself at the feet of Joash.*]
  *Jehoi.* [*while they embrace one another*]. My children, be
    united ever thus!
  *Jehosh.* [*to Joash*]. Thou knowest then whose blood has
    giv'n thee life?
  *Joash.* And who had robb'd me of it, but for thee.
  *Jehosh.* I then may call thee Joash, thy true name.
  *Joash.* And thee shall Joash never cease to love.
  *Chorus.* Why, there is—
  *Jehosh.*                Joash.
  *Jehoi.*                        Hear this messenger.

SCENE V. *Joash, Jehoiada, Jehosheba, Zachariah, Salome,*
*Azariah, Ishmael, the three other chiefs of the Levites, a*
*Levite, the Chorus*

  *A Levite.* I know not what their impious plan may be,
But everywhere resounds the threatening trump,
And amid standards fires are seen to shine;
The Queen is doubtless mustering her troops;
Already, every way of succour closed,

The sacred mount on which the Temple stands
Insolent Tyrians on all sides invest;
And one of these blasphemers now brings word
That Abner is in chains, so cannot help.

    *Jehosh.* [*to Joash*]. Ah! dearest child, by Heav'n in vain
      restored,
Alas! for safety I can do no more.
God has forgotten David and his seed!

    *Jehoi.* [*to Jehosheba*]. Dost thou not fear to draw the
      wrath divine
Down on thyself, and on the King thou lovest?
And e'en tho' God should snatch him from thine arms,
And will that David's house perish with him,
Art thou not here upon the holy hill,
Where Abraham our father raised his hand
Obediently to slay his blameless son,
Nor murmur'd as he to the altar bound
The fruit of his old age; leaving to God
Fulfilment of His promise, though this son
Held in himself the hope of all his race?

    Friends, let us take our several posts: the side
That looks towards the east let Ishmael guard;
Guard thou the north; thou, west; and thou the south.
Take heed that no one, with imprudent zeal,
Levite or priest, unmasking my designs,
Burst forth in headlong haste before the time;
Let each, as with one common will inspired,
Wherever placed, till death his post maintain.
Our foes regard you, in their blinded rage,
As timid flocks for slaughter set aside,
And think that ye will scatter in dismay.

    Let Azariah on the King attend.

*[To Joash.]*

Come, precious scion of a vigorous stock,
And with fresh courage thy defenders fill;
Come, don the diadem before their eyes,
And die, if it must be so, like a King.

*[To Jehosh.]*

Follow him, Princess.

*[To a Levite.]*

Give me thou those arms.

*[To the Chorus.]*

Offer to God the tears of innocence.


SCENE VI. *Salome, the Chorus ..*

*All the Chorus [sings].*

Go forth, ye sons of Aaron, go:
    Never did cause of greater fame
    The spirit of your sires inflame.
Go forth, ye sons of Aaron, go:
'Tis for your God and King this day ye strike the blow.

*One Voice [alone].*

Hast Thou no shafts in store,
    That Justice may let fly?
Art Thou the jealous God no more,
No longer God of Vengeance throned on high?

*Another Voice.*

Where, God of Jacob, is Thy goodness fled?
    With horrors all around us pressing near,

Have but our sins a voice which Thou canst hear?
Wilt Thou on us no more Thy pardon shed?

### *All the Chorus.*

Where is Thine ancient lovingkindness fled?

### *One Voice* [*alone*].

'Tis against Thee that in this fray,
   The wicked set the arrow to the bow;
"Let us destroy His feasts," say they,
   "No longer let the earth His worship show;
Nor his vexatious yoke let mortals longer know,
   His altars overturn, His votaries slay,
      Till of His name and glory
      Remains not e'en the story;
   Of Him and His Anointed break the sway."

### *All the Chorus.*

Hast Thou no shafts in store,
   That Justice may let fly?
Art Thou the jealous God no more,
No longer God of Vengeance throned on high?

### *One Voice* [*alone*].

Sad relic of our kings,
Last precious blossom of a stem so fair,
Ah! will the knife this time refuse to spare,
Which to his breast a cruel parent brings?
Tell us, sweet Prince, if o'er thy cradle hovered
Some Angel that protected thee from death?
Or did thy lifeless form in darkness covered,
At God's awakening voice resume its breath?

### *Another Voice.*

Great God, dost Thou the guilt upon him lay,
That his rebellious sires forsook Thy way?
Is Thy compassion then clean gone for aye?

### *The Chorus.*

Where, God of Jacob, is Thy goodness fled?
Wilt Thou no more Thy gracious pardon shed?

### *One of the Maidens of the Chorus* [*speaking not singing*].

Dear sisters, cruel Tyrians hem us round,
Do ye not hear their trumpets' dreadful sound?

### *Salome.*

Yea, and *I* hear them raise their savage cry;
  I tremble with alarm;
Haste, let us to our place of refuge fly,
  Where God's Almighty Arm
Shall in His Temple shelter us from harm.


## ACT V

### Scene I. *Zachariah, Salome, the Chorus*

*Sal.* What news, dear Zachariah, dost thou bring?
  *Zach.* Double the fervour of your prayers to Heav'n!
Sister, our latest hour perhaps draws nigh.
For the dread conflict orders have been giv'n.
  *Sal.* And what does Joash?
  *Zach.*                   He has just been crown'd,
And by the High Priest with the holy oil
Anointed. Oh, what joy in every eye

Welcomed a sovereign ransom'd from the tomb,
A scar still showing where the dagger fell!
There too might have been seen his faithful nurse,
Who, almost hidden in a far recess,
Was watching her loved charge, tho' none but God
And our dear mother witness'd her concern.
Our Levites wept in tenderness and joy,
Mingling with sobs their cries of glad delight:
He 'mid these transports, all untouch'd by pride,
Gave gracious smiles, words, pressure of the hand;
And, swearing to conform with their advice,
This one his father, that his brother call'd.

   *Sal.* And has our secret reach'd the world without?

   *Zach.* 'Tis known to none beyond the Temple walls
The sons of Levi, in divided bands,
Are ranged in solemn silence at the doors,
All in an instant ready to rush forth
And raise the signal shout, "Long live the King!"
But Azariah has been strictly charged
To guard the Prince's life from any risk.
Meanwhile the scornful Queen, dagger in hand,
Laughs at our frail defence of brazen doors,
Awaits the engines that shall break them down,
And threatens blood and ruin with each breath.
Some priests, my sister, ventured to advise
That in a crypt, dug in the days of old,
We should at least the precious Ark conceal;
"Such fears insult our God," my father said,
"Shall then the Ark that caused proud tow'rs to fall,
That drove the waters of the Jordan back,
And shatter'd to the earth Philistia's gods,
Flee from before a shameless woman's face!"
Our mother, standing near in mortal dread,

Now to the Prince, now to the altar turns
Her wavering glance, yielding to mute alarm,
A sight to make a very savage weep.
From time to time the King, with fond embrace,
Soothes her—Dear sisters, follow in my steps,
And, if this day our King is doom'd to die,
Let the same fate with him unite us all.

*Sal.* What rude hand knocks with quick repeated strokes?
What makes these Levites in confusion run?
Why with such caution do they hide their arms?
Say, is the Temple forced?

*Zach.* Your fears dispel,
God sends us Abner.

SCENE II. *Jehoiada, Jehosheba, Zachariah, Salome, Abner,
Ishmael, two Levites, the Chorus*

*Jehoi.* Can I trust mine eyes?
How did dear Abner find his way to us,
Right through the enemy's blockading camp?
'Twas said that Athaliah, to insure
The execution of her cruel plots,
Had bound in iron chains thy generous hands.

*Abner.* My lord, she fear'd my courage and my zeal,
And worse than fetters gave me for reward,
Confining me within a loathsome den,
To wait until the Temple should be burn'd,
And she, unsated still with streams of blood
Should come to free me from an irksome life,
And cut short days, which sorrows to survive
My princes should have ended long ago.

*Jehoi.* What miracle procured thee thy release?

*Abner.* God only knows how works her cruel heart.
She sent for me; and said with anxious air,—

"Thou seest this temple by my troops beset:
Soon will the vengeful flames but ashes leave,
In spite of all thy god can do to save.
Yet upon two conditions may his priests
Redeem their lives, but no time must be lost,
That in my pow'r they place Eliakim,
With treasure known to them, and them alone,
Amass'd by David when he reign'd of yore,
And left a secret in the High Priest's charge.
Go, tell them on these terms I let them live."

*Jehoi.* What course, dear Abner, thinkest thou the best?

*Abner.* Give her the gold, if it indeed be true,
That in thy keeping David's treasure lies,
And all besides, that from her greedy hands
Thou hitherto hast saved, precious and rare.
Give all; or thou wilt have vile murderers come,
To break the altar, burn the cherubim,
And, on our sacred Ark laying rude hands,
Stain with thy priestly blood the inner shrine.

*Jehoi.* But, Abner, how can I in honour yield
To punishment a poor unhappy child,
Whom God Himself intrusted to my care,
And save our lives by sacrificing his?

*Abner.* Would to Almighty God, who sees my heart,
That Athaliah might forget the boy,
And be content her cruelty to slake
With Abner's blood, thinking thereby to soothe
Her angry gods! but what avails your care?
If ye all perish, will he die the less?
Does God command what is impossible?
When, in obedience to a tyrant's law,
His mother trusted Moses to the Nile,
Almost as soon as born, condemn'd to die;

Yet God, against all hope, his life preserved,
And made the King himself his childhood rear.
Who knows His purpose tow'rd Eliakim?
E'en such a lot may be for him in store,
And the fell murderess of the royal seed
Be render'd sensitive to pity's touch.
Not long ago I saw steal o'er her face
A tender look, that by Jehosheba
Was mark'd as well, calming her wrathful mood.
Princess, the hour of danger claims thy voice!
What! Shall Jehoiada, with thy consent,
For a mere stranger, let his son and thee,
Yea, all this people, fruitlessly be slain,
And flames devour the only spot on earth
Where God is worshipp'd? What could ye do more,
Were he the sole survivor of our Kings,
Your ancestors?

    *Jehosh.* [*aside to Jehoiada*]. Thou seest his loyal heart;
Tell him the truth.

    *Jehoi.*           The time is not yet come.

    *Abner.* Time is more precious than thou thinkest, Sir.
While thou art doubting what reply to give,
Mattan, at Athaliah's ear, demands,
Burning with rage, a speedy massacre.
Must I fall prostrate at thy hallow'd knees?
Now in the name of that Most Holy Place,
Unseen by mortal eye save thine, where dwells
God's glory; howsoever hard the task,
Let us think how to meet the sudden blow.
I only beg a moment's breathing space:
Tomorrow, yea, tonight, I will secure
The Temple, and make outrage dangerous.
But I perceive my words are lost on thee,

Tears and entreaties pow'rless to persuade,
Too strict thy sense of duty to give way.
Well, find me then some weapon, spear or sword,
And, where the foe await me, at these gates,
Abner at least can die a soldier's death.

*Jehoi.* I yield. Your proffer'd counsel I embrace:
Abner, we will avert these threaten'd ills.
'Tis true that David left a treasure here,
That to my charge was trusted, the last hope
Left to the Jews in their calamities;
My watchful care bestowed it secretly,
But, since we cannot hide it from your Queen,
She shall be satisfied, and through these doors
Enter, attended by her officers;
But from these altars let her keep afar
The savage fury of her foreign troops,
And spare the House of God from pillage dire.
Arrange with her the number of her train,
Children and priests can small suspicion rouse.

Touching this child she dreads so much, to thee,
Knowing thine upright heart, I will unfold
The secret of his birth, when she can hear;
And thou shalt judge between us, if I must
Place this young boy in Athaliah's pow'r.

*Abner.* I take him under my protection now;
Fear naught, my lord. Back to the Queen I haste.

Scene III. *Jehoiada, Jehosheba, Zachariah, Salome, Ishmael,*
*two Levites, the Chorus*

*Jehoi.* Great God! The hour is come that brings Thy prey!
Hark, Ishmael.

       [*He whispers in his ear.*]
*Jehosh.* Almighty King of Heav'n,

Place a thick veil before her eyes once more,
As when, making her crime of none effect,
Thou in my bosom did'st her victim hide.

  *Jehoi.* Good Ishmael, go, there is no time to lose;
Fulfil precisely this important task;
And, above all, take heed, when she arrives
And passes, that no threatening signs be seen,
Children, for Joash be a throne prepared;
Let our arm'd Levites on his steps attend.
Princess, bring hither too his trusty nurse,
And dry the copious fountain of thy tears.
          [*To a Levite.*]
Soon as the Queen, madly presumptuous,
Has cross'd the threshold of the Temple gates,
Let all retreat be made impossible;
That very moment let the martial trump
Wake sudden terror in the hostile camp:
Call all the people to support their King,
And make her ears ring with the wondrous tale
Of Joash by God's providence preserved.
He comes.

  Scene IV. *Jehoiada, Jehosheba, Zachariah, Salome, Joash,*
    *Azariah, a band of Priests and Levites, the Chorus*

  *Jehoi.* [*continues*]. Ye Levites, and ye priests of God,
Range yourselves round, but do not show yourselves;
Leave it to me to keep your zeal in check,
And tarry till my voice bids you appear.
        [*They all hide themselves.*]
My King, methinks this hope rewards thy vows;
Come, see thy foes fall prostrate at thy feet.
She who in fury sought thine infant life
Comes hither in hot haste to slay thee now:

But fear her not: think that upon our side
Stands the destroying angel as thy guard.
Ascend thy throne—The gates are opening **wide**;
One moment let this curtain cover thee.

                [*He draws a curtain.*]

Princess, thy colour changes.

  *Jehosh.*              Can I see
Assassins fill God's house, and not grow pale?
Why, look how numerous the retinue.

  *Jehoi.* I see them shut the Temple doors again.
All is secure.

### Scene V. *Joash, Jehoiada, Jehosheba, Abner, Athaliah,*
### *and her Attendants (Joash is hidden behind*
### *the curtain.)*

  *Ath.* [*to Jehoiada*]. Deceiver, there thou art!
Author of mischief, plots, conspiracies,
Whose hopes are all upon disturbance based,
Inveterate foe of sovereign majesty!
Dost thou still lean upon thy god's support,
Or has that flimsy trust forsaken thee?
He leaves thee and thy temple in my pow'r.
Well might I on the altar thou dost serve—
But no, thine offer'd ransom shall suffice;
Fulfil what thou hast promised. That young boy,
That treasure which thou must to me resign,
Where are they?

  *Jehoi.* Straight shalt thou be satisfied:
I am about to show them both at once.

*The curtain is drawn up. Joash is discovered on his throne;
  his nurse is kneeling on his right; Azariah, sword in
  hand, is standing on his left; and near him Zachariah and*

*Salome are kneeling on the steps of the throne; a number of Levites, with swords in their hands, are ranged on either side.*

Appear, dear child, worthy of royal sires.
Queen, dost thou recognize King David's heir?
Observe at least these marks thy dagger left:
Behold thine offspring, Ahaziah's son!
Welcome King Joash, Abner, people all!
  *Abner.* Heav'ns!
  *Ath.* Traitor!
  *Jehoi.* See this faithful Jewess here,
Whose bosom, as thou knowest, nursed him then.
Saved from thy fury by Jehosheba,
Within this temple God has guarded him.
Lo, here is all of David's treasure left!
  *Ath.* Traitor, thy fraud will but destroy the child:
Rid me, my soldiers, of this vile pretence!
  *Jehoi.* Soldiers of God, draw near, defend your King:

*The back of the stage opens: the interior of the temple is shown; and armed Levites enter from all around upon the stage.*

  *Ath.* Treason! Oh, where am I, unhappy Queen!
Weapons and enemies on every side!
  *Jehoi.* Thy search is vain, thou canst not 'scape the toils
Cast round thee by the God whom thou hast scorn'd.
Into our hands has He deliver'd thee;
Drunken with blood He calls thee to His bar.
  *Ath.* My warriors are turn'd craven, numb with fear!
Abner, is this thy coward's snare?
  *Abner.*                My Queen,
As God is witness—

*Ath.*                                                       Never mind thy god

Avenge me.

    *Abner.* [*throwing himself at the feet of Joash*]. Upon
      whom? Joash? My prince?

    *Ath.* He Joash! He thy King! Bethink you, knaves,

That ye are still beleaguer'd by my arms;

I hear my soldiers call me with loud shouts.

Tremble, ye rebels! Succour is at hand.

    Scene VI. *Joash, Athaliah, Jehoiada, Ishmael and all the
        actors in the preceding scene*

    *Ish.* [*to Jehoiada*]. My lord, our foes have left the Temple
      free:

The foreigners are fled, the Jews submit.

As smoke is driv'n away before the wind,

Th' Almighty's voice this army has dispersed.

Our Levites, high above the courts around,

Have Ahaziah's son to all proclaim'd,

Told of his infant life saved from the sword,

And Athaliah's fall into the snare.

The trumpets sounded from all sides at once,

And, mingled with their cries, such terror spread

Throughout the camp as struck with wild dismay

Proud Midian at the flash of Gideon's sword,

The Tyrians, casting arms and shields away,

The first, in all directions disappear'd.

Some Jews, in dazed confusion, shared their flight:

The rest for Joash loudly have declared,

Owning herein the guiding hand of God.

Yea, all the people, with one heart inspired,

Women, old men, and babes embrace with joy,

Blessing Jehovah and the King he sends,

And hymn the son of David raised to life.

All in the holy city execrate
The name of Baal, and destroy his shrine.
Mattan is slain.

 *Ath.*     Jehovah, thou hast won!
Yes, it is Joash. Vain denial now!
'Twas here I gave command to have him slain;
He has the mien and features of his sire;
I trace his kinship with the line I hate.
Thus David triumphs, Ahab is destroy'd.
Relentless god, this is thy work alone,
With hopes of easy vengeance luring me.
And twenty times a day setting my thoughts
In conflict, now remorseful for this child,
Now dazzled with the prospect of rich spoil,
And loath to give it to devouring flames.
Well, let him reign, thy care and handiwork!
And, to inaugurate his sovereignty,
Bid him to direct this dagger to my heart!
This for my grandson is my dying wish,—
My wish, nay, more than wish, my trust and hope;
That weary of thy law, thy yoke contemn'd,
True to the blood of Ahab, drawn from me,
Following his grandsire's and his father's steps,
He, David's heir, shall make himself abhorr'd,
Profane thine altar, rob thee of thy rites,
So avenge Ahab, Jezebel, and me!

   *[Athaliah goes out, the Levites follow her.]*
 *Jehoi.* Out of the Temple precincts have her forth
At once, nor be its holy courts profaned.
Go and avenge your princes massacred,
Whose blood cries out till pacified by hers.
If any venture to defend her cause,
Him let the sword along with her, devour.

SCENE VII. *Joash, Jehoiada, Jehosheba, Abner, and all the*
*actors in the preceding scene*

   *Joash* [*after descending from his throne*]. Thou seest, O
      Lord, the anguish of my soul,
Oh, turn her malediction from me far,
And never suffer it to be fulfill'd!
Let Joash die ere he forgets his God!
      *Jehoi.* [*to the Levites*]. Call all the people, they shall see
         their King.
Let them approach, and fresh allegiance swear.
King, priests, and people, let us all confirm
The covenant that Jacob made with God,
Grateful for mercy, for our sins ashamed,
And with new vows binding ourselves to Him.
Abner, resume thy post beside the King.

SCENE VIII. *Joash, Jehoiada, a Levite, and all the actors in*
*the preceding scene*

   *Jehoi.* [*to the Levite*]. Well, has that monster met with
      punishment?
   *The Levite.* Her guilt has been atoned for with the sword.
Jerusalem, so long her fury's prey,
Relieved at last from her detested yoke,
With joy beholds her weltering in her blood.
      *Jehoi.* By this, the dreadful end her crimes deserved,
Learn, King of Judah, nor this truth forget:—
Kings have in Heav'n their Judge severe, Who to the father-
      less
Is Father, and will punish those who innocence oppress!

**THE END**